Advance Praise

"Mary Eno has enormous firsthand experience in transforming what can be contentious and unproductive interactions into meaningful conversations that make a significant difference in the lives of children and families. Her respect and compassion for all parties in the complicated relationship between families, therapists, and schools permeate every page. She brings her rigor, quest for knowledge, and astutely questioning mind to the thorny dilemmas she's posed and doesn't shirk from confronting the possible roadblocks and pitfalls of the very difficult and delicate balancing act that therapists face. *The School-Savvy Therapist* is a unique and invaluable guide that should be required reading for all clinicians who work with children."

—Frances Schwartz, Ph.D., LCSW, Educational Consultant, and Martha Edwards, Ph.D., Director, Center for the Developing Child & Family, Ackerman Institute for the Family

"*The School-Savvy Therapist* is the definitive guide to decoding and bridging the worlds in which kids live: home and school. Keenly aware of the complexities of the two landscapes, Dr. Mary Eno expertly provides a comprehensive, nuanced, and incisive roadmap for synthesizing them in the therapeutic setting. Her book is essential reading for novice and seasoned clinicians alike, and will empower schools and parents in the crucial task of educating our children while stewarding their well-being."

—Tamar Chansky, Ph.D., Founder Children's and Adult Center for OCD and Anxiety, author of *Freeing Your Child from Anxiety*, *Freeing Your Child from Negative Thinking*, and *Freeing Yourself from Anxiety*

"Any well-intentioned therapist working with children, their families, and schools can easily get lost amidst the dense forest of contemporary education's many challenges—unless you have a guide. Reading Mary Eno's book *The School-Savvy Therapist*, is like being accompanied by a wise inhabitant fluent in multiple languages, who knows where to go, how to get there, and what to avoid. It's the ecology of education at its healing best: a practical, collaborative, systemic, and strength-based path forward that sees the forest and the trees."

—Jay Lappin, MSW, LCSW, Minuchin Center for the Family; Adjunct Faculty, Graduate School of Education, University of Pennsylvania

"Dr. Eno expertly captures the power of a productive collaboration between school and family and provides an accessible guide for how to broker that collaboration by building synergistic family–school relationships. Her strengths-based perspective, peppered with case examples and viewpoints from practicing clinicians and educators, makes this book a tremendous resource for those who are learning to be child or family therapists, and for those who are training the next generation of therapists."

—Mary Rourke, Ph.D., Associate Professor of Clinical Psychology, Widener University

"The School-Savvy Therapist is an action-oriented, comprehensive, and incredibly thought-provoking resource for professionals. Dr. Eno offers practical tips and expertise for therapists who seek to effectively work with schools to foster a positive collaboration between family, school, and child. As a teacher who has worked with dozens of therapists, I applaud Dr. Eno's thorough understanding of school dynamics and her relentless focus on the child and the benefits that can come when families, therapists, and schools work to solve problems together."

—Elena Carlson, M.Ed., Second Grade Teacher, Lower Merion School District

"Mary Eno's insight into the culture and systems of schools and families provides rare and indispensable wisdom and context for therapists working with children. A brilliant colleague to many educators during her lifelong career as a therapist in schools, she has provided a masterful summary of her experience. Dr. Eno's professional skill, compassion, curiosity, and empathy ring beautifully through her writing in *The School-Savvy Therapist.*"

—Rich Nourie, M.Ed., Head of School at Abington Friends School

"Families and schools are often 'worlds apart.' When children have behavior or learning problems, it is vital that the people in these worlds learn how to collaborate. But first they have to get to know each other. Mary Eno's comprehensive, readable guide shows therapists when, why, and how to engage with worried parents, frustrated school staff, and troubled students. The engaging text is threaded with case studies and practical tools, such as checklists of questions to guide interviews and family–school meetings."

—Theodora Ooms, Former Director, Family Impact Seminar

"The School-Savvy Therapist is an invaluable and critical resource for all clinicians working with school-age children and their families. Rooted in systems theory, this seminal work provides effective and practical guidance to assist clinicians in successfully navigating the complex landscape of schools today. Providing a theoretical framework, as well as illustrative case examples and guiding questions, *The School-Savvy Therapist* is the authoritative handbook on how to effectively collaborate with school systems and personnel to foster a truly supportive child–family–school dynamic."

—Eleanor DiMarino-Linnen, Ph.D., Superintendent of Schools, Rose Tree Media School District, Licensed Psychologist, Certified School Psychologist

"Mary Eno's detailed and intimate perspective on working relationships between parents, children of all ages, and educators in all kinds of schools is remarkable. Rich cases cut through professional jargon to examine subjects ranging from homework and bullying to special education and today's anxious school climate. The book is wonderful, and not only for therapists."

—Graham S. Finney, Founding Board Member, Mastery Charter Schools (Philadelphia), Former Management Consultant (Urban Affairs, Education)

THE
SCHOOL-SAVVY
THERAPIST

A Norton Professional Book

THE
SCHOOL-SAVVY
THERAPIST

WORKING WITH KIDS,
FAMILIES,
AND THEIR SCHOOLS

Mary M. Eno

W. W. NORTON & COMPANY
Independent Publishers Since 1923

For information about permission to reproduce selections from this book, write to Permissions, W. W. Norton & Company, Inc., 500 Fifth Avenue, New York, NY 10110

For information about special discounts for bulk purchases, please contact W. W. Norton Special Sales at specialsales@wwnorton.com or 800-233-4830

Manufacturing by Sheridan Books
Production manager: Katelyn MacKenzie

Library of Congress Cataloging-in-Publication Data

Names: Eno, Mary M., author.
Title: The school-savvy therapist : working with kids, families, and their schools / Mary Eno.
Description: First edition. | New York : W.W. Norton & Company 2019. |
Includes bibliographical references and index.
Identifiers: LCCN 2019005757 | ISBN 9780393711905 (paperback)
Subjects: LCSH: School children—Mental health services—United States. |
School psychology—United States. | Clinical psychology—United States. | Family psychotherapy—United States. | Home and school—United States.
Classification: LCC LB3430 .E56 2019 | DDC 371.7/13—dc23
LC record available at https://lccn.loc.gov/2019005757

W. W. Norton & Company, Inc., 500 Fifth Avenue, New York, N.Y. 10110
www.wwnorton.com

W. W. Norton & Company Ltd., 15 Carlisle Street, London W1D 3BS

1 2 3 4 5 6 7 8 9 0

For Dan and my family

CONTENTS

PREFACE

Throughout my years teaching and supervising graduate students, I searched for a book to assign them that would offer practical guidance on how to work with the schools their clients attended. To be sure, there were excellent resources available that addressed various aspects of the topic, but none assembled all the pieces in one place. Because the students were highly motivated and inquiring, they made their way, learning about schools, collaborating with teachers, observing and assessing kids, participating in family–school meetings, and more. Gaps in knowledge were filled in with our collective efforts and cumulative experience. It was their enthusiasm and desire to learn that inspired me to create a resource for future therapists, drawing from my over 40 years of working with schools and the wisdom I've gleaned from so many students, colleagues, and professionals along the way. The result is the book you're holding in your hand.

I began my own professional journey working with children, families, and schools in the mid-1970s, when I was hired to work in the outpatient department at the Philadelphia Child Guidance Clinic as a therapist and coordinator of their services to the public and parochial schools in West Philadelphia. During those years, the clinic was ideally suited—time, place, and theoretical approach—for treating children and families in a community setting. Clinicians and researchers came from all over the world to be trained by and study with Salvador Minuchin, Braulio Montalvo, Jay Haley, Bernice Rosman, Harry Aponte, and others who introduced pragmatic, family systems models for working with children and families. There was a good deal of optimism at the time about the power of these models to transform people's lives. Relatively new to the therapeutic landscape, family therapy brought with it the idea that children's problems didn't necessarily reside inside them but emerged within their very ordinary, day-to-day relationships within their families, schools, and neighborhoods. The approach was innovative, practical and compelling—a way of working with vulnerable kids and families that naturally lent itself to recognizing the inherent value of getting to know children within their school context.

During my years at the clinic, I worked in many schools—public and parochial, preschools, elementary, middle, and high schools. Some functioned beautifully and others far less so. My mistakes were plentiful, and sometimes I was overwhelmed by the poverty and lack of resources I encountered. But mostly I remember feeling uplifted and inspired by the kids and the dedicated teachers and staff, those plugging up broken windows and arranging chairs in maintenance closets so that an impromptu family–school meeting could be held. I consider myself lucky to have been given the chance to grow up as a professional in those schools, to have been afforded opportunities to fail and get back on my feet again. I realize now that it not only takes a village to raise a child but also an equivalent village to train and educate a therapist.

At the PreK–12 Quaker school where I subsequently worked for over 25 years as a consulting psychologist, I was able to see the world of kids and families from the school's viewpoint. I witnessed school representatives bending over backward to understand, support, and educate students, especially those who were struggling. I could see the enormous lengths school representatives went to in order to form partnerships with families, and how therapists became crucial members of those teams. I could see the myriad ways school representatives exchanged information among themselves, collaborating and ironing out their own differing perspectives regarding students. Perhaps, most importantly, I observed something of what it's like for kids to be kids at school—the immense vitality that is evident every day in classrooms, corridors, lunchrooms, and playing fields. I could see the world they inhabit collectively, the world we call school, brimming with their hopes and dreams, conflicts and pathos. Sometimes, seeing all that life and potential simply left me breathless.

All of these experiences led me to write this book and, in doing so, add the voices of kids, families, therapists, teachers, administrators, and student support staff along with those clinicians and researchers who have already contributed to our understanding of how therapists can work effectively with schools. It is abundantly evident that, by engaging with schools, therapists can help strengthen the invaluable networks for kids who have school problems and the families who love and support them.

INTRODUCTION

- Four-year-old Matt is exhibiting increased aggression and disruptive behavior in his preschool classroom, something his parents never saw with his siblings.

- Eight-year-old Danica is refusing to go to school, crying and begging each morning not to go to "that awful place." She is in danger of being held back in the third grade because of her absences.

- School administrators discover that two middle school girls are discussing suicide through social media. Both girls have a history of school problems, and their families have little contact with the school.

- Seventeen-year-old Jose, a formerly high-achieving high school junior, is in the throes of a depression that has sapped his motivation. When asked why he's dropped out of school activities that once gave him joy, he counters with his own question, "What's the point?"

You may recognize some of the school-related problems in the examples above. They represent just a few of the countless problems that bring children and families into therapy. Stressors run the gamut from school violence and suicide, to complex systemic problems rooted in poverty or racism, to the more quotidian challenges of struggling with homework or feeling excluded by friends. Children today face problems largely unknown to their parents' generation—they must learn to navigate the complex, interconnected world created by technological advances, social media, globalization, and climate change.

Families struggling to address these school-related issues come to therapy hoping we can help, sometimes at the urging of worried or frustrated school staff. While you might understand the need to work with the school in these instances, it can be a daunting prospect. Clinical knowledge of children and families does not necessarily translate into knowledge about when and how to contact schools or how to work with them collaboratively.

The purpose of this book is to provide a framework and guidelines for doing so, drawing from foundational research; case examples; and interviews with teachers, therapists, school administrators, and student support staff. It describes what therapists need to know about schools, how they can come to understand the child and family in a school setting, and what they can do to help foster a supportive family-child-school dynamic. Ideally, you will come to see schools as sources of insight and information about the kids you see in therapy, as well as important partners in supporting their development. Understanding that all children's problems are unique and embedded in varied, specific contexts, this book is written with an attitude toward discovery and creative problem solving, rather than as a rigid step-by-step guide or prescription.

A Brief Overview of the Theoretical Approach

This book is anchored in systems, ecological, and developmental theories. To understand this orientation, it's worth looking back, even briefly, to certain research and related practices beginning in the 1960s and 70's. At that time, a new family systems approach for treating children was developed by Salvador Minuchin (1974), Jay Haley (1976) and others that was swiftly put to work in schools. In a groundbreaking article, Harry Aponte (1976) proffered an "eco-structural" approach, which privileged family–school interviews conducted at the school with the child, family, and relevant school staff present. Aponte went so far as to encourage clinicians to begin therapy at the school itself.

During those years, community psychologist Seymour Sarason (1971/1996) argued that our failure to solve children's school problems results, in part, from not widening the lens sufficiently to take into account the context in which they live. Sociologist Sara Lawrence-Lightfoot (1978) also studied systemic problems related to families and schools. She addressed the inherent tensions that exist between families and schools as a result of cultural differences and lack of clear role boundaries. Around the same time, Urie Bronfenbrenner (1979, 1992) introduced an ecological systems theory to explain how children interact within their social environments. He identified five levels of external influence (microsystem, mesosystem, exosystem, macrosystem, and chronosystem) to explain the overlapping contexts in which children live. Bronfenbrenner, along with family systems theorists, not only viewed children as part of a system or ecological environment, but also as unique developing systems in their own right. As children grow up, their cognitive, emotional, social, and physical capabilities evolve, and these changes impact how they relate to others around them. Our expectations of children change as a result. For example, at certain ages, if children can't identify letters of the alphabet or understand another person's perspective, it negatively impacts their ability to thrive within their environment. There is no question that children's development, never removed from context or circumstance, is often a central factor that explains, at least in some measure, why they might be sitting in your office.

As systems theory took root in therapeutic practice, clinicians and researchers at the Ackerman Institute for the Family joined with the New York public school system to develop a model for creating partnerships between families and schools (Weiss & Edwards, 1992). They developed two types of interventions. First, Ackerman therapists developed a format for conducting more productive "family problem-solving meetings" by including both parents and the child as full members of the family–school team. Second, Ackerman therapists worked with public school teachers to revamp routine parent-teacher conferences to insure that the child was an active participant. These were termed "family–school conferences." With the child in the room alongside the teacher and parent(s), children could take greater responsibility for their learning and gain skills in self-advocacy. The Ackerman team discovered that the overall quality of the conversation between the family and school increased. By the early 1990s, Ackerman's well-trained clinicians were working in over 50 schools in New York.

Around the same time, Joyce Epstein and her associates (1987, 1992, 2001, 2009/2018) embarked on years of research and practice to find ways to assist families, schools, districts, and communities in creating sustainable programs and partnerships. By the 2009 publication of her volume *School, Family, and Community Partnerships: Your Handbook for Action*, there were over a thousand schools in 21 states that were actively involved in the National Network of Partnership Schools at Johns Hopkins University working in support of this effort. Similarly, Christenson and Sheridan's edited *Handbook of School-Family Partnerships* (2001) contributed to our understanding of the effect of family–school partnerships on school achievement. Their contributions fostered research and policy initiatives in support of evidence-based practices that help to sustain partnerships between families and schools. Correspondingly, Sheridan and Reschly (2010) researched practices that strengthen family–school bonds, especially when applied to diverse populations. The extensive research and practice of all of these researchers and clinicians has advanced our understanding of how families, schools, and communities can work together to support the education of all children.

Fundamental to all of this is a child's sense of place and self. Everything about a school—its teachers, administrators, support staff, classrooms, facilities, and general location—converges to create a message about who one is within that world. Kids who feel confident about themselves as students tend to get the message that they're respected by the school community and that they belong to it—a fundamental human desire (Baumeister & Leary, 1995). To belong to a place that's bigger than yourself (and that isn't your own family) is an important part of finding your way in the world. Kids might feel that they mostly belong to their families, but for some, problems at home can make school a safer place, with ties that are stronger, fairer, and less complicated. The luckiest kids feel that they belong to both worlds and that these worlds are relatively harmonious and overlap in significant ways. Kids who are especially vulnerable don't feel they belong to either world.

These insights and contributions can help to show today's therapists how to consider the wider circle of influence beyond the child—where kids fit in among their peers, how teachers view them, the culture of the school in relation to the family's values, and more. Without considering these wider-optic contexts, educators and therapists might fail to see the contributing factors to a child's problems, and thus limit the range of possible interventions and solutions that would follow. Though widening the lens necessarily adds enormous complexity to the issue, the therapeutic challenge is for us to not only try to make sense of this complexity but also to consider it an essential part of the work we do.

The Role of the Therapist

So where do we, as therapists, fit in? Therapists are uniquely positioned to help foster a successful child-family–school dynamic. We are trained to ask probing questions, including about kids' relationships with their family, teachers, and friends. We know how to engage and connect with people who need help. We know how to build on a child's and family's strengths and resources and look for the goodwill present in most situations. We know the value of persistence and how an intervention today can lead to lasting change down the road. We can connect the purpose and goals of therapy with the purpose and goals of a child's education. If, in addition to these clinical skills, you learn how to work well with schools, you will be able to assess and treat a child's problems even more effectively. As one experienced therapist said, "With schools, we do what we already do with children and families. There are just more people in the room."

By working directly with schools, therapists are better able to understand how school is a key context in their clients' lives: a space that can shape children's sense of efficacy and worth, a place where they face the challenges of "learning to learn," and a social world where they interact with peers and adults who are not their parents. Through observations, assessments, conversations, and meetings, therapists can begin to "see" the child at school—what motivates and excites him, what interferes with his learning, how he gets along with his classmates, what "a day in the life" is like, what his teachers are like, who's advocating for him, what frustrations he encounters and why, and much more. By working with the school, therapists can broaden the conversation about a child, which can greatly enhance the therapeutic work.

All of the school personnel interviewed for this book spoke of the value of working with outside professionals who are skilled at collaboration. One psychologist at a large, suburban public school raved about his work with a therapist who, he said, begins every conversation with the words, "How can I be helpful to you?" A school social worker in a midsized school district said that a therapist with whom she works "never fails to make the connection between the family and the school." The principal of an alternative high school spoke enthusiastically about one therapist who, he exclaimed, is a constant "team player." A school psychologist who works in a school for kids with special needs said, "Some therapists understand the impact of their client on the school system. That makes such a difference." And one experienced public elementary school teacher asserted that she "welcomes the opportunity to work with a third party who is less emotionally involved." Such accounts go on and on. Working independently, therapists and schools are necessarily limited in their knowledge and abilities, but when they collaborate, some of those limitations can be overcome.

Structure of This Book

This book is broadly divided into four main parts. The first part (Chapters 1–4) provides therapists with the basic building blocks for working effectively with schools, by introducing them to the world of schools and their role in relation to them, including how to conduct school-focused therapy sessions. The second part (Chapters 5–8) lays out what therapists actually do when working with schools, including the ins and outs of school observations; best practices for attending family–school meetings; and how to review homework, testing results, and other relevant data. These chapters examine the why, how, and who of reaching out, illustrating how to establish collaborative and productive relationships. The third part (Chapters 9–10) reviews specific challenges that a therapist may encounter, and how to respond to them constructively. Common problems like anxiety, blaming, and so forth are covered, as well as more complicated situations like racism, natural disasters, and other crises. The final part (Chapters 11–12) reviews how parents can better advocate for their children and what the therapist needs to know about helping them navigate school systems and special education services. The Conclusion (Chapter 13) provides ways that therapists can explore new opportunities working with schools.

Terminology, Focus, and the Use of Case Material

This book is clinical in nature and written for mental health professionals of all theoretical backgrounds who work with school-age children. It is family oriented, strength based, and assumes that, when it comes to kids, forming collaborative relationships with others who know and work with the child—especially in schools—is an essential part of providing the best standard of care.

The term *therapist* is used to capture the broadest possible range of mental health professionals, though I occasionally use the terms *clinician, behavioral specialist,* or *practitioner* as well. I have also chosen to use the term *client* rather than *patient,* reflecting a broader, nonmedical approach to working with kids. The word *child or children* is used to refer to those who are 18 years of age and younger.

In this book, the word *family* rather than *parent* is deliberately employed to use the broadest possible term for describing the potentially wide array of people in a child's life. This may include one or more parents, extended family members (e.g., siblings, grandparents, aunts, uncles, or cousins), as well as those people who function as nonbiological or adoptive family members, such as caretakers or very close friends. By doing so, I give recognition to the fact that many children are raised by people other than their biological or adoptive parents. Sometimes, I have explicitly chosen to use the term *parent* in reference to the person (or persons) who is *most* responsible for the child. This person may or may not be related to the child biologically. The chapter on parental advocacy (Chapter 11), for example, assumes that the person advocating for the child is whomever assumes the most responsibility or has legal responsibility for the child.

When speaking about *public schools,* this includes magnet and charter schools as well. The terms *private, independent,* and *nonpublic* schools are used interchangeably, depending on context. For the most part, I have chosen to use the term *student support team* to represent those professionals who together support kids' adjustment at school; it covers *behavioral* support teams, *multidisciplinary* teams, *instructional* support teams, *student study* teams, and others.

Throughout this volume, to protect anonymity, all case examples are composites drawn from multiple sources, and all children's names are pseudonyms to protect confidentiality.

Many problems kids have at school are the result of complex societal problems—parental mental illness, trauma, poverty, racism, and inequality. While these are acknowledged as serious issues (see Chapter 10), they are complex and far-reaching and not the major focus of this book. Similarly, though recognized as profoundly problematic, I've not proposed specific solutions to the large systemic issues that plague many schools (such as inadequate funding, racial discrimination, teacher turnover, and poor building maintenance). Neither have I focused on specific childhood disorders (such as ADHD or other learning disabilities) and the common clinical interventions used to treat them (such as cognitive behavioral therapy, family therapy, attachment based therapy, etc.). Rather, my focus is on providing a general framework that will help you become more aware of the role you can play in the complex, ever-shifting child-family–school dynamic, no matter the type of school or the nature of the child's problem.

Ultimately, it is my hope that this book will serve a number of purposes:

- Expand the dialogue between educators and mental health professionals who work outside the school.

- Offer a practical resource for therapists to use when assessing when and how to reach out to schools.

- Build on our knowledge of the child-family–school dynamic and the role therapists can play when working at this intersection.

- Inspire therapists to have greater interest in schools and how they work.

- Provide therapists with the skills and confidence needed to work with school personnel in support of vulnerable kids.

- Strengthen the reliable networks available to kids who have school problems and to the families who are trying to support them.

"We've Tried That Before and It Didn't Work": A Call to Action

Early in my tenure at the Pre-K–12 Quaker school, where I worked as a consultant, I was blown away by the enterprising faculty and staff who knew no limits when it came to helping kids. In one instance, I was sitting at a table with a division director, the dean of students, a learning specialist, and an advisor, discussing what to do about a student's persistent problem keeping his aggressive behavior in check. This was no small matter, since many interventions had been tried already. Under a cloud of collective discouragement, the new dean of students began to propose ideas to which one or another of us would, in some variation, say: "We tried that before and it didn't work." No matter how often we declined her suggestions, she simply went on to the next idea in the spirit of, "Okay, so that didn't work, what about this idea?" I had never seen anything like it. The goodwill that was created by the sheer force of her commitment and the quantity of her ideas drew us all in. We finally agreed to try an intervention that was, if I remember correctly, effective.

"We've tried that before and it didn't work," is a common refrain when dealing with children's persistent school problems. It is echoed in our offices as well as in meetings at schools. Once spoken, we may feel frustrated if not immobilized, whether the refrain comes from our own mouths or others. But thanks to the enterprising dean, I learned to see this statement as a place from which to take off, rather than a place to stall or quit. Because of her persistence, we were forced to look at the child's problem in an even more nuanced way—at all his unique qualities, the classroom culture, the family relationships, the variability of his behavior in different settings, and more. In that conversation, it became clear that the oh-so-common refrain reflects something vital in our work with kids: it shows how fierce our commitment is to helping vulnerable kids (even if some efforts are unsuccessful). It also shows that the better we understand the overlapping spheres of influence that impact a child's life, the better are the solutions we can formulate. Remembering this reality can be a source of profound inspiration even in the most trying times.

Though there is no substitute for your own experience, my hope is that this book will provide you with the resources and confidence necessary to be similarly emboldened rather than discouraged when hearing, "We've tried that before and it didn't work." I encourage you to recognize it as evidence of the galvanizing good that has come before and as a call to approach the problem with a sense of discovery and conviction that can expand your engagement with your community.

PART I

The Basic
Building Blocks

CHAPTER 1

What Therapists Need to Know About Schools

When I ask educators and student support staff, "What should outside therapists know in order to work more effectively with your school?" one of the most common responses I hear is that therapists need to know more about schools in general—how they work, what makes one school different from another, and so on.

What exactly does it mean to heed this advice? We all went to school for at least 12 years, and more if you include pre-K or nursery school, kindergarten, and higher education. Doesn't this fact afford us the knowledge and credentials we need to work with schools in our role as therapists? Aren't our personal experiences and the bits and pieces we glean from the news, our colleagues, or our own children's experiences enough?

While it's true that we all know something about what it means to go to school, every school has its own unique culture and cast of characters, from the teachers, principal, and guidance counselor, to the social worker, psychologist, occupational therapist, and other support staff. School type and socioeconomic context also matter a great deal; school quality and culture vary enormously by differences in demographics, district funding, personnel, resources, maintenance, parental involvement, organizational structure, and more. Therapists who take the time to learn about these differences in culture and pedagogy will have a distinct advantage in making recommendations for kids, enlisting school-based support, strengthening the relationship between the family and school, and knowing how to participate effectively in collaborative relationships. In turn, these relationships help us provide more comprehensive and effective care to children and families.

Discovering Your Own Biases

Part of learning more about schools requires reflecting on some of the things you already believe to be true about them based upon your own experiences. Most of us can remember something of what it was like to walk down a school hall-way, facing a crowd of peers and teachers. We know what it's like to sit at a desk, to dreamily stare out the window, to grapple with a devious math problem. We can call to mind what it felt like to admire or dislike a teacher or to have heart-pounding moments as we waited for important test results. In addition to what we learned in school academically, we are deeply imprinted psychologically by our own experiences as students.

For better or worse, we judge schools partly or primarily on the basis of this imprinting. As therapists, we are also at least intellectually aware that our own singular experiences do not tell the whole story. We are trained to see that ours is not an objective perspective but rather a quite narrow and individualistic one. We hope we come to know ourselves well enough to wrangle with those moments in sessions when we recognize that we're speaking from the confines of a bias or belief, failing to see a wider world.

However rigorous our course work and clinical training, most likely it didn't include a comparably hard look at our biases and beliefs about schools. As a result, most therapists have not stopped to ask what backpack of beliefs and biases they carry with them when working with children and families in this con-text. Sometimes, we might notice that we react with negative or positive biases toward schools that are very different from our own experiences, based on their size, resources, and other factors. We may see things that make us uncomfortable, as well as qualities of schools that suit us well. Kahneman (2013) termed this the "availability heuristic," referring to the mental shortcut we take when we evaluate an issue based on the immediate examples that come quickly to mind in compa-rable situations. As a way to begin to reflect on this further, consider some ques-tions that are designed to help you understand your underlying beliefs and biases about schools. (See Box 1.1)

Box 1.1: Questions to consider concerning your experience and biases about schools

1. How did you emerge from your educational experience: feeling affirmed, nurtured, injured, ignored, taught effectively, or some combination of the above and more?

2. When you think about your education, what were the most important things you learned over the years about the subjects, the world, yourself, or others?

3. Picture yourself in your elementary, middle, and secondary schools. Describe the first images that come to mind. What do they represent about your schooling? Your family of origin? Your current beliefs about school today?

4. If you are thinking about your own children, what aspects of your school experience would you like them to experience? Not experience?

5. Think of a teacher who influenced you positively or negatively. What stands out about those experiences? What would you want to say to those teachers at this point in your life and why?

6. Reflect on the last case you had with a child who had problems at school. What do you remember thinking about the school the child was attending? Did your thoughts about the school precede the child's or family's experience, derive from it, or both? Given what you thought about the school, how might that influence whether you would reach out to the school or talk to the family about the school? How might that influence the interventions you recommend?

Examining a School's Reputation

If you've been working in one geographical area for a while, you're likely to be familiar with the school a child attends. As time goes on, it's easy to assume that you know the differences among that area's schools, yet part of our job as therapists is to learn about each particular child's experience in the classroom and in the school as a whole. It's also possible that you're completely unfamiliar with the school and therefore bring few if any preconceived notions to the conversation.

Those who work in schools are aware of their school's reputation, for better or worse. Some know what it's like to have their school characterized in a way that doesn't fit their lived reality. One teacher said that the independent school in which she teaches is often described as "unstructured" when, in fact, the structure is simply different in design from its neighboring public school. An urban magnet school is widely criticized for having "too much homework," when, compared to schools similar in size, socioeconomic status, and student body, its homework demands are identical and in some grades less than in other schools. In yet another case, over the course of a decade, a small, suburban public school was first considered "soft on bullies" and then "rigid and unforgiving" after a student was expelled for threatening another student. And haven't we all heard such comments as, "Kids in that school are cliquey, mean, elitist, or violent" or "Teachers in that school are incompetent, don't care, yell at the kids, or don't set limits"?

Schools' reputations rise and fall and grow and contract for any number of reasons. In some cases, reputations stick even when a school has made significant changes. Like everyone else, therapists can slip into oversimplifications based on hearsay instead of standing back and making their own determinations. To go one step further, therapists can also be guilty of adding to an inaccurate portrait of a school by subscribing to a common view of a school's reputation that's been left unexamined.

It's often true that negative reputations and rumors travel faster and carry greater weight than positive ones, but all reputations must be subject to the same scrutiny we apply to generalizations that are made about the children and families we treat. A therapist who has spent much of her career working as a school psychologist and also as a private clinician said, "It's not that you can't come to know a school well. You can, but only with time and a lot of care."

Given how reputations are formed and maintained, it is important for therapists to step back and use their own skills to learn more about a school. This knowledge can come indirectly from children and families or from colleagues who have a history of working closely with the school. In such cases, you are learning about the school from others and will understand the information as such. You can also learn about the school by contacting school personnel directly or, better yet, from actually visiting the school to observe a child in the classroom, assessing for yourself what the teacher and other students are like. The first step, though, is to ask the child and parents you see to talk about their experience in the school: what they've learned, what has worked for the child and what hasn't worked, and what they think *you* need to know. Keep in mind that, as one school principal said, "School is not a generic thing. It is a very personalized experience for every child." School is the child's experience in the classroom and hallways and lunchroom every day. Additionally, children's experience of any school is mediated by attributes they and their families bring to the school (e.g., attitudes, behaviors, expectations).

Understanding a School's Culture, Rules, and Expectations

More important than understanding a school's reputation is learning about and understanding its culture and the rules and expectations that are embedded in it.

At the macro level, school culture partially derives from school type. As of 2016, roughly 90% of children attend public schools—including magnet, special education, vocational, and charter schools (U.S. Department of Education, 2016). Even so, there is a significant population of students who attend private, parochial, private special education, and faith-based schools, or who are homeschooled (a growing population, yet outside the scope of this book). The vast majority of schools divide children into formal developmental stages or educational levels: early childhood, primary or elementary, middle or junior high, secondary, and higher education. Different types of schools have different pedagogical approaches. They might have different classroom models, disciplinary tactics, levels of formality between students and teachers, and uses of testing as a means of assessing a child's progress (see Appendix A for further details on school types and pedagogies). All of these factors may impact the culture of the school with which you work.

Nonetheless, every school has its own unique culture that may manifest in different ways despite broad similarities (e.g., buildings, teachers, administrative personnel, classrooms). For example, a Roman Catholic school in one part of town may be quite different from another Roman Catholic school only a mile away. These distinctions likely relate to socioeconomic, ethnic, racial, and regional differences, but also to particular features of the school such as its personnel, history, relationship to the larger community, expectations of parents, and so on. From your vantage point as a therapist who works outside the school, you might not be able to discern many of these distinctions, but you can learn to distinguish certain key components of a school's culture. These include its rules, organization, reputation, and expectations in addition to the ways school personnel relate to families.

All schools have rules and expectations for students, teachers, administrators, staff, and even parents. Though applied variously, some rules are explicit, fixed, and accessible for perusal, such as the legal guidelines for receiving special education services or what constitutes harassment or bullying (Jacob, Decker, & Lugg, 2016). Other rules and expectations are more implicit and informal, reflecting the particular school culture, such as whether kids are expected to greet visitors in the hallway or how they are expected to address their teachers. Such expectations and practices may not be overtly explained or taught; they have developed over time and become consolidated as everyday norms. Some of what's most striking about a school relates to these less explicit rules and expectations and can help explain what brings a school to life or leaves it constrained. Therapists will do well trying to understand both the explicit and implicit rules and expectations in order to fully grasp the child's experience at school. One thing therapists need to know is that kids (or families) often don't know or understand the implicit or explicit rules of the school or the teachers' expectations. Kids, especially the kids we see in treatment, can miss the subtle cues and behaviors exhibited and understood by others that reflect the written and unwritten rules of the school.

Sometimes, rules are inadequately explained, and when kids bump into them there is friction that can convert to skepticism or mistrust. Sometimes, when the rules are pointed out, kids find them annoying or offensive. People working inside schools can also be confused about the rules or not fully align with them, causing further disruptions and misunderstandings. In addition, kids or their parents might disagree with the school's rules and expectations or see them as arbitrary and rigid or too soft and inconsistently applied. It's important to note that school rules are rarely arbitrary, even if they can sometimes appear rigid or poorly defined. When working with kids who clash with people in positions of authority, seek to clarify the school's rules and how to work within them. Kids' oppositional behaviors are often rooted in a sense of hopelessness they feel themselves or that others feel about them (Brooks & Goldstein, 2009). In these cases, explore interventions that reinforce the student's self-efficacy and empowerment and that the school can help develop and maintain. Sometimes, it's simply enough to clarify expectations held by the student, parents, and school.

The case of Grace, a high school freshman at a small public high school, is a good example of the importance of understanding a school's rules. Grace had been in therapy off and on for years, given her family and behavior problems, though her problems at school never rose to the level of needing special education services. As her freshman year began, there was general concern that Grace might not be able to manage the workload, resulting in negative educational consequences. By October, when the list of unfinished work piled up, coupled with several incidents in which she was late to class, Grace's advisor contacted the family and her therapist to set up a meeting at school.

What soon became clear in the meeting was that adjustments that had been established in Grace's middle school were no longer workable given the rules and expectations of the high school. Grace's parents were angry and demanded that certain expectations regarding homework be changed so that Grace could substantially reduce her workload. When the principal stepped in to demarcate the limits of what could be done to support Grace in that setting, the conversation broke down. Only then did the therapist realize that neither she nor Grace's parents had adequately checked out the school's homework expectations prior to the meeting; doing so perhaps could have prevented the meeting's discord. Later, the therapist had a chance to help Grace's parents see that fighting that particular battle wouldn't serve their daughter well. Instead, the therapist worked with

Grace's homeroom teacher, school counselor, and Grace herself to devise a plan for how to maximize the time she had free during the day, including periods when she could meet with her teachers.

When relevant, it can sometimes make a big difference to a parent or a child to hear about school policies, including those that address issues of academic expectations, detention, suspension or bullying. Sometimes, clarifying the reasons why the policies were established and what purposes they serve can cut through a thicket of problems. Therapists can help facilitate the explication of rules and policies in family–school meetings or in other conversations with school representatives. They can also be helpful by encouraging parents to stay attuned to the school's rules and expectations and how they are being applied in a given circumstance. In addition, many public schools have special programs that address expectations for kids' behavior. Discovering the limitations of what a school is able or willing to do can sometimes lead parents and older kids to take a strong advocacy role, a topic to be discussed in Chapter 11.

Each school also has expectations of parents: whether and how they'll be involved with their child's homework, school meetings and activities; what it means to be a member of the school community; and how wide and deep that community is. Though the mandate has been clear for decades—schools should promote family involvement and engagement—schools vary in how well they do this. The expectation that schools must reach out and connect with families corresponds with research that has documented the positive impact of family involvement in schools for kids with disabilities (Lines, Miller, & Arthur-Stanley, 2011), for school achievement and behavior (Patrikakou & Weissberg, 2001), and for the scope of services available to children (Clarke, Sheridan, & Woods, 2010). We know that family–school partnerships and parent engagement and involvement in schools make a difference in the lives of kids, families and school personnel. As therapists working with kids with school problems, we can pay attention to the ways school personnel interact with families (and us) to better understand their expectations. It's wise to refrain from drawing conclusions prematurely, but it's important to be aware that the quality and types of relationships school personnel form with families are relevant factors in how kids adapt and perform at school.

Learning About a School's Organization

All schools are organizations that have a structure of accountability for all personnel. This is true for even the most egalitarian, parent-cooperative schools. Each school has a built-in hierarchy of roles and offices that determine the work each person is supposed to do. Typically, public schools have a hierarchical structure that's replicated across many schools in a district, since divisions of function and purpose are necessary for handling large numbers of students. Regardless of the type of school, the strictness of the school's hierarchical and power structure varies and is another factor to consider when working with schools.

School flow charts reveal the level and direction of responsibility, much as in business or other noneducational organizations. That said, as therapists we are unlikely to be privy to a particular school's administrative flow chart. Even so, we can and should think of the school as a system with component parts that are organized in a way that makes sense of the diverse demands of the entire system. Being even somewhat familiar with a school's structure can be helpful in our work with a school or the guidance we give to a family.

The division of responsibility in a school as outlined in its flow chart may not necessarily be the one operating in practice. For example, a small public elementary school in an urban district brought in a newly minted principal every three to four years, as it served as a kind of launching pad for these individuals' careers. As a result, a highly competent school counselor who worked at the school for decades was the go-to person for all manner of problems and advice. Some dimensions of a school system structure may remain inherently complicated. Take, for example, the role of the school psychologist who works in a public school. She reports to the school principal but also to her supervisor at the district level; at times this leads to tension or conflict as well as opportunities for valuable collaboration and reexamination of issues.

Teachers are at the center of the child's experience

Many of us have heard our friends or family members say something to the effect, "If it hadn't been for x teacher, I would never have (select one or more of the following): graduated from high school; chosen my professional field; made it through middle school; survived my family life; sought the help I needed; believed in myself enough to try harder; known I could learn to do math." We also have heard stories of kids being derailed by a particular teacher or set of teachers. The influence teachers have over the lives of children (and children over the lives of their teachers) is enormous. Yet, we may lose sight of this reality when we are working with kids who have problems at school. There are several ideas to keep in mind when reflecting on and working with teachers.

First and foremost, teachers are the ones who most often know the child best, and often it is the teacher who is the first person the therapist will contact in the school, especially for younger children. The very fact that teachers spend roughly 35 hours a week with children in elementary school, in contrast to a therapist's typical 1 hour a week in office sessions, illuminates something of the impact teachers can and do have on a child.

Second, because teachers observe children with other children where common demands are placed on their time and attention, teachers have an important perspective to offer based on the comparisons they make among all the children in their classrooms. In fact, experienced teachers develop a keen sense of what is normative for a particular age and stage of development and, therefore, how and where a particular child fits into that spectrum. Therapists can benefit from this wisdom by asking the teacher questions about how a particular child is doing in relation to other students.

Third, the vast majority of teachers care deeply about the students they teach and their work as educators. Consider the comment by a teacher after the school shooting in Parkland, Florida: "We do, as teachers, everything that we possibly can to help these children, we truly do" (Craig, Brown, Larimer, & Balingit, 2018). Not only is the teacher's caring communicated in that statement, but the pathos and pain as well. Reflecting her dedication to her students, an art teacher in a large suburban high school said, "You have to have strategies, to have them like you and you have to try to like them. If you lock horns with a mean kid, even if you have good intentions and a lot to offer, you're at risk of getting into a ditch that's hard to get out of. It's not easy being a teacher."

As professionals, teachers do not always receive the respect and credit that is their due. Of course, there are legitimate complaints about teachers as there are about all professionals, including therapists. However, it's worth looking at the context in which teachers often work. Concerns range from low salaries, lack of safety for kids and themselves, poor working conditions, lack of parental involvement, too much emphasis on testing, and lack of professional status. Some of these contextual factors will be at play in your work with teachers.

Fourth, as the head of a private school stated, "Teachers' responsibilities are diffuse and complex, based on a different matrix of priorities and demands." They must attend to many individual children and to the successful functioning of the class as a whole. They also assume responsibility for the way students in their class interact with other students and faculty in the school at large. Most teachers also establish relationships with parents of the children they teach and with other faculty members, administrators, and student support staff. In that swirl of activity and set of responsibilities, teachers are also expected to work with outside professionals like us who bring our own expectations to the relationship.

Fifth, for teachers, there's a lot of variability in the job. "There's a semester where there's good chemistry in the class and another semester that doesn't work as well . . . each class has its own personality," an art teacher stated. Teachers' own lives vary as well. A teacher whose father was ill spoke about her diminished ability to connect with the students during that rough year of anguish and the additional family-related responsibilities she had to absorb. Several teachers spoke about the impact on their teaching during major national and international crises or events. Local community problems or tensions within a school can affect how teachers teach as well. Personnel in a school can shift and there can be "lag time," as one teacher said, "as the culture shifts with new leadership or until the newbie 'catches' the school culture."

Sixth, a big factor in how kids do in school relates to the *fit* between teacher and child. Some teachers, for instance, work more effectively with kids diagnosed with attention deficit hyperactivity disorder (ADHD), while others may not. There are kids who thrive in classrooms with strict teachers and other kids who wilt under the perceived pressure of following rules and expectations they feel they can't meet. Sometimes, a child's placement with the right teacher can make all the difference in the world to the child's success or failure.

Finally, forming a relationship with a particular teacher who shares the same concern about a child as you can be a deeply rewarding dimension of your work. Through conversations and school visits, therapists can get to know teachers and the educational opportunities they provide, thereby enriching the therapist's own professional world while finding ways to support a child who is struggling.

What teachers want you to know

Teachers with whom I spoke had consistent stories to tell and advice to offer therapists working with schools. Many of these ideas will be expanded on in later chapters, but it's worth being introduced to the most essential ideas as you begin to think about working closely with your clients' teachers. The following is a list of 10 common themes that arose again and again in conversations with teachers:

1. **Make an effort to speak directly to the teacher.** This depends on school policy and the family's preferences. Solicit their opinions to find out what's working and what's not, and engage in give and take.

2. **Generate concrete, specific, pragmatic recommendations.** These should correspond to the context of that classroom and school and are best made in collaboration with the teacher or student support staff. When making suggestions, ask what's possible. Be flexible when an intervention doesn't work.

3. **Communicate regularly and always follow up.** Be prompt and

specific about how and when to reach you. If you say you're going to do something, do it or let the teacher know why not.

4. **Do not wait for a problem to emerge.** Reach out early in the year to see how the child is doing, and keep lines of communication open. Encourage teachers to let you know early on if things are becoming more problematic for the child.

5. **Respect teachers' time as well as the reality and constraints of the situation in which they work.** Be aware of the differences in pace between work in your office and life at school.

6. **Make a sincere effort to learn about the school.** Learn its philosophy, expectations, rules, and culture. Explore the specific roles people have in the school as well as in the child's life.

7. **Recognize and acknowledge differences in how things work depending on the setting.** A plan that works in one setting—at home, in your office, or at school—may not work in another. Recognize and acknowledge that the teacher's situation differs from the therapist's. If possible, observe the child in the classroom.

8. **Be an advocate for the child without being adversarial.** When needed, help the family advocate for the child and the child advocate for him or herself.

9. **Be available in a crisis.** When kids' problems become severe, it is important for therapists to be available to coordinate interventions with relevant school personnel.

10. **Help parents strengthen their ties with the teacher and others in the school.** When tension or conflict exists between teachers and parents, look for opportunities to find common ground.

In certain cases, these themes emerged in response to negative experiences teachers had with therapists even as therapists sought to achieve similar goals in support of a child. Some teachers felt criticized or analyzed by therapists, or that the therapists "acted as a mouthpiece for the parents," undermining the relationship between the teacher and the family and child. Some felt that therapists cast them as "the villains in the kids' life." Incorporating guidance offered above can support your efforts to build relationships with teachers and the school.

Student support staff: Helping kids adjust

Except in small or severely underresourced schools, there are school personnel whose job it is to identify and find ways to support children's adjustment, and they are often people with whom you'll connect. They are called by various names: student support teams, student therapeutic services, student behavioral teams, and others. For the most part, they consist of familiar players: the school psychologist, school counselor, school social worker, learning specialists (math, reading, science, etc.), occupational and physical therapists, home-school liaisons, and so on (see Appendix B). Each has a prescribed role, though how those roles are carried out may vary by district and school).

One social worker in an urban public school spoke about a student who had suffered multiple traumas and was being treated by a therapist in a local children's clinic. After collaborating closely with the child, therapist, and foster family for most of the year, the social worker was encouraging the child to view key people at school as emotional resources. As part of the process, the therapist came to the school on several occasions to meet with the child, the school social worker, the parent engagement liaison, and various teachers in an effort to create a system by which the child could find a *safe space* at school when she was feeling sad and overwhelmed. Upon successful completion of this transition, the school social worker said, "The kid was so excited because the therapist was so collaborative. [The child] could see that someone else would be taking on the mantle and the kid would be okay and the therapist made that happen. The therapist gave her social capital to us!"

When you consider reaching out to schools, in addition to thinking about teachers, keep in mind that there will likely be a student support team or the equivalent whose job it is to identify and support those students who are struggling with behavioral, medical, emotional, academic, or other problems that interfere with their learning and success at school. Seventy-one percent of high schools nationwide had student support teams in 2014–2015 (U.S. Department of Education, 2017). Members of the support teams work collaboratively within the school and are oriented toward solving problems. Team members are often the school representatives with whom you will work and who will be present for family–school meetings. Make sure that you check in with the family and child about the school's support team in order to gauge your involvement with them.

The rhythm of the school year

Schools operate on academic calendars, as do the children whose school problems are brought to our attention. We're all intimately aware of a school calendar from our own experience as students, but we're not necessarily aware of what sort of rhythm and pressures the school calendar places on those who work in schools. One thing to keep in mind is how the child's situation is embedded in the roughly ten months' flow of events in the life of the school. How might this awareness affect your work with children and families?

Take the example of a middle school student who is new to the school and hasn't had experience taking midterm exams. Neither the parent nor child is familiar with what it means to adequately prepare for what will be a grueling experience for the child, given his significant learning disabilities. The parents ask their son's therapist when and how to reach out to the school for information about the exams and how best to prepare for them. In this case, the advisor at school was disheartened to hear from the therapist the week before exams were scheduled; her suggestions couldn't be reliably followed in such an abbreviated time period. In another instance, the teacher just scratched her head when a therapist contacted her immediately before an extended holiday when extra pressures made it difficult for the teacher to respond promptly if at all.

Another calendar-related issue relates to therapists who work with a child from one academic year to the next. In these cases, the therapist will want to be in touch with the school in the fall, renewing permission from the family and ensuring that the new teacher(s) and student support team are informed of the therapist's work with the child. Each fall, not only will the students likely have a new teacher or crew of people with whom they're involved but also they may change divisions or even schools. If they enter a different school they will encounter a different school structure, culture, and resulting educational expectations.

Parents are obliged to operate according to the school schedule and calendar as well, which can be a challenge given their work schedules or family demands. Then there's the issue of the speed with which parents engage the school with a problem or concern, another time-related factor. For instance, some parents need to learn how to either slow down or speed things up when it comes to their involvement with their child's school. One therapist spoke about parents who, "sit back and seethe". They may call the therapist or the teacher after they are already deeply distressed or furious, which could have been avoided had they been more active earlier on. Other parents may react to just about everything they see that causes them concern. In these instances, parents need to learn how to slow down, gather their thoughts, and determine positive, timely ways to contact the school.

Therapists are in a unique position to help parents gauge the timing of calls or emails and advise them whether to hold off or to step in. This again is something that needs to be determined case by case, school by school, even teacher by teacher, keeping in mind the arc of the academic year. By actively working with parents to assess the advisable level and type of engagement with the school, therapists can provide an educative function, helping parents increase their awareness of the impact their involvement has on the teacher and the school, for better or worse.

Therapists will do well to be aware of different timelines as they relate to the child. In addition to school schedules for children, there are parent agendas and timelines that matter. The parent role may vary based on whether it is taken by a parent, an extended family member, a friend, or whoever. Therapists have schedules and timelines, too, even lives of their own! And, often such timelines create competing demands. By being aware of the timeline of the school year, the therapist will be able to better navigate the challenges a school calendar creates.

What Schools Might Not Know About Therapists and Therapy

It may not be obvious to teachers, administrators, and school staff that therapists often work with kids directly around what's happening at school. In other words, when kids have school problems and parents seek outside help, most likely, school problems are what's being discussed in the therapist's office. What may seem obvious to us may not be obvious to those who work in schools. Perhaps this is a result of the strict rules of confidentiality surrounding the therapeutic relationship, or because therapy is thought of, for good reason, as happening behind closed doors, both literally and figuratively. It's not that people in schools don't see the value of therapy, because schools are often the source of referrals. But rather the assumption may be made that, by referring the child to therapy, the child will improve; the child will become less anxious, more productive, better behaved, and so on. As the child improves, it is assumed, those psychological gains will translate to enhanced performance and better adjustment in school.

On a day-to-day basis, teachers and others in schools are probably not thinking about the child's therapy. They are thinking about how to instruct, support, and engage the child at school. What therapists need to know is that teachers and others in schools will benefit greatly from learning about the direct connection between the work in the classroom and the therapy in which the child and family are engaged. Therefore, as a therapist, it's important to be explicit in describing the therapeutic work so that those at school can understand and make the connection. For example, the therapist might say, "Grayson and I are working on ways that he can manage his afterschool time better since I know he's been late at getting his homework in" or "Since Sheila thinks that her teachers don't like her, we're working on how she can examine this belief based on a kind of therapy that looks at how our thinking impacts our actions and feelings."

Therapists can work across the divide by letting teachers and others know that if the child's problem is happening at school, therapy will focus on the child's school life. This will be an enormous help in setting up a direct link between what's taking place in the therapy office and what's happening at school. "It's one line of connection," an experienced former teacher and learning specialist said. As therapists, we are looking for these lines of connection with those who are part of the child's life, especially the family and the school.

REVIEWING THE BASICS

Through training and experience, therapists know a lot about children and families. What we haven't typically learned is how schools work, how to access and evaluate information about how kids are doing in that setting, and how to maximize the potential to support vulnerable kids by collaborating closely with those who teach and work in schools. To review:

- Try to unpack your own beliefs and potential biases about schools in order to widen the lens you use to understand your clients' own particular school environments.

- Every school has a different culture, reputation, organization, and set of explicit and implicit rules and expectations. It's important to try and understand the different nuances of the schools in your area.

- Teachers are often among the most important people in your clients' lives, and often the first people with whom you'll work at a given school. It's worth taking time to figure out what works and what doesn't when collaborating with them.

- Members of the student support team are also key people you'll likely work with after contacting a school.

- Remember that schools have particular rhythms and schedules, and try to keep this in mind when you reach out and plan interventions.

- Let teachers know that the therapy you're doing in your office will often be directly related to the problems the kids are exhibiting at school.

CHAPTER 2

Conducting School-Savvy Sessions

Parents reach out to therapists about problems with their children for all sorts of reasons: a child is complaining about stomachaches, overwhelmed with work, or engaged in activities that are risky or downright dangerous. But no matter what the problem is or who brings the child to your office, it's necessary to know something about how the child is doing at school. School-related problems may manifest as defiance at home, and problems at home may result in the refusal to go to school. Regardless of the root of the problem, knowledge of the child's school life is crucial for understanding the child as a whole and how the child is faring in his or her world. Even if the child is, by all reports, doing fine in school, this is important and useful information to gather.

Whether a child is referred to you by a teacher or school counselor or from another referral source, this chapter will provide some of the tools to help guide your inquiry into a child's life at school. This is a fundamental part of the initial assessment process, even when school issues are not the primary focus. Since all therapists are trained in how to conduct first sessions, we'll focus primarily on how to understand the child's life *at school*, rather than how to conduct initial sessions more generally.

First Contact with the Family

Therapeutic relationships begin when a parent contacts you. From the outset, it is important to try to understand why the parent is calling and what conclusions parents have drawn (or others have drawn for them) about the nature of their child's problem. Kids' school problems can be long-standing, episodic, incidental, or sudden. Whatever the duration, it's safe to assume a threshold of some sort has been crossed that made picking up the phone a necessity. Perhaps a daughter's struggle to make friends transformed into a teacher's complaint about her being mean or bullying others. Or a son's school avoidance began to look more like depression after a week of struggling to get him to school. Parents may be pushed or pulled by others: complaints from teachers, worries expressed by the school counselor, or disciplinary action taken by the assistant principal. Sometimes, parents call because they're fed up with a teacher or some aspect of the school and don't know where else to turn. Whatever the reason, you'll become grounded in the parents' perspective about what they think is going on with their child. It reminds us that, except for those cases in which the teenager contacts the therapist directly, parents are often the first *authors* of their child's experience; from their account of their child's struggles, you'll begin to formulate your understanding of the issues at hand.

During an initial phone conversation, ask for concrete, real life examples that illustrate why a particular label or description was used to characterize the child. Questions such as, "When you said that your child is nervous about going to school in the morning, can you take a minute and describe what happened, say this morning?" or "Could you describe what happens when your child is having problems with his homework, maybe what happened last night or sometime this week?" Generally, a narrative account will flow from these questions, but not always. When it does, you can start to form a picture of events that can aid in your understanding of the problem. It will help you decide whom to invite for a first session, guided partly by your particular therapeutic orientation. If there appears to be explicit tension between the parents and the school, you may decide to discuss this situation initially without the child present, so as not to unnecessarily burden the child. Sometimes, parents have a difficult time describing what is going on; that, too, is important information to know.

As you begin, you may hear about differing views regarding what is going on with the child. For example, "The teacher said that my daughter was doing really well in school, but I can see how she struggles with her homework at night and is nervous about going to school in the morning." Similarly, the therapist may learn that one parent thinks one thing and the other something different. It's not just parents who might disagree, but also other family members or caregivers who are involved in the child's life, say a grandparent, uncle, or aunt. Hold on to those different ways of seeing the child. Don't make up your mind yet. As we'll see, multiple vantage points are keys to understanding the child. Typically, it is part of the diagnostic process to determine whether the differences of opinion are run of the mill, or are significant and even explanatory—indeed, possibly at the root of the problem.

When we learn that the parent is seeking help at the recommendation of someone at the school, we're in a position to ask not only what prompted the call from the parent, but also what the person making the recommendation said about the problem. Don't assume that these are one and the same. Especially for a school-related issue, try to figure out all the motivating narratives that led the parent to seek your help; this information will aid in how you intervene.

Beginning the Therapeutic Process: A Practical Framework for Understanding School-Related Problems

In order to construct this multifaceted understanding of a child's situation, therapists need to develop and utilize a framework for asking about the problems that brought the family into therapy. Regardless of your theoretical orientation—psychoanalytic, attachment-based, family systems, cognitive-behavioral, ego or self-psychology, or other—inherent in any protocol or system of inquiry are the "Who, What, Where, When, Why and How" questions. They are asked with an eye toward identifying patterns of behavior that you, as the therapist, seek to understand about the child. Looking for patterns of behavior requires paying close attention not only to what people say but how they respond to your questions: their language, nonverbal behaviors, and interactions.

As a means of guiding these inquiries into a child's life at school, this chapter presents a framework of seven major areas: the child's school, academics, relationships with peers, relationships with teachers and other adults, emotional and behavioral functioning, health, and extracurricular activities. Case vignettes are used to illustrate common problems that bring children to therapy, and specific questions are listed to help guide the task of formulating and testing hypotheses. The natural trajectory of initial sessions will clarify what to focus on, since it isn't possible or advisable to cover all areas exhaustively or mechanically. Some areas have not been addressed: drug and alcohol use, suicide risk, developmental and family history, antisocial or violent behavior, threats of violence and problems with the law, sexual identity and activity, child abuse and neglect, and more. Yet, having the following topical areas in mind can serve as a way of checking yourself to see if you've missed something about a child's school life that warrants review.

A small matter worth mentioning up front relates to how to quickly calculate what grade the child is in. One way to associate a child's age and their grade in school is to start with the child's age and subtract five, and that's the grade, or close to it. No such calculating system is perfect, since some school systems use a September 1 cutoff while others use December 1 or 15 as a cutoff date for starting kindergarten. No matter what the child's age or grade in school, there are basic areas to cover when assessing kids' school-related problems. Box 2.1 is an outline of these areas.

Box 2.1:	Basic areas to cover in assessing school-related problems with parents and kids

1. **The school:** its culture and larger social or environmental context, the family's and child's history with the school, and their beliefs and biases about schools

2. **Academics:** school performance, past and present, learning difficulties, if any, and motivation to work

3. **Social relationships:** peers and friends

4. **Relationships with teachers and other adults at school:** coaches, tutors, administrators, afterschool mentors, etc.

5. **Emotional or behavioral problems**

6. **Health concerns and related school attendance and lateness issues**

7. **Extracurricular activities, inside and outside school:** clubs, sports, theater, after-school and religious activities, etc.

Each topic area begins with a broad, open-ended question. By starting big-picture, the therapist will have the opportunity to see where the parent or child directs their attention, what's of greatest concern, and, perhaps, what's prompting the family to seek professional help. Therapists will need to listen carefully to the parent's construction of the problem, not only to know where to begin in asking follow-up questions but also in terms of what will propel the family to fully engage in the assessment phase of therapy, further developing and maintaining their motivation.

Note that in each area of inquiry, there are two sets of questions—one set directed to parents and another to kids. The questions are not meant to be exhaustive, and not all will be necessary in every case. There are many excellent resources for therapists to learn sound and basic interviewing skills (McConaughy, 2013; Morrison & Flegel, 2016). These questions are designed to give you a chance to think about the range of issues that you might want to discuss as you begin to determine what might be going on for the child at school.

What About the Child's School?

Adopted shortly after birth, Darren was admitted to the fifth grade in a small private school and struggled academically from the start. Previous psychoeducational testing that was done when he was a second grader in his local public elementary school revealed both learning and attention problems that had been successfully addressed through the school's student support services. Buoyed by the progress he'd made, Darren's parents thought he would benefit from a more demanding academic environment and were delighted when they found a way to pay the tuition costs associated with private school education.

Darren's parents were surprised when the school psychologist contacted them in the fall because their son was caught cheating on an important math test. As a result, they sought professional help. Speaking with the therapist, they wisely surmised that Darren's difficulty and resulting frustration learning math led him to cheat and then lie to the teacher when he was caught. Less worried about Darren's cheating specifically, given their confidence in his good values and behavior, they were very worried that he might not be able to keep up with the other kids. They also were fearful that he would be asked to leave the school given that, unlike the public school he'd attended, this school wasn't required to keep him on.

Since the school was new to him and them, they weren't sure how to move forward, fearing that they might inadvertently make things worse by saying or doing the wrong thing. They also knew that Darren needed extra help and wondered whether there were sufficient resources and commitment on the part of the school personnel, in light of the fact that he'd cheated on a test and lied to his teacher. Darren's parents were sorry and somewhat embarrassed that they hadn't invested time in getting to know his teacher and the school in general and wondered whether the school might not be a good fit for them and him. As a result, much of the session was spent reviewing differences between public and private schools and also how and whom to contact at the school. During this process, Darren's parents revealed that part of their hopes for Darren involved being able to provide for a private school education financially given their detrimental experiences attending large public schools in which they had felt anonymous or worse.

Being able to talk with parents about the broad and specific environment of a child's school is important. Parents will have thoughts about the teachers, curriculum, and school that you will want to explore as it relates to the presenting problem. Sometimes, the parents' experience and attitudes can create a bridge to involvement and interventions, and other times those attitudes and beliefs can impede the child's progress. Keep in mind that one of the best predictors of a child's success at school is the quality of the relationship between the family and school (Clark, 2015; O'Malley, Voight, Renshaw, & Eklund, 2015). Here's where the therapist's knowledge about schools and particular schools can be very helpful. The questions below are designed to help you explore the parents' views of their child's school as well as their own school experience as students.

THE SCHOOL:
Questions for PARENTS

1. What kind of school does your child attend?

2. Did you choose this school for your child and, if so, why?

3. How long has your child been at this particular school? What other schools has your child attended?

4. What do you think about the school?

5. What is the school's reputation and what do you think about it?

6. What do you think about your child's teacher(s)?

7. What do you think about the curriculum and ways of teaching?

8. What general resources are available for your child at school? What about art, music, physical education, sports, tutoring, Internet access, library support, and afterschool activities?

9. What student support services are available at school? Is there a school counselor, school psychologist, school social worker, special education resource, speech and language specialist, nurse, or occupational or physical therapist? Are there groups for kids with special needs, such as children of divorce, children surviving the loss of a loved one, children needing help with social skills, etc.? Has your child ever participated in such a group?

10. How does your child get to and from school each day, and what's that like for your child?

11. In what ways are you involved in your child's school?

12. When problems come up in relation to the school, with whom do you talk or who is accessible to you?

13. What ways are there for parents to get involved at the school?

14. What are you hoping for your child this year at school?

15. What was it like for you when you were in school?

When the therapist met with Darren in the following session, he was distraught about what had happened, especially the pain and disappointment he'd caused his parents. Prior to the cheating incident, he hadn't felt that he could tell them how uncomfortable he was in this new school setting or say much about the math challenges he faced. He was afraid to raise questions in class because everyone would think he was "stupid." He could see his classmates learning math with greater ease and facility, which also translated into comfortable peer relationships that he didn't seem able to join.

Kids have feelings not only about what it's like to be a student in a given classroom, but also about the school itself. They see what seems to work well and where it falls short for them or others. Most importantly, they know what it's like to walk in the door each day, encountering peers who are like-minded or differently minded, teachers in favor of them personally or not, and instructions that work or don't. Kids are aware of an environment that feels relatively safe, or is unsettling, or is worse. They experience a building structure that either supports their learning or leaves them feeling uncared for as paint chips land on their desk or the heating system fails to keep them warm. Kids may feel alone in their perceptions and experiences, or they may gain a sense of camaraderie with their classmates by sharing similar perspectives about the school.

For kids and parents who are unhappy with the school, it's important to find out why. Perhaps it's a momentary unhappiness, for instance, the child doesn't like the teacher this year but has done well with previous teachers. Or, the teenager is new to a school and finds this new environment less congenial than the previous one. Part of what you may discover is that kids who are unhappy at school often don't feel a sense of belonging. They may not speak of the problem in those terms, but it's important to assess the child's ties and attachments to people in the school and whether they've been able to establish some kinship with a teacher, administrator, school counselor, coach, peer, or friend. There are many questions that you can ask kids about the school to further your understanding, some of which are listed below.

THE SCHOOL:
Questions for KIDS

1. Tell me about your school and what it's like to go there?

2. How long have you gone to the school? What schools did you attend before this one? What were they like?

3. What do you like about the school? Dislike?

4. Describe a day in your life at school.

5. What's the school's reputation, and what do you think of it?

6. If you could change something about your school, what would you change?

7. Tell me about your teachers. What are they like?

8. What's it like in your classroom (for younger kids)? Can you describe it to me? What classes do you enjoy (for older kids) and why? Not like and why?

9. What's it like in the cafeteria, gym, or your common areas?

10. What do your friends or other kids say about the school?

11. Is there someone you feel you can talk to? Tell me about him or her. Do you ever talk with the school counselor, psychologist, social worker, or another adult at school? If so, how does that go?

12. How do you get to school each day? What's that like?

13. What do you think your parents think about the school? Tell me something about parent-teacher conferences. How do you think they go?

14. What goals do you have for yourself at school?

How Is the Child Doing Academically?

James' problems learning to read first appeared at the end of kindergarten, when he attended a large, urban public school. Described to the therapist as a bitter moment in the life of his family and their relationship with the school, they couldn't understand why he was so unhappy at school and why their efforts to figure out what was wrong were unsuccessful. Everyone who knew him at school said that he was bright and articulate, outpacing his peers in comprehending books that the teacher read to the class and gifted at building complex structures with blocks or other materials. Why was he faltering in his grasp of some of the basics? Through a psychoeducational evaluation that was administered at the beginning of second grade, the family learned that James had dyslexia. As a result, he entered into a small, school-based program designed to help kids with reading problems, and soon made significant progress. Unfortunately, now in fourth grade, James is struggling again. Despite multiple resources that have been put in place, he has become discouraged.

In the first two sessions with the therapist, James' parents came in without him to review his history and discuss their frustration with his school. They were unhappy watching him face such obstacles again and worried that the teachers and learning support team would not be quick to respond to his needs, as had happened the first time around. As parents, they were aware of their frustration with the school and weren't certain how to proceed. They knew that James' self-esteem was affected by his recent lack of progress and were, at times, angry at him for not keeping up. They wondered whether part of the problem was James' own failure to take his schoolwork seriously and how much was a failure of the school to help him step up to the challenges he faced as the reading demands grew. This wasn't something they could determine on their own, so talking to an outside professional made sense.

When talking with parents about their child's academic issues or problems with learning, there is a range of things to consider. Problems may have existed for a long time and gone unidentified or undiagnosed. Problems may be recent, and their suddenness becomes a source of stress and even panic. Problems may also have occurred at one stage in a child's life and been successfully addressed, only to reoccur at a later stage, such as the case with James. In addition, parents and kids may be frightened about the idea of identifying a learning problem where the child could be labeled and stigmatized as a result. Finally, and perhaps most importantly, many problems that kids have are multidetermined and variously expressed. An academic or motivational problem may be due to underlying emotional issues, or, conversely, a learning issue might first appear in the form of a child acting out behaviorally (a typical presentation with which most therapists are familiar). Keep in mind that roughly one out of every six children has diagnosable learning problems, so questions about learning will necessarily include consideration of this possibility (Pullen, 2017).

In many instances, you will want to review the child's past report cards or sample homework assignments to better understand the child's current academic struggle. Be sure to ask for report cards going back multiple years and review them with an eye toward finding common threads or pinpointing the first time the problem was identified. This takes time, but is well worth the effort (see Chapter 7).

One question to ask is whether the child has had a psychological evaluation and, if so, what learning problems may have been identified and how the recommendations have been incorporated into the child's learning plans at school. Younger kids are generally less informed and aware of services that have been put in place. Older kids will be directly involved in determining the range and types of accommodations and how useful they've been. If there has been no previous testing and there is reason to suspect that the child has learning problems that extend beyond the occasional struggles inherent in normal childhood development, then exploring testing as an option becomes a central part of what you'll discuss during sessions. How to work with schools around the issue of testing—when it should be done, who should do it, how to involve key people in the process, motivating the child to engage in the testing, reviewing findings, determining appropriate interventions and follow-up strategies—will be addressed in Chapter 7. For now, the questions listed here cover a range of topics to explore when talking with parents about academics and learning.

ACADEMICS:
Questions for PARENTS

1. Tell me about your child at school. How is he or she doing academically? What comes easily? What's hard? What classes or subjects does your child like or not like? What most concerns you?

2. What do teachers say about this? How do they communicate with you?

3. Tell me about your child's homework—the volume, your child's motivation, and what gets in your child's way in completing the assignments or doing them accurately.

4. What grades does your child receive and what do you and your child think about them?

5. If there has been testing, what did it reveal about your child? What do you think about the findings? Does your child have a diagnosed learning problem? If so, tell me about it. When was the problem identified and how?

6. What supports have been put in place to support your child at home and at school? What seems to be working and what isn't? What would you like to see happen?

7. Who conducted the testing? If it was done outside the school, is the school aware of the testing? If not, why not? Who might be aware: current or past teachers, a school counselor, a psychologist, or an administrator?

8. If your child has been diagnosed through a psychoeducational evaluation, may I review it? May I talk with the person who did the testing or speak with someone at the school about the testing?

9. If you think your child has a learning problem that has not been evaluated, why not? What do you think is the next step in moving forward? How will you know if or when the time is right to do an evaluation?

10. Does anyone else in the family struggle with a learning problem?

Only during the third session did the therapist meet with James, who was able to describe in some detail how hard he had tried at school and how things no longer made sense to him. He liked his teacher but he didn't think the extra supports were helping anymore. He said that he loved when the teachers read to the class, but the books were too hard for him to read alone and sometimes he was teased by his classmates when he was asked to read aloud. James was clear about his likes and dislikes—math problems that involved pencil and paper calculations were fine, but word problems of any kind were "impossible." Saying so left him tearful and less communicative. The obvious distress he felt illustrated why his parents were worried about his self-esteem and confidence, both having taken a hit, they said. It's at just such intersections that therapists often explore the relationship between a learning issue, such as dyslexia, and a child's emotional or behavioral struggles (explored in a later section).

Often, problems that the child and family present in your office will involve a range of learning, emotional, and behavioral issues that will require thoughtful assessment and close collaboration among the child, family, and school. Knowing what issues to cover with the child will be an important part of the assessment process. The following questions focus on what you can explore with the child regarding academic struggles the child may be having. Remember to seek information so that you get a grasp of the child's strengths as a learner since you'll inevitably build on those strengths as you discuss various interventions. Again, keep in mind that life at school is outside the realm of what's visible to you or the child's parents. This makes it all the more important to listen and learn about what is going on at school and to identify what information you will likely need to secure from those people who observe and relate directly to the child in that setting.

ACADEMICS:
Questions for KIDS

1. Which subjects are hard, which are easy, and why? Which do you like or not like? What about school gets you excited or motivated?

2. What was school like last year or the years before?

3. What do your teachers say about you as a student? What do you think about this?

4. Tell me something about doing homework. What's that like for you? What's hard and what seems to come more easily?

5. How are your grades? What do you think about them?

6. What do your teachers or others at school do to help when you need it? How do you let them know that something is

> hard or that you need help? How does that go? What do you think they should do to help even more?
>
> 7. What do your parents do to help? How do you let them know that something is difficult? How does that go? Are there ways they can help even more?
>
> 8. What do you think about the evaluation you had (for those kids who have had formal testing)? What did you learn?

How Is the Child Doing Socially?

Anna, a 10th grade student at her local public high school, always seemed young for her age, her mother told the therapist. Even though Anna does well enough academically, she has had trouble making friends and is visibly awkward in social gatherings. When Anna returned home from school this week, she was quite sad and discouraged. Her mother worried that she was becoming depressed. Though Anna was reluctant to get help from an outside professional, her mother insisted she come along with her for at least one session with a therapist. Anna agreed as long as her mother was present. The therapist was willing to see Anna with her mother for the first session in an effort to sort out what was going on and also try to make a connection with Anna, abetted by her mother's presence.

During the session, Anna's mother provided a brief overview of the situation, including her worries about Anna's mood. The mother assumed that this related to Anna's difficulty connecting with other kids at school, which Anna was only able to do with the structure of teacher-directed, classroom projects. Even in those instances, Anna had a strong sense that she was the least desirable group member and only the "nice kids" befriended her, and only temporarily at that. For her part, Anna said that other kids made her nervous since she never seemed to know what to say to get a conversation going or how to respond to a comment directed to her. Forlornly, she claimed that her only friends were her two older sisters, both of whom were out of the house now, leaving her feeling more alone than ever. Both Anna and her mother wondered whether the absence of her sisters was precipitating the increased distress and sadness she was feeling.

While Anna's struggle to make friends was intense, all children have to adjust and struggle with peer relationships over the course of their school life. Therefore, asking about a child's peer relationships is an essential part of any inquiry the therapist makes about a child or adolescent. The quality of peer relationships and choice of friends is predictive of many aspects of successful adjustment such as: steering clear of addictions or antisocial behaviors (Miller-Day, Alberts, Hecht, Trost, & Krizek, 2014), forming close bonds, learning how to deal with conflict and disappointments, regulating behavior, withstanding the inevitable hardships and challenges of life, avoiding isolation and loneliness, maintaining healthy self-esteem, and so on (Brown & Larson, 2009). Though kids don't need to have many friends to be well-adjusted socially, they do need some friends, especially those with prosocial skills and inclinations (Van Harmelen et al., 2017). In addition, they must learn how to manage and negotiate friendships using social media, with the gains and risks associated with their use. Anna's case was fairly extreme because she seemed to have sidestepped friendship formation throughout her school years, a worrisome feature of her life.

There are questions we can ask parents in order to understand their child's social world. One reason to do so is because parents' knowledge of their child's social activities and peer relationships is linked to lower levels of risky behaviors (Lippold, Greenberg, Graham, & Feinberg, 2014). In particular, note the questions related to whether the child has siblings and, if so, how those relationships work. Siblings are children's first peers and, as such, give them ample opportunity to develop social skills in the inevitable daily exchanges they share (Downey, Condron, & Yucel, 2015). Furthermore, with older children, such as Anna, parents have had many years observing them interacting with peers and, in Anna's case, with her older siblings as well. Siblings may also have friends in common and may know at least some of their siblings' friends unless there is a significant age difference between them. The following questions for parents will guide you in learning more a child's social world.

SOCIAL RELATIONSHIPS:
Questions for PARENTS

1. Tell me about your child's friendships and peer relations. What's she like with her friends? How important are her friends to her? What problems arise, and how does she handle them? What do you think of your child's choice of friends? Is she dating and, if so, how is that going?

2. Has your child ever been rejected, bullied or victimized by peers? What happened as a result? Have you ever thought that your child bullied other children? What happened as a result?

3. Describe your child's use of social media. How important is social media to your child's friendships? What sorts of issues or problems have come up for your child as a result of using social media? How have you handled them?

4. What do teachers, other family members, coaches, neighbors, and others say about how your child gets along with peers and friends?

5. How does your child get along with siblings (if applicable)? What do your children enjoy doing together? How are conflicts resolved, and what role do you play in helping to resolve conflict? Do your children sometimes include their sibling(s) when they're with peers or friends and, if so, how does that go?

Speaking with kids about their friends, peers, and social difficulties is a substantial part of what we do in our offices, with or without parents present. We talk with kids about whom they interact with at school and what they think about their friends and peers. When kids are thriving socially, we likely witness animation and attention to detail when they speak about their group of friends. Particular friends will come alive in your office, especially as the child enters the middle school years and beyond. After a while, you may feel you know these other kids, too, since they're spoken of so often. Not surprisingly, when kids are struggling in their peer relationships you will begin to see the way their friends may be struggling, too.

One psychologist claimed that he "would love to interview everyone's best friend." Inherent in this assertion is a crucial notion—a systems-based derivative—that we operate in different spheres of influence and attachment and that these spheres constitute, in good measure, who we are, for better or worse. No child is simply "the child who can't sit still at circle time," "the student who is excellent at math" or "the teenager who antagonizes his peers." A best friend has a unique perspective on the child, a perspective that would be valuable to the therapist, though interviewing your clients' friends is clearly neither practical nor ethical, except under unusual circumstances. So why does this idea resonate? Think about yourself for a minute. Outside your family, who would you most want to reflect on your character, habits, or foibles than your closest friend? Even by *contemplating* a friend's view of the child in your office, we're better able to consider how we might incorporate additional viewpoints, including asking the child what a friend would say about him or her or what the teacher would say. The point is that it's the therapist's job to corral as many relevant perspectives as possible, thinking hard about who might have the most valuable angle by which to understand the child.

There are questions that you can ask the child about his or her relationships. Most kids are able to say what it's like to be someone's friend and what it's like to lose a friend. In elementary school, kids can describe who they think brings out the best in them and maybe the worst, and what they make of this. They will have their own ideas about how kids do and don't get along with each other and what role they play in the various friendships that form and dissolve over the years. Even in preschool, children can say why this or that person is their friend. It's rudimentary in the early years: "we're friends because we like to play with blocks" or "we live next door to each other." Children grow in their ability to define, develop, and maintain ties to others outside the family and to grasp the depth of meaning and purpose they derive from having friends who share mutual interests, affection, and trust.

In Anna's case, the absence of friends was a very painful part of her life; this was profoundly evident after her older sisters, her true confidants, left home for college. Her insecurities and social awkwardness seemed to necessitate her mother's presence in the first session, where both Anna and her mother spoke about Anna's difficulties making friends and feeling uncomfortable with her classmates. She confirmed what her mother said about how she was funny and articulate at home, especially with her sisters, and clammed up when she was at school. Both agreed that Anna was temperamentally shy and that her shyness had grown rather than subsided in high school, when having friends mattered more to her.

Questions below can be directed to kids either alone or with their parents and serve as a framework for the information you will need to understand more fully what is going on for the child socially. Keep in mind that asking questions of kids who feel they have no friends can be painful, so asking more general questions about the social scene at school, such as what they notice about social groups, can be useful. In order to learn about a child's relationships with peers and friends, a range of questions are listed below.

SOCIAL RELATIONSHIPS:
Questions for KIDS

1. What's it's like for you at school with your peers and classmates? When do you feel like you are part of a group, and when, if ever, do you feel like an outsider?

2. Tell me about your friends: What are they like? How do you get along? What happens when you're not getting along with your friend(s)? What would your friends say about you if they were here? Your best friend? Have you ever been rejected by a friend? Have you ever been worried about a friend? Have you ever had a friend become very ill or die?

3. For kids who say they have no friends: Are there kids you sometimes hang out with? Tell me about them. Are there kids you'd like to be friends with? Where do you sit during lunch? Whom do you play with at recess or hang out with at school?

4. If you could change something about your relationships with your peers or friends, what would that be? Have you tried to make those changes? If so, what happened?

5. With siblings: How do you get along with your sibling(s)? When you're not getting along, what's that like? How much help do you need from your parents when you're not getting along? Do you ever include your siblings in the things you do with your friends, or do your siblings ever include you? How does that go?

6. For older kids: Are you dating? What's that like? Are you seeing someone regularly? How is that going?

7. What do your parents think about your friends and the kids you hang out with? How involved are your parents with your friends? What's that like for you?

How Does the Child Get Along with Teachers and Other Adults?

Sixth grader Lucas stormed out of his small classroom in a private school without permission from his teacher. When the teaching assistant found him in the bathroom, he yelled at her and said he refused to watch a health-and-wellness video that was being shown that morning. Since Lucas had recently been arguing with his teachers about other classroom activities he disliked, the teacher contacted Lucas' father to discuss what might be going on. In the meeting at school with two teachers, the school psychologist, Lucas' father, and Lucas, the father, a recent immigrant, actively supported Lucas' right to reject certain activities and lessons. Though he didn't want his son yelling at the teachers or abruptly leaving the classroom without permission, for religious reasons he also didn't want him participating in values or health education. Lucas' father expressed deep appreciation for the general education his son was receiving, but he disagreed with some of the ideas that were promoted by the school. In his mind, he wanted Lucas to have the freedom to reject the educational experiences that diverged from his family's values and beliefs. With a real desire to find common ground with Lucas' father in the meeting, the teachers and school psychologist were able to modify curricular expectations and arrange for alternative educational options for Lucas. Despite this achievement, Lucas continued to behave defiantly, resulting in a referral for therapy.

In the first session, the therapist could see how upset Lucas was with his father as well as his teachers. He sat sullenly in the chair and spoke in monosyllables, giving nothing away to his father or the therapist except the sense that he was unhappy to be there. Though his father grew increasingly impatient, Lucas refused to talk. The therapist eventually decided to meet with the father alone while Lucas sat in the waiting room. Subsequently, the father reported that Lucas was not only failing to cooperate with his teachers at school, but he was also disruptive and disrespectful at home. He said that Lucas always knew how to stand up for himself and had been this way since he was a small child, a characteristic he'd been proud of in his son. Now, Lucas's way of standing up for himself was defiant and, as a result, the father was at a loss to determine what to do. He was embarrassed by Lucas's behavior in the session and angry and fearful, too, worried that if Lucas didn't start to behave himself, he would get into more serious trouble in the neighborhood, where people were less understanding and patient than his teachers at school.

Children's behavior in relation to those in positions of authority is a critical issue to consider. We know that there are many reasons why kids become testy or oppositional with their teachers or other adults. At different points in their lives, most kids will question people in positions of authority or challenge them in an effort to determine their legitimacy or the limits of control they have. Some kids come into therapy having been betrayed by adults, including their parents. In these cases, it is especially important to inquire about personal and family history in order to better understand their behavior. Furthermore, families vary enormously regarding what is acceptable behavior with adults. This is often determined by cultural, ethnic, and individual differences. In Lucas's family, for instance, he was rewarded at home for standing up for himself, since those behaviors were considered a sign of strength and self-determination given the family's immigrant background. Thus, when kids come to therapy with problems getting along with adults at school, there are a number of questions to ask to clarify what might be going on, such as those listed below.

RELATIONSHIPS WITH ADULTS:
Questions for PARENTS

1. What kind of relationship does your child have with teachers and other adults outside your family? Do you have any concerns about how your child gets along with adults?

2. When problems arise between your child and a teacher or any adult at the school, how does your child handle them? How did you respond to your child? The school?

3. How does your child get along with coaches, tutors, club leaders, or other people who oversee your child's activities?

4. What are the similarities and differences in how your child relates to adults in the family and those outside the family? What's your sense of why that is the case?

Talking with kids about their relationships with teachers, administrators, and other people in positions of authority at school can be complicated. On the one hand, kids can minimize their difficult behavior, blame the adult, or fail to see the impact of their actions on others. Alternatively, they can blame themselves, miss the ways that they may be unfairly singled out, or feel misunderstood and defeated. This is one of the areas where working closely with the family and school has the biggest payoff in terms of understanding the nature of the problem and what to do about it. One of the key elements in sorting this out is by talking with the child or adolescent.

At the outset of therapy, it was nearly impossible for Lucas to talk about school, including what he thought and felt about his relationship with his teachers. When he did speak up, he was angry, fighting back tears and expressing a sense of hopelessness. Though he had liked his teachers in past years, he was unable to see how they could be helpful to him now. Clearly, something had changed, either for him, them, or both. It took time, a visit by the therapist to the school, and a number of sessions with him and his father to grasp the depth and meaning of his frustration. One thing that emerged was that Lucas felt deeply about his family's values and couldn't reconcile them with the school's practices. He hadn't been able to connect with his teachers about how uncomfortable he felt. He was torn between the loyalty he had toward his father, expressed at school by challenging his teachers and bolting out of the room, and the loyalty he felt toward the school, expressed at home by defying his father. With no safe place to land, he lashed out and grew sullen. It became clear to the therapist that a lot of family history went into Lucas's plight, something the father recounted in the initial sessions when he spoke about being a single parent, speaking English as a second language, and the brutal struggle he had leaving his country of origin and making his way to the United States.

Being able to talk with kids about what is going on with their teachers (or coaches or other adults at school) is critical. Kids will have feelings about what it's like to be a student in a teacher's classroom or on a team with a particular coach. They may feel alone in their perceptions and experience, adding to their isolation and frustration. Or they may share with other team members the perception of a coach that "nobody likes" because "she's mean," which creates camaraderie, and with it, some consolation.

When a child feels valued by a teacher or other adult at school, much can be accomplished in terms of the child's learning, overall success at school, and self-esteem. However, when a child has negative feelings about a teacher or other adults at school, the effects can be serious. It is important to figure out what is going on and work with the child, family, and school to improve the situation. The following questions are designed to facilitate discussion about how the child gets along with teachers and others in positions of authority at school.

RELATIONSHIPS WITH ADULTS:
Questions for KIDS

1. Tell me about your teacher(s). What's he or she like and how do you get along? Do you have a sense of what your teacher thinks of you? What makes you think so?

2. How does your teacher relate to your whole class? When there are problems in the classroom, how does your teacher handle them? Can you give an example? Do you speak with anyone about this?

3. What was it like for you with your teachers in previous years? How do previous years compare with this one?

4. What's it like for you with your coach, school counselor, principal, or other adults at school?

5. What's it like for you with other adults in your life? Is there a Sunday school teacher, boss, club leader, or other adult who oversees your activities? Is there anyone you really like? What do you like about that person? What isn't working as well as you'd like with these adults and why?

Does the Child Have Emotional or Behavioral Problems?

When Maria entered high school in the ninth grade, she and her mother were well aware of the problem she had managing her anxiety. This first appeared when Maria, then 4 years old, spent six months crying every morning when her mother dropped her off at the neighborhood day care center. Maria's mother found ways to support her first and only child over the years when her anxiety flared up, especially during stage-of-life transitions, such as entering preschool. Beginning high school was a defining transition since, for districting purposes, Maria's closest friends ended up attending another high school in the area. Not only was Maria anxious about going to school, she became irritable at home and standoffish with her old friends. It was this combination of factors, coupled with a conversation Maria's mom had with Maria's former middle school social worker about anxious behaviors she'd seen over the years, that led the mother to reach out to a therapist.

In the initial session with the therapist, Maria was distressed, demanding that her mother get her admitted to the high school her friends were attending, eventually protesting the need to go to school at all. Initially, her mother responded sympathetically and later threw up her hands in anger and disgust, not only with Maria but with the whole school system and the restrictions imposed by district boundaries that didn't take into account student or family preferences. It was a tense and painful session, revealing Maria's anxiety and fragility regarding her ability to adjust to the new school, and also her mother's frustration. The mother's quick-to-anger response seemed to paralyze both of them, making it difficult to pursue a course of action.

There are emotional and behavior correlates for kids' school problems that you may observe in your office. They may correspond well to the depth and nature of the school problem they are having, or they can be the cause of the problem, or both. For example, Maria struggles with anxiety, although she found ways to manage and cope with difficult situations that arose over the years. The transition to high school proved too steep, increasing her anxiety and, in turn, activating her mom's anxiety and anger at her and the school. Anxiety regarding entering a new school would be expected, but in Maria's case, it was more than she could handle. Her anxious responses provoked her mother's reaction and a cycle of fear, frustration, and a kind of shutdown resulted.

Therapists are inevitably exploring how kids (and their parents) are feeling in relation to the presenting problem. This sometimes necessitates the evaluation of an undiagnosed emotional or behavioral problem, such as Maria was experiencing. Finding out how people respond emotionally and behaviorally to situations is the therapeutic ground on which we stand as we engage kids and their families. Questions such as those listed below run through the course of most if not all of the work you do with modifications based on many factors, including the child's age and stage of development.

EMOTIONAL OR BEHAVIORAL PROBLEMS:
Questions for PARENTS

1. Tell me about your child. Describe how your child responds to things emotionally and behaviorally at school and at home. How do you know when your child is happy? Upset? Angry? Confused? Joyful? (Etc.)

2. Have you noted any changes in the way your child responds to things emotionally or behaviorally? If so, when did the changes occur? What might have precipitated the changes?

3. Has anyone expressed concerns to you about your child's behavior or the way they react to situations emotionally or behaviorally at school? If so, what were the circumstances and what happened as a result?

4. What would your child say about how he or she handles things emotionally or behaviorally at school and at home?

With the help of the therapist, kids can feel a sense of relief that their experiences at school are taken seriously and may tell their therapist things that they did not tell their parents. When kids share their thoughts, feelings, and experiences with you, as part of your assessment of their isolation or connections to others, be sure to check out whether you're the only person to know. In Maria's case, though she was dismayed, she was able to talk about her frustration and feel heard by the therapist and her mom, too. Over time, the therapist helped Maria become aware of the importance of being able to talk about her anxiety now that she's older. She had remembered feeling awful about her preschool, but hadn't made the connection between what she called having "nerves" and what she was experiencing now, as she faced a transition that precipitated intense disappointment, fear and worry. It became clear that Maria's problem largely related to her generalized anxiety and the way it became entangled and stoked by her mother's heightened reactions, a not uncommon situation (Chansky, 2014).

There are any number of emotional and behavioral problems that can arise for kids, some quite serious and others less so. Getting to know what kids feel and how they behave is, again, the mainstay of the clinical work therapists do. The specific questions below designed for kids are but a small range of the possible questions you might ask while helping them feel safe and comfortable enough to describe what they are doing, thinking, and feeling, especially as it relates to their lives at school.

EMOTIONAL OR BEHAVIORAL PROBLEMS:
Questions for KIDS

1. What's it like for you when you're happy? Sad? Other feelings? What do you do when you're feeling this way?

2. What's that like for you at school?

3. What brings you happiness? What kinds of things make you sad? Upset?

4. What is going on at school that is bothering you? What's going on that's working well?

5. When things aren't going well at school, what do you do? How do you feel? Whom do you talk to? How does that go?

6. Do you ever talk with the school counselor, psychologist, social worker, or another adult in the school? If so, how does that go? If not, why not?

Does the Child Have Any Health Problems?

Jerome, a senior in his fall semester, suffered a concussion playing football with his high school team. It was one of several concussions he'd had playing sports over the years, and this one was considered moderate to severe. Despite his coach's advice to stay home, he went to school the following morning and had to leave shortly thereafter, feeling overwhelmed by the demands of the school day. Exhausted and unable to concentrate, he stayed home to rest for a few weeks. Given that he was already a student who his teachers said just "squeaked by," Jerome fell behind in his coursework and became despondent. His father worried that he was depressed. Even though Jerome lived with his mother, his father agreed he would contact a therapist to secure the help he needed.

When Jerome went to the first appointment with the behavioral specialist at their local clinic, the therapist was alarmed by his behavior and mood. Jerome had withdrawn from all contact with his friends and teammates and hadn't been able to keep up with his work that a homebound tutor was monitoring. The therapist determined that Jerome was suffering from major depression. With the help of both parents, a caring younger brother, the therapist, and, eventually, the support staff at his large public school, plans were made to help Jerome begin to do his work incrementally while simultaneously starting on a trial of medication. Concussions are not uncommon, yet are but one of many medical problems kids can have that may interfere with their schoolwork and life (Cantu & Hyman, 2012).

When a child is having problems at school, or anywhere, for that matter, it's important to find out whether they have any suspected or identified health problems. In Jerome's case, there was a clear precipitant to the problems he was having that led to his depression. However, medical problems may not be part of what's initially presented to the therapist, so it's our job to ask the questions that will elicit information about the child's overall health.

When there are medical concerns, whether related or unrelated to the presenting problem, there are issues to consider. For instance, in the case of chronic asthma, a common problem for kids especially in urban settings, a child might have problems related to safely functioning in the school setting. Typically, there are guidelines for proper care and attention that must be followed by the teacher, coach, and school nurse. For children with metabolic disorders, parents, the physician, and possibly the therapist will need to coordinate whatever interventions are needed to stabilize the child in an emergency. Obviously, it is not the job of the therapist to monitor medical care unless the therapist is a physician, is trained in health care delivery and services, or is part of a clinical team in which the therapist has a prescribed role. Nonetheless, there are some basic questions to keep in mind when talking with the parent or child. These questions are relevant for understanding health care needs, since they may impede a child's functioning and progress at school. Keep in mind that it's important for children to understand and, as much as possible, take responsibility for their health-related issues in age-appropriate ways. Knowing when to reach out to others, and to which others, is part of that process. Exploring these issues with the child and family through the questions listed below, gives you an opportunity to further the child's growth in self-understanding and personal efficacy.

It's important to add that, if there are health problems, the child will likely benefit from having the therapist work collaboratively with the physician, school nurse, or other health care professionals who are treating the child.

HEALTH ISSUES:
Questions for PARENTS

1. Does your child have any health or medical issues? If so, can you describe them? How long have they been going on?

2. How do you think the health or medical issues may be impacting your child at school? At home? How worried are you about your child's health?

3. Is your child taking any medications for these problems? If so, what are the medications, who is the prescribing physician and (when indicated) is this someone with whom you, the therapist, can collaborate?

4. What's being done at home and school to manage these issues? Is it effective? When problems arise, what happens?

5. What happens when your child isn't able to do schoolwork as a result of the health concern? How often does this happen?

6. How often and for what reasons does your child miss or arrive late for school (or work) due to these problems? If your child is late for or missing school, what happens? At home? At school? How often does that happen?

7. What have you tried to do to get your child to school,? Help your child get to school on time? Help your child with their schoolwork? What works best?

HEALTH ISSUES:
Questions for KIDS

1. Do you have any concerns about your health? If so, what are they? How long have they been going on? What's that like for you? How concerned are you?

2. Who helps you with the problem? If you see a doctor for the problem, what does the doctor say about it? How does that go?

3. How does this problem affect your life at home? At school? What do people at home and school do to help you? How does that work?

4. Are you sometimes unable to do your schoolwork because of this problem? What happens then?

5. Do you ever miss school or go to school late because of this problem? What happens then? How does that work for you?

Is the Child Involved in Extracurricular Activities in or out of School?

Kara was feeling lonely and left out among her peers in middle school, so her grandmother decided to speak with her pediatrician about the issue, especially since Kara was not engaged in sports or any other extracurricular activities through which kids often make friends. Kara's grandmother followed up on the pediatrician's referral to a local clinic that provided mental health services and accompanied Kara to the first appointment. In the initial session, it became evident that, in addition to her social difficulties, Kara sorely needed extra learning support given the problems she was having with writing assignments, which took precedence over her difficulty making friends.

Among other school-based interventions, the therapist and grandmother identified an afterschool tutoring program at the local library, and Kara enrolled in sessions twice a week. Kara's grandmother was relieved, since she would often return home after a long day at work and feel overwhelmed by the prospect of helping Kara with her homework. Progress was slow on her acquisition of writing skills, partly because the tutoring wasn't as consistent as needed. Nonetheless, Kara became a regular at the library. She befriended several librarians who came to rely on her for various jobs that needed to be done, and she found a place among other kids who came to the library.

Though the therapy was short-lived, Kara eventually began to help other students at the library, which strengthened her social skills and, importantly, gave her a social field—the library's reading tables—where she was appreciated for the contributions she made, thereby increasing her confidence and sense of belonging.

Children's lives extend beyond the walls of the school and home. How far and wide depends on many factors related to the availability of and access to extracurricular activities, the child's interests, and the family's ability or willingness to do what it takes to help their child participate in these activities. Extracurricular programs, clubs, and sports might be school-sponsored or entirely independent of the school's offerings. Parents are often familiar with what's available in their community, but in some instances they aren't, given the many demands on families today. In the instances when families don't have the resources to support their children's out-of-school activities, sometimes the therapist can work with parents or the school to help figure out what's available through neighborhood associations and services, especially given the fact that afterschool supervision is a protective factor for kids (Biglan, Flay, Embry, & Sandler, 2012). Therapists are also in a position to think through options in light of the child's wishes, needs, and the demands on her and her family's life. In Kara's case, tutoring services at the local library provided additional support for her, but were also a lifeline for her grandmother, the sole guardian whose full-time job limited her ability to help.

Families with knowledge of available resources and the means (both logistical and financial) to utilize them may report "chauffeuring fatigue" from driving their children to soccer practice and piano lessons with dinner to follow. Listen to what some parents and kids have to say about their overscheduled lives and the worries that accumulate regarding whether their child is doing enough to achieve their college aspirations. Typically, these are the complaints of families privileged enough to be able to arrange and afford such special interests, unless the child is involved in public-funded, school-based activities, which can, of course, be equally pressing. When there's so much going on in a child's life that the child is frazzled and exhausted, exploring this issue with a therapist can be illuminating, especially when examined in the context of what brought the child into therapy in the first place. Sometimes, the problem the child is having is a result of being overscheduled.

Extracurricular activities that are ideally chosen by the child or adolescent based on true interests, maybe even passions, can add sparkle, coherence, diversion, and meaning to their lives. Just by asking questions, you can learn about possible jobs they have outside the home and the activities they do that animate their lives. These activities are frequently done in conjunction with peers and caring adults, establishing extracurricular communities that can balance school pressures and generate a sense of belonging. Therapists often hear kids say, "I don't have good friends at school but I do have friends in my religious youth group or local theater crew." This extracurricular peer group can be deeply affirming for kids for whom relationships with kids at school have been less than adequate.

Kids can act one way at school and be quite different in their outside activities, as we all know. Learning about a child's different worlds can be extremely useful to the therapist who is trying to determine what isn't working for the child and why, but also what *is* working and why. While school may be a source of frustration and failure, there may be places where the child is happy and thriving, or at least feels competent and has some sense of belonging. In those instances, figuring out what's working can be part of the foundation for what the child needs at school. If children aren't flourishing in either world, then the therapist has more cause for concern. In such cases, we might ask is the absence of a positive space, in school or out, a function of family problems, a sign of depression, anxiety, or of inhospitable surroundings that make it hard for the child to safely and confidently navigate from home to school to extracurricular activities? Therapists have an opportunity to examine this part of a child's life by gathering information from parents and kids, asking questions such as the ones that follow.

EXTRACURRICULAR ACTIVITIES:
Questions for PARENTS

1. What does your child do outside the regular classroom activities at school (such as sports, afterschool programs, clubs, religious activities, performing arts, volunteer work, jobs, etc.)? Are these at the school or in the community?

2. How does your child feel about these extracurricular activities now and in the past? What activities bring them pleasure or excitement? Challenges?

3. Do you have concerns about their activities? If so, what are your concerns? What have you done to support your child in these activities? What has worked? What hasn't?

4. What extracurricular opportunities exist for your child in general?

EXTRACURRICULAR ACTIVITIES:
Questions for KIDS

1. What activities do you do outside of class (such as sports, after-school programs, clubs, religious activities, performing arts, volunteer work, etc.)?

2. How's it going with other kids in these activities? Do you have any good friends doing this with you?

3. How do your extracurricular activities fit with what's expected in school?

4. Do you ever feel like you're doing too much? What would you prefer not to do? Is there more you'd like to do and, if so, what kinds of things would you like to do that you aren't already doing? For older kids, are you concerned about activities to list on college applications?

5. What do your parents think about your activities? How do your parents help you with these activities? How is that working?

REVIEWING THE BASICS

Considering the range of questions and topics to cover in the first session or over several sessions can be daunting, so it makes sense to review some of the key takeaways for conducting initial sessions when the child is struggling at school.

- Parents or guardians are often the first to describe the child's problem at school. They listen to their child's concerns, consider their circumstances, and seek to understand what might be going on. However, parents' understanding of how their child is faring at school is naturally limited. Those who know the child in the school and other settings can provide valuable input as you seek to understand the child's problem and how to intervene effectively.

■ It's important to consciously implement a framework for understanding a child's life at school. Though not exhaustive, this necessitates asking kids and parents about seven key areas of the child's school experience: the school itself, academics, relationships with friends and peers, relationships with adults, behavioral and emotional problems, health problems, and extracurricular activities.

CHAPTER 3

The Case for Contacting the School (and Why You Might Not)

Now that we have reviewed some of the tools to help guide your exploration of a child's school problems, it's important to examine and enumerate the compelling, important reasons why you might reach out to the child's school in the first place, and also focus on the reasons, both clinical and personal, why you or the family might choose to hold off. Contacting the school can benefit all parties who have a stake in a child's therapy—from teachers, to parents, to your own clinical practice—and, of course, the kids themselves. First, we'll delve into the key reasons for reaching out, before listing a number of the reasons (for better or worse) why therapists might refrain from contacting the school directly.

Five Key Reasons for Reaching out to Schools

It provides a fuller understanding of the situation

The therapist's office is a tiny window into a child's world, and without information from the school that *you* gather by observing the child or talking with teachers, support staff, or administrators, you will necessarily be limited in your ability to understand the full scope and context of the child's problem. You will miss both the big and small pictures, that is, what's going on in *that* school at *that* time that includes an up-close, on-the-ground view of the child.

Even though there are portions of a child's school day that aren't observed by the adults who work in the school, much of it is. This is true even if a particular incident such as a mean-spirited taunt from a classmate or an older student's intolerant aside isn't witnessed by teachers or others who work in the school. They know the students, the types of problems that typically occur, how other kids respond to similar situations, the vulnerabilities and strengths of the student in question, and what steps might be taken subsequently to figure out a solution. A psychologist who consults with a small independent school said that many teachers think that "the therapist is in a bubble and [doesn't] value the information [the teacher] has to provide." By reaching out to the school personnel and showing respect for their opinions, you will step outside your bubble and receive valuable input.

Additionally, for many reasons, kids and parents sometimes have a difficult time answering the basic question, "What's it like for you and your child at school?" And even when they do provide solid information, it's often not enough to understand the full story. For instance, when Jorge, a third grade child, complained that he was being bullied, it was hard to determine the severity of the problem without knowing how people at the school perceived the situation. At worst, the case could involve serious issues of safety. At best, the problem may stem from Jorge's misperceptions of difficult daily interactions with his peers. Or it could be some combination of both. Though, as a therapist, you will surely seek to understand what happened from the child and parents' perspectives in your office before contacting the school, hearing from a teacher or other personnel can provide essential information in determining what steps to take and with whom.

In other words, there may be dimensions to the problem that simply aren't visible unless you contact the school. For instance, in Jorge's case, the teacher reported that when Jorge transitions between the two homes of his divorced parents, he comes to school disconsolate and antagonistic, especially with his peers. His mother and stepfather hadn't been aware that this was occurring until it was reported to the therapist in a brief phone call. The concern about bullying wasn't fully explicated by this information, but the picture was expanded to include a dimension of Jorge's life that hadn't previously been brought to anyone's attention.

It helps the school support the child

Teachers, school counselors, or coaches may notice that a student is struggling in ways that they find puzzling or worrying, but they might not have enough information to act or intervene effectively. Your involvement might clarify the child's struggles and open up a dialogue about what's going on and, most importantly, what to do about it.

Take, for example, an instance in which a middle school teacher was frustrated because a particular student wasn't completing her homework. What the teacher didn't know was that this preteen was charged with the task of taking care of her two younger sisters throughout the evening hours since her father had been deported and her mother had acquired a second job. Once the situation became known, the therapist and school counselor worked with the student to help her find ways to maximize her free periods and collaborated with the teacher in order to adjust the student's workload.

It strengthens the partnership between the family and the school

For any number of reasons, some ordinary and others more serious, the key people in a child's life at school may not have a constructive or positive relationship with the family. Likewise, the family seeking outside professional help may already be at odds with the school, and the incident or particular circumstance that resulted in a referral has simply exacerbated that strained relationship. One of the central, overarching ideas to keep in mind when collaborating with schools is to support the relationship between the family and the school in any way necessary. As research has shown, facilitating better communication between these two parties is paramount to a child's ultimate success (Grant & Ray, 2018; Sheridan & Kratochwill, 2010).

To offer a case example, Jeanine, a ninth grader in a small charter school, was questioning her gender identity and as a result found herself increasingly at odds with her family and friends. Her mother reached out to a therapist recommended by the school counselor who, in turn, listened to Jeanine talk about her struggles. A real source of her worry involved figuring out what information to share with her peers or trusted adults at her school. Jeanine and her parents agreed that the therapist could reach out to her advisor to seek advice, resulting in a family–school meeting to discuss the issues. Over time, the family made the school an ally in exploring ways of moving forward together. In this case, it involved encouraging the entire family to seek guidance through a local agency specializing in LGBTQ (lesbian, gay, bisexual, transgender, questioning and queer) issues. This partnership eventually included collaborating with the agency's social worker, who became part of the team supporting Jeanine and her family.

Helping one child may benefit the whole school

As any teacher can tell you, one child's learning, emotional, or behavior problems can disrupt the development and progress of the entire class. Not only are classrooms impacted by children and teens who struggle, but the lunchroom, hallways, locker rooms, and other common areas are also places where problems can emerge and escalate. Keeping problems as small as possible is itself an important goal. When you step in decisively and thoughtfully, you can indirectly help maintain the safety and well-being of all students in the classroom.

Let's again consider the case of Jorge, who said he was being bullied. In order to proceed, it was essential to get a clearer picture of what was going on between Jorge and his peers at school. His teachers initially reported that they'd observed Jorge behaving aggressively toward his classmates at times. As the situation evolved and more details were gathered, the therapist and teacher determined that Jorge's aggressive behavior was partly in response to a peer who was, indeed, actively bullying Jorge. Now there were at least two children at risk—the bullied and the perpetrator—with possible long-term, adverse consequences for both, as research has shown (Garandeau, Vartio, Poskiparta, & Salmivalli, 2016). In this case, the therapist, Jorge's parents, and the school were able to validate and support Jorge while also intervening with his classmate and the class as a whole. Your efforts, when carried out with skill and evident goodwill, can bring attention to issues that are important to the quality of experience for the child's classmates as well as your client.

Additionally, one of the least-recognized realities is that good ideas travel. Not always, of course, but more than would be apparent to those outside the school setting. Therapists can positively impact not only the child in therapy and a given teacher or classroom but also the entire school. One of the great benefits of my having spent many years working in one school is discovering the swift, recursive, and additive way that ideas transit among teachers, in student support meetings, with parents, and in meetings with faculty and parents.

It can be as simple as this: In one instance, a local therapist recommended an intervention about how to manage a middle school student's disruptive behavior, and it worked. The intervention popped up in the middle school faculty meeting some weeks later when discussing a second child who was struggling with similar issues, and the intervention was applied and made a real difference. Not long after, there was an incident with a high school student whose school counselor was also part of the middle school student support team. The school counselor suggested using the same intervention that turned out to be equally effective with this particular high school student. Suddenly, the idea became a go-to intervention for students who exhibit disruptive behaviors. Consider the impact such effective classroom interventions can have as teachers master and disseminate them—once a teacher has a good handle on a particular problem, the entire classroom can function more smoothly when the problem inevitably crops up again.

Therapists are unlikely to know that a recommendation they suggested for one child would have such a positive impact in the school long after the work with the original child ended. While it's true that your ideas might have some lasting effect, it's important not to approach a school with an outsized view of your knowledge and influence and thus the notion that what you suggest will have a definitive, far-reaching impact. Yet, as you collaborate with those in a school system, keep in mind that when good ideas are cooked up in your office or in collaboration with the school, they may help others who, in turn, help shape the educational experience for other kids in the school. At the very least, try to help generate ideas that are convertible and reusable in the hands of those implementing them.

It energizes, strengthens, and renews your work

Clinical work can often be isolating, especially for those in individual or small group practices. One of the great pleasures of working with other professionals is the creation of common bonds and shared goals with others who care about a child. This is one major benefit of working with families, of course, but it also applies to close collaboration with school representatives who, like you, want to do whatever they can to help a child be successful at school. Furthermore, by working with those who know the child at school, you will enhance your own skills and knowledge. The school will come to respect the work that you do with its students, leading it to refer other students to you. Ask any student support person in any type of school and you'll hear them talk about their stable of trusted outside professionals to whom they turn when the services they offer a child or family are insufficient and a referral is needed.

Reasons Families Might Not Want to Contact the School

As described above, a strong case can be made for engaging with schools as a matter of course at the start of a child's therapy. That said, there are valid reasons why therapists may decide to wait to contact the school or not contact the school at all. The most basic reason is that the child or family doesn't want the school to know the child is in therapy. Period. The decision to contact school staff is, ultimately, in the hands of the older child and family, as we know from studying the ethical and professional guidelines in our respective fields. This reality can be difficult to accept at times, though it's important for therapists to consider some of the reasons why families might make this choice.

Timing is off or trust is missing

As therapists, we're privileged to have total strangers walk into our office, sit down, and tell us their problems with the implicit hope that we'll be able to help solve them. As every therapist knows, understanding the nature, breadth, and depth of a child's problem often takes time. This early stage of therapy is one of building trust and forging a partnership among the child, family, and therapist.

Even though the early stage of therapy is often the best moment to reach out and collaborate with others, there may be times when it makes sense to wait to make that connection. It could be that you aren't clear about the direction the therapy is going, or you may think that it's premature to reach out to the school in light of the presenting problem and the family's own culture, predilections and sensibilities. It could also be that you're insufficiently connected to the child or family and trying to persuade them to contact the school will erode their confidence even further. Children and families who have suffered trauma, for example, can understandably be reactive and hypervigilant and unlikely to believe that working with the school will benefit them. Here's where you don't want to push too hard, but rather work slowly and carefully to establish mutual trust, further examining the pros and cons of contacting the school at some later time.

Some therapists say that they typically begin treatment with the assumption that they will contact the school and only later change course in the face of a family's reluctance or disagreement. Consider making this your default, too. If you do, make sure to communicate at the outset that this is your standard practice and, at the same time, remain open to changing course when the situation warrants a delay or suspension of what is otherwise a routine intervention. If the child or family is reluctant to have you contact the school directly, or if you think it's too early in the process of getting to know them to make this request, hold off until you're on firmer footing.

Families are concerned about their privacy

Think of privacy (as opposed to confidentiality) as a characteristic that varies among families, something to understand as you would other dimensions of family legacy and interpersonal dynamics. Some families are simply more private than others. For them, contacting the school crosses a boundary they do not wish to cross. In particular, cultural differences can often influence parents' felt sense of privacy in both general and very specific ways (Fahey, 1995). Therapists also have their own sense of what should remain private and what should be shared based on their personal and professional histories, cultural backgrounds, and perhaps even their own stage of professional development. Such differences in personal boundaries can create a complicated brew of opposing styles, sensitivities, and beliefs swirling around the decision to contact the child's school.

If you think it's important to contact the school but the family thinks their privacy will be violated as a result, you must support their decision. Try to find a way to understand and, ideally, respect their choice, even if it differs from yours. Make sure to carefully explain your point of view in addition to listening to theirs, in order to come to a shared understanding that everyone can endorse. You might encourage the family to gather information about their child or share relevant information with the school via a phone call or meeting. Together, you may be able to help shape questions or concerns that, by reaching out to the school, empowers them to collaborate more effectively.

There may be instances in which you believe the necessity of working with the school is so strong that you're no longer able to support the family's wishes. Under these circumstances, it's important to fully discuss your disagreement and encourage the family to reconsider their decision in light of the value of collaborating with the school in order to support the child in that setting.

The child or family is embarrassed or afraid

Shame or fear may be at the root of a family's reservation to let you engage with the school. Parents may be embarrassed that they had to see a therapist, even if the school itself made the referral. When examining why parents are reluctant to have you contact the school, be sure to ask whether they or their child feel that they might be seen differently as a result of the school knowing that the child is in therapy. If so, explore the nature of their concerns in order to determine the best path forward.

One fear or concern that parents may have is that the school's perceptions of the child will change if they know the child is in treatment. Despite significant societal advances, in many groups, communities, schools, and families there can be and often is a perceived stigma associated with seeking help from a mental health professional. Parents sometimes say that they fear their child will be treated differently once a loaded word or label is assigned to them, such as ADHD, depression, or OCD (obsessive compulsive disorder). They worry that such labels can blind teachers and school personnel to seeing their child as a separate, unique, and whole individual. In some instances they are right. Of course, it's more likely that school personnel will be pleased and even relieved to know that the family takes the child's problem seriously enough to seek professional help. As one experienced psychologist said, "In many, if not most schools, teachers and staff will think better of the family for having sought professional help." Part of your work will involve examining whether it is worth taking this risk. To do so, it will be important to review the child's and family's prior experience with the school, examining the basis for their worries and making your own assessment. If you and the family decide to move ahead and inform the school of your involvement, part of your job will be to try to assess in an ongoing way how the school is using this information to ensure that everyone is moving forward productively.

In one case, Gianni, a junior in a large public high school, was adamant about not informing his advisor that he was in therapy because he was certain that he would be treated differently as a result. He'd recently been diagnosed with major depression and was still struggling to accept the need for therapy and medication. Informing his advisor seemed like a humiliating prospect, so the therapist, Gianni, and his parents agreed to put the idea on hold. However, the therapist needed to address how Gianni and his family could respond to concerns his new coach had about his missed practices and provocative on-the-field comments to his teammates, manifestations of his depression-based fatigue and irritability. The therapist was aware that the decision wasn't irreversible; they could revisit the idea of contacting the school at a later time as the therapeutic relationship developed. In the meantime, the therapist could track Gianni's progress via his and his parents' assessments, as well as well as through his upcoming report card.

The child or family has had negative experiences with schools

It's not unusual for a parent or teen to come into a therapist's office and register complaints about a school or schools in general. All such complaints must be taken seriously. Clinicians and researchers have been addressing the issue of dysfunctional relationships between families and schools for decades (Cutler, 2000; Lawrence-Lightfoot, 2003). Past bad experiences can become a barrier to collaboration, and there is no end to the variety of negative experiences one can have. Along with parents and therapists, school staff are naturally subject to human error. We make plenty of mistakes over the course of our lifetime. Those who work in schools, especially teachers, will often say that much if not most of what they know they learned on the job.

Mistakes made by a teacher, administrator, or staff member might be the source of a parent or child's negative experience, especially if what broke down wasn't adequately repaired. Sometimes, the school as a whole systematically fails its constituencies, and this fact may not be transparent to many either inside or outside the school. Fortunately, flagrant transgressions by teachers and schools are rare. Most educators hold deeply idealistic convictions and place a high value on children, education, and the basics of our democratic society (as represented by the constant striving for a robust public school system that tries to meet every child's educational needs). Nonetheless, therapists need to be aware that things can go wrong in a school, sometimes very wrong.

Parents' own adverse experiences of being a student can have an impact on their children and their relationship with the school. This is especially true for parents who struggled or failed academically or socially, attended less than adequate schools, were victims of bullying or other forms of prejudice or racism, or experienced personal trauma at home or school. They may enter the school with "generational echoes" from their past that reverberate in confounding and intrusive ways (Lawrence-Lightfoot, 2003). It may be helpful to take the time to examine these past harmful events with the parents or discuss what might have happened at school that resulted in their mistrust of the institution more generally. These conversations may not only be illuminating for them and their child; they may also be therapeutic and a source of connection and shared understanding between them and the therapist.

The work parents do with you and the school may engender a corrective emotional experience that can positively affect their relationship with their child's school. For example, in a recent family–school meeting, a flustered, somewhat indignant mother said that she came prepared to argue her case in defense of her teenage son's extensive absences. As the meeting unfolded more congenially than the mother had anticipated, she revealed that she'd expected her son would be judged harshly given her own adverse experience in high school. Like all of us, parents arrive with a set of preexisting experiences and beliefs. Their experience working with you and with their child's school may help them overcome at least some of their reservations and antipathy, and allow them to collaborate more effectively.

Finally, in the past, parents may have shared information about their child with someone from the school that was misused or misunderstood. As a result, they may be understandably hesitant to try again. It is important to note that schools and individuals vary in their ability to hold information responsibly. This is a factor to consider when helping parents and kids decide what to share and with whom. You, too, may have had an experience with a school where common norms associated with respecting the privacy of their students and families were violated. It's wise for therapists to remember that, even with the best of intentions, people talk and others listen. This is especially true for information that by its nature is easily transformed into gossip. In the ongoing effort to maintain the highest professional standards, it will be the therapist's job to work with the school to understand and reinforce the boundaries associated with information that is shared. This includes being intentional and thoughtful about how and what ideas are expressed.

When families have had negative experiences with the school, examine each situation carefully and seek to determine what might be done differently this time around. Understanding what may have gone wrong in the past will make it more likely that you'll be able to help the family work with the school in a way that respects their sense of privacy, shares information carefully, and establishes mutual goals that address the current problem. Over decades, national and international research has demonstrated that most parents care deeply about their child's success at school (Benner, Boyle, & Sadler, 2016; Wentzel, Russell, & Baker, 2016). Tap into that reserve of goodwill and look for possible building blocks to facilitate eventual collaboration.

The parents disagree with each other

Sometimes, especially if the parents are divorced or separated, there can be differences of opinion within families as to whether or not you should reach out. One parent might be enthusiastic about the idea, while the other is reluctant to share something that he or she fears will become a source of gossip or judgment. Sometimes, parents disagree because the disagreement is part of a larger set of problems in the relationship. When there is disagreement between the parents, it's the therapist's job to slow down the process and review the reluctant parent's perspective. The therapist must avoid the appearance or reality of taking sides, especially before fully understanding the reasons that one parent may not want the therapist to get involved with the school. Often, there are legal stipulations associated with a separation or divorce that require therapists (and others) to secure the permission of both parties.

If the parents' views are not too entrenched, conversations about whether to contact the school can be not only useful but also enriching, further clarifying the goals of therapy and, ideally, enlisting the support of all family members. It's possible that, over time, you'll all come to an understanding about the value of contacting the school, even after the initial hesitation or disagreement.

Reasons Therapists Might Not Choose to Contact the School

Apart from a family's hesitation or decision, there are five additional reasons why therapists sometimes choose not to contact a child's school. These come up consistently. Some are practical or logistical, while others relate more to the therapist's own therapeutic orientation or sense of the job's parameters. Sometimes, a child's school problems can be addressed in the therapist's office without contacting the school because of the nature of the problem or short-term work that is needed. Finally, sometimes therapists can coach or support parents to work with the school directly. It's important to reflect on the reasons why you, as a therapist, might not raise the possibility of working directly with someone at the child's school, and what the implications or trade-offs of this decision might be.

Time constraints

Perhaps the most common reason why therapists don't reach out to a child's school is lack of time. Therapists are busy people. Some therapists have heavy caseloads, leaving little free time to make calls, write emails, or visit schools. Then there are the instances when your life or the system in which you work does not allow you to spend time observing kids or attending family–school meetings. On top of this is the glaring fact that for most therapists who work with children, our day begins when the teacher's day ends, with little overlap. Those therapists who work during the evening hours are understandably unsure what might be considered intrusive for the person at school. Furthermore, coordinating discussions with a teacher during the school day might be difficult, perhaps even impossible, given the demands on a teacher's time and yours. Despite busy, often conflicting schedules, email and other digital forms of communication can be incorporated into your practice to make or even sustain contact as you coordinate efforts with the school.

Lack of information about how to make contact

Sometimes, it's neither clear whom to contact at a child's school nor the best way to contact them. A school social worker working in a charter school said she's "surprised how infrequently outside professionals reach out to the school." She wondered whether therapists simply didn't know enough about the school, or about charter schools in particular, and therefore don't realize that there was a support staff ready and willing to collaborate. When in doubt about whom to call, it's important to seek advice from the parent or child. In the next chapter, we'll review steps to take in making initial contact with a school, which could diminish this concern.

Worries about additional responsibilities

Sometimes, therapists don't reach out to the school because we recognize that, once we do, we'll be responsible to an even broader network of interested parties. This is worth considering for a moment, given the pressures we feel to do good clinical work, pursue continuing education opportunities, maintain professional peer relationships, secure additional supervision when needed, manage records, do billing, and perform other assorted jobs associated with the practice of being a clinician. So, one might ask, "Now you're saying that I need to keep in touch with my client's teacher or school social worker, too?" It's a prospect that may feel burdensome, even if clinically indicated. Keep in mind that with the additional responsibility come many benefits for your client and you, from access to information you wouldn't get otherwise, to relationships that will ultimately benefit the child, the family and you.

Doubts about the skills required to work with schools

As therapists, we sometimes lack confidence in our work, wondering whether we're doing all that's needed to support the child (and family) we're treating. Especially for those of you just starting out, you will likely face such concerns as you grow into your role. Self-doubt can interfere with calling the school, since we'll surely be asked questions about our assessment of the student and what we're doing therapeutically, as well as questions about what teachers or student support staff can do to solve the problem—questions for which we may not have answers. As one therapist states, "If you don't have a background in education, don't know what an IEP is, or know what to ask about what services are given through the school, it's scary to broach." As therapists, we can check in with our own insecurities and see whether they relate to an absence of knowledge, skill, or our temperamental characteristics, all of which can be overcome by attempting to address the issues we uncover that prevent us from doing our best work.

Therapeutic orientation

Some therapeutic orientations are less oriented toward outside collaboration. There is a long tradition of psychodynamic child therapy, for example, in which transformational change occurs through a corrective therapeutic relationship between the child and therapist. In some instances, direct input from others may be seen as interfering with the child's therapy. If you practice a type of therapy that deemphasizes collaboration, and if a parent asks you to talk with someone at the child's school, it will be important to reconcile the therapeutic model with the parent's request for outside collaboration.

Two problems can arise. First, it can be difficult to create a common language about the child; communication missteps can leave everyone confused and frustrated. Second, the focus on the past or underlying psychodynamic issues can conflict with the pace and orientation of educators. In one instance, a therapist, in speaking with a school counselor, referred to how the child's school problems were due to the child's internal conflict and losses associated with her mother's depression when the child was young. The therapist explained that the child was parented poorly at a critical time in her development, and he was trying to help her deal with deep, unresolved feelings resulting from that loss. Given what the school counselor knew about the child's history, the therapeutic formulation for this child made sense. However, it was not useful in solving the day-to-day problems that the child was having getting her work done in several classes and determining whether the child would be able to move on to the next grade level. The past was relevant to the child's problems, as was the exploration of the issues in therapy, but not necessarily to those at school; they were seeking more immediate solutions.

If you are using a therapeutic framework that is less oriented toward outside collaboration, consider using the following guidelines when working with schools.

1. **Discuss your therapeutic orientation.** Discuss your therapeutic orientation with the parent and child to decide whether and how to move forward in light of the school's immediate concerns. Inform the school representative about your therapeutic orientation, how the therapy works, and what your goals are for the child. Search for common ground in moving forward.

2. **Clarify the school's perspective, and use the school's language (when possible).** Ask the teacher or school representative to describe what the school sees, clarifying anything that might be confusing. Teachers with whom I spoke reported feeling frustrated or put down at times by a therapist's use of clinical terms that were outside the norm for them as educators, so make every effort to use their language when discussing the child. Such lack of congruence can impede progress for you and them in your efforts to support a child.

3. **Be willing to adapt your timeline to match the needs of the child and school.** Keep in mind that the teacher's pace and your pace may be quite different. Think about how you can maintain your goals in light of the child's more immediate and sometimes urgent needs at school.

4. **Be open to involving other therapeutic resources.** In the face of serious conflict between your goals for treatment and what needs to be addressed at school, discuss this with the parents and child. Consider drawing from integrative approaches the might bridge the divide (Rudenstine, Wright, Morales, & Tuber, 2018; Wachtel, 2004), consulting with trusted colleagues who share your therapeutic orientation, or adding someone else to the team who can work with the school to solve problems in that setting.

REVIEWING THE BASICS

There are many reasons why a therapist might choose not to work with the school directly. However, each of these concerns can be effectively mitigated with the right tools, techniques, and mindset. Collaborating with the school can greatly enhance your work and correct misperceptions you've acquired by the distinct limitations inherent in talking only with the child and parent.

- In most instances, it's a good idea to contact a child's school when a child you are seeing in therapy has problems at school.

- Contacting the school will often give you a fuller understanding of the child's problem and can also help the family (and caregivers) and school personnel in a child's life be more supportive.

- Working with the school on one child's problem can have positive reverberations throughout the whole classroom, or even the whole school. You never know how far your good ideas will travel.

- Sometimes, the family you're working with will want you to hold off on contacting the school for various reasons, sometimes related to their discomfort with telling the school that their child is in therapy. Always make sure your efforts are in line with the family's wishes and decision making.

- With reluctant families, you can always revisit contacting the school as the therapeutic relationship develops.

- You might feel ill-equipped or unable to add "working with schools" to your long list of to-dos, or you simply might prefer not to due to your clinical orientation. Ideally, this book can mitigate some of those hesitations or insecurities and, at the very least, allow you to better understand and clarify the choices you make.

CHAPTER 4

Building a Collaborative Relationship with the School

Given the inherent complexities of working with children, families, and schools, there are no fixed linear steps to follow that would encompass every type of problem or type of collaborative relationship. Yet, generations of educators and therapists have found ways to collaborate effectively, resulting in a store of experience and knowledge that derives from research, practice, and good common sense. This chapter will outline a framework all therapists can use to build collaborative relationships with children's schools, no matter the type of institution or clinical issue at hand.

A Framework for Building a Collaborative Relationship with the School

Effective engagement with schools follows an iterative path. The figure below illustrates how to start thinking about building a positive, productive relationship with any school.

Typically, good collaboration starts with establishing a shared perspective about the problem and outlining steps that can be taken to help the child who is struggling. Once this is accomplished, interventions—at home, at school, or in your office—are implemented. As interventions are tried, feedback is solicited from relevant sources in order to reflect on and determine what has worked and perhaps what hasn't. Ongoing conversations can further enhance the shared perspective going forward when needed, and interventions can be refined and repeated accordingly.

What you will find as you go through this process is that, as you work with the child, family, and school, you will help create a system of support for the child. Perhaps you will become part of the school's support team or, together, you will help create a system of support for the child. This may happen naturally and with-out forethought. In fact, many of you will look back on your collaborative work with schools and see yourselves as part of a number of child-family–school teams. By becoming aware of everyone's role in this process, you can evaluate your work in light of the larger systems and resources that are functioning to help the child in need. Ultimately you will develop and enhance the solutions you implement. Using Figure 4.1 as the model, we'll review the four parts of this approach.

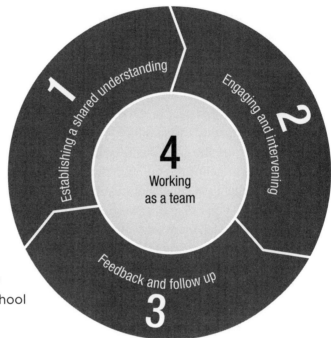

Figure 4.1: Approach to building a collaborative relationship with the school

Source: the author

Establishing a Shared Understanding

To support a vulnerable child, it is essential that everyone involved in the child's care shares an understanding about the problem at hand. If not, the therapist might be working on one facet of the issue and the teacher another, at best con-fusing the process and at worst creating friction or conflict. That's not to say that there aren't often multiple problems to address at a given time, but unless you share an understanding of some kind, it's possible you could be working at odds with the other supportive figures in the child's life, rendering your interventions ineffective or muddling the process. The shared understanding that you create becomes the foundation on which conversations and interventions rest until a new understanding is needed to explain what's going on in the ongoing process of supporting a child. Establishing a shared understanding involves actively seeking multiple perspectives, learning about the school, and recognizing that you may be working with different types and sources of information across stakeholders.

Seek multiple perspectives

To begin, it's important to listen actively to what others have to say about the child, including the family and teachers. Therapists should pay close attention to the expertise and biases each person brings to the situation—especially their own. Each party enters the conversation with a set of feelings, expressed or not. For clinicians, the therapeutic enterprise consists of paying attention to the emotions, language, and nonverbal behaviors of our clients and the people in their lives. We also need to pay attention to beliefs, perceptions, and ways of life associated with cultural, ethnic, religious, and other differences, including our own. Listen to the way that people at the school talk about the child. Hear their level of frustration, empathy, and familiarity with the child; their ways of thinking about the problem; and the solutions they have tried. Continue to look for overlap or discontinuity in cultures, parenting practices (Lareau, 2011; Lawrence-Lightfoot, 2003), and other contextual features related to the family and school. When possible, everyone is heard in this process, laying the groundwork for a shared understanding from which plans and interventions follow.

Sometimes, after parents and teachers hear each other speak about a particular child, someone will remark, "It seems we're talking about two different kids!" This experience of disjointedness is a familiar one for therapists who work with children. Differing views are endemic to the work we do; they involve us unequivocally, once we jump into the fray. Keep in mind that having different perspectives should ultimately be reassuring. It reflects the likelihood that people are speaking independently and generating a more rounded, full picture of the child. Children who become familiar to you in sessions may behave quite differently at school when they're hanging out in the hallway with their friends or interacting on the field with a coach. The school counselor may report that a particular student makes nonsensical comments in class and randomly lobs insults at those who don't agree with him. But in your office, this young man may be polite and deferential to his parents, to you, and in the way he talks about his teachers at school. It can take a while to make the connections that explain the different kid that each person sees. Listen carefully to what teachers or other student support people report, initially asking questions to clarify rather than forward your own thinking about the child.

While seeking out the views of those who know the child best, keep an open mind as you listen. Be willing to change your perspective as a result of what you learn along the way. Good listeners have "a capacity not to be thrown off course by, or buckle under the weight of, information that may deeply challenge certain settled assumptions. Good listeners are unfussy about the chaos which others may for a time create in their minds; they've been there before and know that everything can eventually be set back in its place" (de Botton, 2016).

Also, be prepared to share your ideas with others as needed. Assembling a perspective about the child based on varying reports and your own experience is your job as the child's therapist; it develops over time. Your clinical perspective and judgment will be the basis for the recommendations you make and collaborative relationships in which you engage.

The story of 16-year-old Jody illustrates the importance of seeking multiple perspectives on a child's problem. In Jody's case, the school counselor had emailed home to say that Jody was falling asleep in class and wondered what might be going on. When Jody's mother called the therapist, she revealed that Jody had suffered from anxiety and depression for years and was now having trouble sleeping. The mother expressed concern that Jody's grades would suffer, which would affect her GPA and thus her college options. It also became clear that there were long-standing pressures at home due to what Jody's mother described as "difficult family dynamics," related, in part, to the parents' preoccupation with an older, disabled sibling. Though Jody's depression had led the parents to seek help for her in the past, current concerns about Jody's future college admission were the tipping point in securing professional guidance. Interestingly, when Jody herself spoke about the problem in the initial session, she had an altogether different worry. She was afraid that her lack of sleep was symptomatic of a serious mental illness, the type her uncle had, which she said had ruined his life.

It's not unusual for a parent to be focused on one set of concerns (Jody's school performance and college prospects), the school representative to be focused on something else (what falling asleep in class might reflect about the student's overall health and well-being), and the client, in this case Jody, to be upset about something different (fear of having a mental illness). Had the therapist gone with only one person's perspective, the therapeutic intervention would have been necessarily limited, given how much was at stake for Jody. Jody's worry about her mental health factored into her lack of sleep, but was not evident to her mom or the school counselor. Falling asleep in class impacted Jody's classmates and the teacher's perception of her; it might have resulted in a disciplinary response had the counselor not become involved. Jody's mother's anxiety about college admissions prospects likely added to Jody's worries, so the therapist needed to direct some of her attention to Jody's mom, who was often overwhelmed by her daughter's difficulties and disabled son.

Inevitably, there are layers of motivation and concerns that are uncovered in the course of assessing and treating problems. Sometimes, the problems eventually line up; that is, they tell a coherent story of the child, family, and school, as they eventually did with Jody. In other instances, the different reports are contradictory and people are at odds with one another over which account is more accurate. It is your job to understand the problem definitions in a wide enough context in order to uncover what matters most to the children and families you see. Equipped with that understanding, together you can determine the direction therapeutic interventions will take. Co-constructing meaning not only clarifies what is going on and therefore what might be at stake but also allows you to work in concert with others. Indeed, the process of co-constructing meaning to shape up the formulation of the problem mirrors the process of problem solving collaboratively.

Learn about the school

As explored in Chapter 1, every school is different, so part of establishing a shared understanding will be familiarizing yourself with the type of school your client attends. Knowing something about what it's like for the kids you see in therapy to walk into a classroom each day or sit down at the lunch table is invaluable. Client families will greatly appreciate this familiarity and knowledge as they try to engage their child's school more effectively. School staff will come to know you and your work, adding to the trust and confidence that grows between you. Getting to know a school is simply a good clinical investment for those who treat children and families. Going to a school to observe a child, talking with a teacher, or attending a family–school meeting are some of the ways that you can accomplish this. Over time, as you engage with different families, you'll become increasingly aware of whether you're on the right track in your thinking, assessing ever more effectively what works in which school.

Recognize that you may be working with different types and sources of information

A shared understanding will not necessarily be achieved in your initial contact with someone from the school. Keep in mind that you are not seeking agreement across all aspects of the presenting problem. As one experienced clinician said, "When not all information is shared, it can be complicated and challenging to juggle." For example, all parties may be concerned about the third grader, John, who doesn't seem able to settle down and get his work done in class. At the same time, through your work with John and his family, you're aware that his mother has just been admitted into a rehabilitation program for drug addiction following a stormy period in which his parents repeatedly separated and reunited. As the therapist, you have been focused on helping the family find the resources they need to stabilize life at home, such as having his mother's sister move in to help with maintaining routines. This family thoughtfully declined to inform the school about the larger family issues. Therefore, it was the therapist's job to keep this information confidential and, along with his aunt focus on how John could get his work done at school.

Those who worked with John at his school understood his problem from a different vantage point. The school's support team knew that they were dealing with a new teacher at the school, a teacher whose lack of experience led her to inadvertently antagonize John when he was less engaged and unproductive. A senior teacher in the school was working behind the scenes to mentor the teacher, though this was a slow process and not one to be resolved right away. Understandably, the school team decided not to share this information with the family.

Particular circumstances or the so-called back story may not be transparent, yet a common understanding about the child's problem or part of the child's problem can still be identified. In John's case, all parties agreed that John needed help staying focused in class and to do so meant temporarily modifying expectations of his performance and having the school's learning specialist observe him in class. "You may not be working with the same set of variables," one clinician said, "just one or two that overlap." It will be your job to listen to how the problem is being addressed at school and at home to catch the overlapping variables or depictions. On the basis of this overlap, large or small, your work can advance. However modest a goal, some shared view of the child—in this case, John's problem focusing in class—is essential, otherwise you will not be able to determine a course of action or judge whether what you are doing is effective.

Engaging and Intervening

The core of the work we do with schools involves two things: First, figuring out what's working and what's not and second, trying something new or modifying what's already in place. Once you've developed a shared understanding, the task is to help design interventions that support the kids you're seeing in therapy. Plans can be small and brief, such as in John's case when the decision was made that the school's learning specialist would observe him in the classroom that week. Or they can be more involved, like having the child tested by the school psychologist for a possible learning disability or setting up a series of therapy sessions with the child to strengthen her social skills. Some interventions are classroom-specific. For example, in collaboration with the therapist, a teacher could decide not to respond to a child who keeps interrupting her classmates to see whether the absence of reinforcement diminishes the child's disruptive behavior. Effective engagement and intervention involves an ongoing search for good ideas and resources and a commitment to true collaboration with and empowerment of the child and parents.

Three levels of engagement

When you first contact a school, more often than not you won't know in advance the level of your eventual engagement. All you know is that you're reaching out because of your involvement with and concern about the child (and family) you are seeing. In some cases, a single phone conversation with a teacher will do the job. In others, you may find yourself emailing or talking regularly as interventions are introduced and revised. Or you may be involved in a multiyear commitment, given the child's and family's deeply rooted and pervasive problems. As you continue in your practice over the years, it's possible that you will see multiple children in the same school or give presentations to faculty or parents in your area of expertise. In short, it's hard to know where the first contact with a school will take you. In light of these different possibilities, three levels of engagement will be reviewed.

One contact (or so) is enough. In many instances, you'll talk with a teacher, carry out a classroom observation, or exchange emails with a school psychologist, and that will be the only contact you'll have with that school. It can be that straightforward, if not always that simple. All that was needed, perhaps, was a nod from you about a planned intervention. Or you might have solicited information about a child or sought clarification about a teacher's expectations that were confusing. In short, you may have found that the question you had or the problem that was presented was resolved in one favorable phone conversation.

Sometimes, a classroom observation serves a specific purpose, and there is no more reason to contact the school. Therapists who do testing, for example, sometimes need to talk with a school representative only once in order to gather the necessary information. In addition, there are many times when parents decide to handle issues at the school themselves after your phone call with a teacher, administrator, or school representative. Parents may decide to pick up where you left off and, with or without your advice or coaching, work directly with the school. In fact, parents who work well with the school may need only minimal if any direct involvement between you and the school.

There are cases where something about the way the person at the school interacted with you left you feeling that further contact would not be productive or helpful. Not every school representative has experience working with outside professionals or, if they do, desires collaboration. In those circumstances, try to keep the door open with a comment or two about your availability and willingness to work together. In some cases, in discussion with the child and family, you might consider contacting a different school representative. In such instances, talking with the parents about how they can best work with the school is essential.

Regular contact while working with a child. Regular contact with the school involves sharing and receiving information about a child in an ongoing way. Contact might be with one person or more, depending on the problem and circumstance. This level of engagement includes a good proportion of the work you'll do with the schools your clients attend, especially those cases in which the child is struggling in that setting and the family has actively sought your help in collaborating with the school. In these cases, you will stay in touch with a school representative until the child is functioning better or whenever the school-related part of the child's problem is resolved. The expectation is that at the end of treatment your contact with the school will end, too.

Multiyear collaboration with the school. In some instances, you will form lasting, multiyear relationships with schools; these collaborative relationships can be a source of deep satisfaction and productivity. The relationship may form because you see multiple clients from the same school or because you have provided services over the years such as workshops, presentations, or consultations to students, faculty, and parents. Sometimes, you are one of a handful of therapists who offer expertise in an area that's related to a particular type of school or student population and are brought in from time to time.

Over the years, you may become one of the therapists who knows the teachers, administrators, and staff of the school. They get to know you, too. In these instances, you may give priority to receiving referrals from the school, and they come to rely on you to try to fit someone into your practice when possible. Schools need therapists like this—those with whom they know they can work well.

In my role as a consultant to a school, we often relied on therapists who knew how to work with the students and families in the school and, as importantly, when and how to collaborate with us. We knew that if a child was working with a particular therapist, a collaborative relationship with the school would likely be established and excellent clinical care provided. I also know as a therapist working with children and families that my most satisfying and enriching collaborative relationships are with the schools with which I've worked for a long time, even decades. Even though personnel may change, there is a continuity that deepens over the years and brings with it an increased confidence in being able to help.

Search for good ideas and resources

Regardless of your level of engagement, schools can offer a wealth of ideas and resources to support interventions designed to help the student, if you know where to look. Those of you with experience working in schools know what it's like to have a school representative respond to your request to become involved with unequivocal delight since the staff may have run out of ideas about what to do next. Here's where your past work with children and schools and your specific work with a particular child and family can yield productive insights and ideas that will unstick a tough situation. As someone who knows both the child and the larger family unit, you're able to see what turns the tide when the family gets stuck and what can be leveraged for change within that system.

The converse is true, too. There may have been times when the child, family, and you have run out of ideas and through a conversation with someone from the school you heard something new that might never have occurred to you, something uniquely attuned to the child you see in your office. Through my experience working with schools I have witnessed the transformative energy that comes when a teacher or school counselor runs through a half dozen ideas to consider in support of a student. School staff have seen what works and can extrapolate from those instances by applying their knowledge to the particular child. Meeting at this intersection is one of the true pleasures and morale boosters of this work.

People working in schools are also often quite savvy about getting kids involved in various activities. For example, one school counselor described a situation in which he invited a high school student to his office to talk about joining a support group for children of divorce. The student declined. Later, the counselor met with the student about her poor grades in math, and they agreed to meet weekly to try to sort out what might be the problem. After the student grew more comfortable with the counselor in discussing math, she began to talk about her home life as well. The transition to reconsidering the divorce group naturally followed; this time, the student agreed to attend the meetings.

Part of what therapists can do is search for new ideas and resources, both within and outside the school. For example, many schools have groups for kids who struggle with social skills or reading. Schools also have clubs and activities that meet a range of needs and interests. Keep in mind that kids of minority status may be seeking activities that represent their interests rather than those of the majority population. School social workers and others can help identify neighborhood resources and how to access them, and can also work directly with parents to facilitate referrals and provide follow-up assistance. Some of what's available may be easily known and accessible, and other resources may take some digging to uncover.

Finally, you might offer to do programs or workshops at the school on various topics such as stress management, resilience, childhood anxiety and depression, social media, or a topic about which you have expertise. In this way you can become one of the school's resources and sources of support.

Make sure your involvement is truly collaborative

As much as possible, speak with someone from the child's school before you make specific recommendations related to the school. In one case, this did not take place, and the child suffered as a result. A therapist, working with a teenager, advised the school counselor to discontinue her weekly meetings with her client because it would "dilute the therapy" she was doing with the student. By not seeking information about the counseling sessions nor attempting to collaborate with the counselor, the therapist inadvertently undermined what was a steady and valuable relationship the teenager had formed with someone at school who was there to step in when problems arose or debrief situations that hadn't gone well on a given day. It wasn't clear if this reflected a conflict of therapeutic paradigms or a failure of the therapist to reach out and become better informed. Either way, the teenager lost out as a result, as the recommendation undermined the relationship she had with her advocate at school—the school counselor. By contacting the school, the therapist can better tailor advice and interventions to the child and the problem, as well as to those who will be carrying out the interventions. Also, find out what's been tried before and how it worked. If an intervention has been effective in the past, see whether it can be adapted. Learn what adjustments are needed to fit the current circumstances.

It is important to keep in mind that the child who entered your office is there because what she, her parents, and the school were doing wasn't working or wasn't working well enough, even if each person thought the other was the one falling short. It is your job to assess the situation and build on the resources and strengths of the individuals and surrounding systems to seek solutions that move the child along a better pathway. Every client, family, and school must be understood in its own uniqueness. Plans that are made must relate to *that particular child, family,* and *school* and not some abstract or idealized version of them.

Look for ways to empower the child

As we know, children and teens need to have a sense of control over their lives in order to develop self-esteem, personal efficacy, and self-determination. Part of our job as therapists is to maximize opportunities for children to develop these skills and habits, whether children have school problems or not. The therapist is in a unique position to help children develop self-advocacy skills in the school, beginning with the simple act of listening to what they have to say. As the child's perspective becomes clear, the therapist can help the child, especially a preteen or teen, to articulate his or her views to those people who are most able to help. By facilitating this kind of self-advocacy, the therapist can support the child in being able to avoid saying, "My dog ate my homework" and instead say something like, "I couldn't do my homework last night because I didn't understand it."

Even though the child we see in therapy is at the center of the conversation we're having, sometimes the child may not be at the center of the decision making. The therapist can look for ways to bring the child into those situations when decisions are being made about possible interventions. For example, Kevin struggled to complete his homework at night, even when there were minimal requirements. Home life was chaotic even with best efforts on the part of his large, extended family. Eventually, Kevin's therapist suggested that she meet at the school with Kevin, his mom, the lead teacher, and the parent liaison to discuss the problem. It was Kevin who came up with the idea of his staying after school to do his homework there, returning home on the school bus with those who stayed late for sports practice. By working with the mother and the school, the therapist helped bring the child to the table and thereby become an active and able participant in figuring out what he needed. Being allowed at the table is not only about character building. The child's measure of buy-in relates directly to the likelihood of an intervention being successful.

Empower the parents, too

Parents and caregivers need to develop skills for working with their child's school to maximize the possibility for mutual support and collaboration. Often, this involves helping parents expand their role, sometimes involving a learning curve on the parents' part. It might also involve helping parents repair and build stronger relationships with key people at the child's school (see Appendix B). Typically, this is a process rather than an educational moment. It begins with sorting out the family's history of involvement with the teacher and school. Then, the therapist and parents can figure out what role the parent can take in engaging more effectively. This involves reassurance and care as well as planning and problem solving. (See Chapter 11 for more about parents as advocates.)

Therapists can look for opportunities to facilitate these connections. For example, recommendations can be made to parents about what they can do in a given situation, such as recommending that they contact the administrative assistant to confirm that they'll be coming to the school for a meeting. Modest gestures such as this can help to replenish and restore confidence and goodwill. In instances where there is a history of miscommunication, antagonism, or a significant breakdown in trust, more time and effort will be required to build connections or at least minimize further erosion of respect and mutual reliance. As one therapist adamantly affirmed about his work with families and schools, "We're going to make this [family–school] relationship as good as possible!"

Sometimes, you may be in a position to help the parents adjust their expectations and "make peace with a teacher," as one therapist said. This is not an unusual situation, in fact. Based on what you've heard from the teacher or observed in the classroom, it may become clear that the teacher is trying his or her best to support the child. Through your involvement, you may have learned how missteps were made by the various parties, leaving everyone at odds with one another with varying degrees of grievance or discord. In such situations, reviewing what happened and helping the parents accept what the teacher has to offer can facilitate a more amicable (or less antagonistic) relationship that may be more sustainable through what remains of the academic year.

Based on conversations a therapist had with the parents and teacher of an elementary school student, he could see that the disruption that occurred in the family–school relationship was repairable, given each party's resolve to help the child. Relying on the trust that the mother had in the therapist, a plan was put in place for the mother to attend the next family–school meeting to propose to the teacher that they have a fresh start. The teacher responded well to this, and both relaxed into a more productive conversation.

Advice and recommendations from therapists can help parents relate more constructively with school representatives, not a small thing. Kids benefit from knowing that their parents get along with their teacher as well as with others at school and, if that's not possible under the circumstance, that the parents are willing to try to make the best of things for their child's sake. However, sometimes making the best of things requires that parents need to actively advocate for their child in order to try to remedy a situation that they have determined is at odds with their child's best interest and needs. Again, this topic will be explored in Chapter 11, on parental advocacy, and Chapter 12, on helping families navigate special education systems.

Sometimes, through developing a relationship with their child's school, parents can have a restorative emotional experience. Here are some examples: A mother who felt alienated from her peers in high school discovered friendships materializing from years sitting on the bleachers watching her son play baseball each spring. Likewise, a father who dropped out of school found that shouldering the responsibility for his asthmatic elementary school daughter with a caring and devoted fifth grade teacher altered his unfavorable views about teachers formed when he was young. Another parent, whose daughter couldn't seem to grasp the principles of graphing in her geometry class, could see that the teacher's patient instruction revealed that, "She wasn't only interested in teaching the smart kids."

Feedback and Follow-Up

The most important aspect of feedback and follow-up is that it happens. You simply won't know whether a planned intervention is working unless you hear back from those who are carrying out the intervention—be it the parents, teacher, school counselor, advisor, or nurse—or are there to observe what's happening. Therefore, you will need to stay in touch with someone from the school as a means of giving and receiving feedback, making it possible to assess the effectiveness of what's being done. How often, with whom, and in what fashion (by phone, email, text, or via meetings at school) will depend on the situation and your planned level of engagement.

What good follow-up looks like

Good follow-up is prompt, reliable, respectful, and child-focused. It's important to make every effort to do what you say you'll do or inform the school otherwise. This is worth noting, because a common complaint that teachers and student support staff convey about therapists is that they don't follow up in the ways they said they would. Keep in mind that your credibility depends partly on your ability to follow through with the plans you've made with the school, so don't promise too much (an easy mistake for us to make in this profession when our desire to help may exceed our capabilities). People in schools who make referrals to outside therapists will recognize the difference between the professionals who follow up as promised and those who don't. Being aware of this issue can help us avoid problems, such as constantly having to begin emails or phone calls with the words, "I'm sorry I didn't get back to you sooner."

There are many ways to assess the progress a child is making, including formal behavioral assessments that are designed to determine the effectiveness of interventions. If using such assessments is part of your practice, make sure that they are fully understood by those who will be using them with you. Others will check in more informally, asking questions and receiving input from whoever is involved in making or carrying out the plans. In some cases, a particular outcome can be determined by hard data, such as better grades, a reduction in the number of absences, a return to activities, or the absence of suspensions for behavioral problems.

Closing the loop

As you work with others to make and alter plans to fit the needs of the situation, it helps to think of this process as a natural strengthening of your common understanding of the child. This means that you grow in your understanding and that, in turn, feeds into future planning and interventions. Often, the resolution of one problem leads directly into trying to solve another, and even another, since the problems many children face are complex and multifaceted. By seeing your work in this recursive, additive way, you can further clarify what roles people can play and how best to support the child and family.

Working as a Team

By its nature, the therapist's job is finite (time-limited), circumscribed (occupies certain functions and parameters) and facilitative (with and between families, children, and schools). You may be able to participate in, support, and strengthen a team of people who are working together to support the child and family you are seeing in therapy. This depends on a number of factors: time spent working with a school, the existence of a team framework in a school, the school's capacity and willingness to be involved and work with you, and the family's and child's willingness to permit you to work with the school. It's important to look at this phenomenon from different angles.

Understanding your role and the roles of others

In some cases, you will be valued simply as another outside resource because of your work with the child and family. This tenure may be short-lived or not. It may involve a widening circle of people who coalesce in their efforts over time to assess a problem and seek solutions. Whatever level of engagement or breadth of people involved, try to think of yourself as a part of a team working together to solve problems as energetically and creatively as possible. It may not feel like a team to you, stationed as you are in your office each day. But if you ask those who work in schools where teamwork and collaboration are the norm, you'll find that you're viewed as a valuable member of the assembly of people they depend on to support a vulnerable student.

Over time, the ties that are formed become discernable to you during conversations, email exchanges, or school meetings. Then, if you add to this the idea that every person on the team is an expert in their own sphere of involvement and influence, you have an even greater chance of building and strengthening the team. Regarding the latter point, one therapist said, "It helps to be explicit about the idea that everyone is an expert because there can be competition in the stew."

Therapists are in a good position to understand this reality and recognize the validity of everyone's perspective and expertise about the child.

It may be useful to think about the following analogy: When you or someone you care about has had to face a tough medical situation, there are multiple people involved: the primary care physician, a medical specialist, someone who assists with scheduling appointments, and so on. These people, linked to one another through a very real problem or crisis, not only coexist in real time and space but also in shared consciousness. When this collective is capable, focused, and collaborative, we begin to see them as part of the circle of people who share the desire and determination to help make things better for us or our loved ones. Our confidence grows and perhaps even our sense of optimism about the overall outcome. When a collective energy is harnessed with steadiness and skill, opportunities may increase, even with stops and starts along the way.

A school social worker working in an elementary school made this point clear when she said, "We need a therapist who gets it that we work together." When queried again, she said, "What advice do I have for outside therapists? Come to the school! See the kid in class. Meet the teacher. Let the social worker or others facilitate this." Her enthusiasm for this process spoke volumes about the inherent value in working with the school and becoming part of the team. One caveat: When you work with a school, not only might you become part of a team but, as a team member, you might inadvertently become part of the problem rather than part of its solution. Systems are powerful, and dysfunctional systems bring with them potential pitfalls for the therapist (see Chapter 9).

Strengthening the family–school relationship

Therapists are in a unique position to help strengthen the relationship between the family and the school. Plenty of research documents the value of this; kids do better when families and schools partner together (Sheridan & Kratochwill, 2010), and those who work in and with schools know this experientially. We also know that there is a strong link between parental involvement and a child's academic achievement (Christenson, 2004). Positive impact derives from partnerships between families and schools, even though they may be hard to form and sustain.

For example, at times there can be damage from previous insults and injuries that has resulted in mutual distrust and hostility. In these cases, the therapist can look for ways to try to bridge the differences. Being attuned to the sound of blaming (that is guaranteed to further alienate both parties), the therapist may have the opportunity to interrupt and redirect the conversation. You may be able to find common ground; resolve problems; or recognize the frustration, sadness, or worry from which the blaming may have originated (see Chapter 9). It sounds like a tall order, but it happens all the time when working with schools. Of course, therapist involvement doesn't guarantee that things will work out well, but due to their training, therapists can think in terms of what amplifies and corrects difficult conversations and relationships.

Building relationships of trust and respect between the family and school is both a goal and a potential outcome of your work. Even when there is conflict and gaps in understanding, you'll be looking for ways to build trust grounded in the realities of the problem and the context, gauging people's limits and strengths as well as your own. You'll need to be patient, since mistrust and animosity may not subside until the child is doing better. As Patterson, Grenny, McMillan, & Switzler claim in their best-selling book *Crucial Conversations* (2011, p. 49), "When it's safe, you can say anything," and mutual trust is built on feeling some degree of safety.

You may also help strengthen the relationship between the family and school by remaining positive and professional and keeping an open mind. You don't need to have the answers to all questions; in fact, it's better to enter into a conversation aware that you likely won't have all the answers. What you can bring is a willingness to explore, examine, and seek to answer them.

REVIEWING THE BASICS

Forging a good working relationship with a school is an important dimension of working effectively with kids who have school problems. In doing so, it's important to maintain hope that something can be changed to improve the life course of the child and the family. To review:

- Seek everyone's perspective on the situation and ask how they've come to the conclusions they've made. The child needs to be an active part of the process.

- Hold on to the different ways of seeing the child since they are keys to developing a shared understanding.

- Be open to different levels of engagement with the school, depending on the situation.

- Look for ways to empower the child and family, including identifying what's worked in the past. Parents may not recognize the ordinary things they do that make a difference.

- Don't forget to follow up with teachers, student support team members, or other key personnel after interventions are implemented.

- Except in unusual circumstances, the therapist is almost always going to make every effort to find a way for the family and the school to work together effectively, with an agreed upon framework, toward a goal that all parties believe makes sense. Keep in mind that one of the best predictors of a child's success at school is the quality of the relationship between the family and school.

PART II

Establishing Collaborative Relationships

CHAPTER 5

Effective Practices for Contacting the School

In this chapter, we'll walk through a protocol for contacting a school, as well as review basic principles to keep in mind while talking with school representatives. Your thoughtful, ethical handling of this process will help parents and kids understand the importance of your involvement with the school. Ultimately, it will reassure them of your professionalism and high standard of care. That begins with seeking permission to reach out to the child's school.

Securing Proper Permission and Documentation

Securing permission and proper documentation is the first step for any outreach to the school. It should follow from a conversation about the nature of the consent that you have with the parent or a child who is old enough to give consent. Though the consent can be oral or written, it's better to have a signed, written release of information form. However, if time doesn't permit, you can secure oral permission that's documented in your records and followed up with written documentation. This agreement involves establishing the parameters of confidentiality—who can speak to whom and about what issues. You'll need to discuss the reasons for contacting the school with the family and formulate an understanding about what information will be shared and sought. In particular, check with the parents about whether there is something that has been discussed with you that they do not want the school to know. Asking the parent to inform the appropriate school representative that you'll be contacting them will facilitate the process and strengthen the connection between the family and school. It's also good practice to inform the family (and older child) following an exchange of information with someone at the school. Discussing these issues is a fundamental part of building trust and creating a collaborative model for addressing a child's school problems.

Release of information forms should indicate the person or persons with whom the therapist can exchange information. In many instances, it's advantageous to secure general permission, though this wider scope of permission can be determined at any point along the way and later documented in your release of information form. Similarly, if the chosen contact person at school is away or a decision is made to change the contact person with whom you're collaborating, make sure that permissions are updated. Remember to specify that this is a two-way exchange of information agreement. If the school wants a copy of your release of information form, be sure to send a copy of it. If the parent or child (who is old enough to give consent) signed the school's release of information form, ask the school representative to send a copy of the form to you. As with all release of information forms, be sure to note the expiration date on the form, typically one year from when it was signed. Also be sure to keep these documents up to date, even if you've been working with a child and school over many years.

In situations where the parents are separated or divorced, most states require that the clinician receive permission from both parents to confer with the school (Glosoff & Pate, 2002). Since you likely addressed and resolved this issue when seeking consent for treatment for the child whose parents are separated or divorced, assume that the same rules and guidelines apply in the case of obtaining consent to work with the school. This may involve having both parents sign a release of information form when they give consent for treatment.

The federal government, through the Family Educational Rights and Privacy Act (FERPA), mandates that, "Educational records are defined as any records maintained by the schools that are directly related to the student." (U.S. Department of Education, 2001). This is relevant to therapists because information you share with the school in writing—emails, texts, summaries, reports—can be held in a student's record. The extent to which these records are kept varies from school to school, but it's important to know that what you send can be kept in a student's file. Again, here's where you will want to have established with the parents and older child what information will be shared, with whom, and in what form. All records can be court-ordered for release, and biological parents have the right to look at the records until the child is 18 years of age. Stepparents can have access to the records with permission from the biological parent.

A note about emails

When considering using email as a means of communicating, it's essential that you follow Health Insurance Portability and Accountability Act of 1996 (HIPAA; Centers for Disease Control and Prevention, 2003) and other professional guidelines. Rather than go into detail about the requirements here, I would recommend contacting your professional organization for guidance in this regard. Be aware that maintaining digital records requires following guidelines designed for that purpose as well (Pfohl & Jarmuz-Smith, 2014; Reamer, 2013). Furthermore, you will want to determine with the parent and child beforehand whether you will be using email as a means of communicating with the school. Because emails are not a secure form of communication, you need to discuss this with the family and older child and come to an agreement about what you will be communicating by email with them as well as with the school. Be sure to indicate this understanding in your records or through a written email agreement to be signed by the parents and older child.

There is durability to anything you've put in writing that outlasts a real-time conversation. That's not to say that you shouldn't communicate in writing, but rather that you should do so consciously and fully informed of the ethical and legal implications associated with such communications, including the fact that all records can be subpoenaed, including emails.

When you do use emails, be specific, data-oriented, and respectful. There's no room for venting or processing experiences. It helps to ask oneself, "Since I can't control who may read this, what do I want to put in writing?" At times it may be helpful to check with a trusted colleague regarding any questions you have about an email you plan to send. Remember that sometimes a conversation is better than an email—quicker and less complicated, especially after the exchange of several emails or when there are questions that need further clarification.

Many therapists with whom I spoke indicated that, once they communicated with the school representative by phone, subsequent communications were often conducted via email. In the absence of complicating factors, it allowed for a quick and easy exchange of information on a timeline that was commensurate with the needs of both parties. A psychologist who is an expert in treating anxiety disorders in children said that typically she emails the teacher whatever plan they discussed, highlighting key recommendations for working with an anxious child, and sends additional email updates as needed. Sometimes, therapists are asked by the family or school to write a summary or report to be sent to the school about the child they are seeing. If this is indicated in your clinical judgment, consider whether to send this as a hard copy or through email.

Figuring out the Best Person to Contact

Once you've agreed to reach out to the school, you'll want to decide together whom to contact and how (by phone, email, or other method identified). It's usually best to start by asking the older child or the parent whom they think would be best to contact. Here's another opportunity to give older children as much control and ownership over the process as possible by exploring this issue with them. The priorities that follow from whom the parent or child designates should include consideration of the presenting problem(s), the source of the referral if it came from the school, and what you know about that particular school (see Appendix B for a review of Who's Who at School).

It may be helpful for the parent or older child to let the school representative know that you'll be reaching out, empowering them to make the first connection. If you are uncertain about whom to call, you have some options, as shown below:

How to decide whom to contact at the school

1. First, ask the parents or older child if they would designate a contact person at the school.

2. If the family is unsure, consider the referral source. If it was made from someone at the school, you might reach out to that person directly.

3. Another option is to reach out to someone in the school's student support team. For example, if the child has already been meeting with the school counselor because of problems making friends, you might reach out to the counselor first.

4. Finally, you might look for advice on whom to contact from a colleague who's worked with the school in the past, or more broadly for guidance about how to engage the school.

Preparing for the Call

Before you make the first call, it's important to find time to collect your thoughts and prepare for the conversation. Try to identify specific concerns and questions that reflect the issues addressed in your work with the child. This may only take a few minutes, but it will greatly improve the quality of the conversation. When preparing for the call, there are a number of questions you might ask yourself, as listed below:

Questions to consider before contacting the school

1. Why am I calling?

2. What gaps in my knowledge do I need to fill in?

3. What specific questions do I have about the child?

4. What do I need to know about the school and how the faculty and staff work with outside professionals in order to better understand the child's problem or make recommendations?

5. What might I need to know about the family's relationship with the school?

6. What hypotheses do I have that might explain what is going on with the child at school, and what questions best correspond to those hypotheses?

7. What does the school need to know about my professional background and the work I am doing with the child?

8. What ideas do I have about best supporting the child at school?

9. What goals or interventions can the school help coordinate?

Once you're clear about the purpose of the call, be sure to think through the exact information you want to acquire and share. For example, in an initial phone call with a teacher, you might say, "As you know, Lin has been diagnosed with a learning disability and I wanted to check with you about how she's doing in her math and science classes." If you know Lin is struggling with a particular math unit, you might ask what her teacher has noticed about how things are going and what seems to be working or not. In this case, if you've first answered the question, "What do I need to know about how Lin is doing in math?" you'll be in much better shape to secure additional information you need from her teacher or other student support team members.

Using another case example, you might be calling the school psychologist to find out how best to support a teenager, Kaylee, whose father recently died. In this instance, the conversation could begin with, "I'm calling because I wanted to talk with you about Kaylee, whose mother brought her to see me after her father died after a long illness. I understand that she's having a hard time at school and I thought it would be helpful for us to talk about how she's doing." Here, you've made it clear that you're looking for ways to work with the teacher or advisor to help Kaylee adjust to her loss.

The Format of an Initial Phone Conversation

There are four basic parts of an initial conversation with a school representative. They may be obvious, certainly for the experienced clinician, but they are worth reviewing here to ensure that when you do reach out, you use the time wisely.

Four parts of an initial conversation with a school representative

1. Introduce yourself, state the purpose of the call and clarify with whom you'll be speaking.

2. Offer a brief description of or question regarding the child and the problem.

3. Listen to the school representative's view of the situation and ask questions accordingly.

4. Seek to create some form of shared understanding and plan for how to move forward, including when and how to follow up.

When you reach out to someone at the child's school, you are further extending an outreach that began with the family reaching out to you. This is no small matter, since by reaching out you can widen the circle of care and concern in order to secure the information and support needed.

When we introduce ourselves, we might say something like, "I am the therapist working with Josef and have permission from him and his parents to talk with you about how he is doing at school." The next step is to think about how to state the purpose of the call in light of the child's issues. Possibilities might include stating that you'd like to:

- Talk with someone at the school about how the student is doing, whether there are concerns and, if so, what they are

- Open up lines of communication with key people at school

- Answer questions about the child based on my experience working with the child and family

- Collaborate with the teacher or school's student support team.

Once you've developed a relationship with a school, there will be less need to clarify your role and professional background because certain assumptions will be made about you and your clinical work and, ideally, your ability to work collaboratively and effectively with those who work there. However, personnel and positions change often, so you'll want to begin afresh with each new contact, perhaps adding something about your prior work with the school, if applicable. Therapists often get to know the administrative staff, too, those who answer the phones and serve as gatekeepers to the faculty and staff. The staff can become your allies when trying to reach someone who is busy or may not return phone calls promptly. Remain friendly and open if you have to call a second or third time. Schools may not have the resources to convey information efficiently, so it's your job to be patient and find ways to connect. If this fails, discuss the situation with the child or family and determine how they might step in and facilitate the connection. Don't give up.

Once you reach the intended person, make sure to focus on the central problem and avoid discussing peripheral information. Remember that your primary obligation is to the child and family and your shared understanding about what will be discussed. For many reasons, we can become sloppy, indirectly seek confirmation or justification for the clinical work we're doing, or reveal information that has no bearing on the situation in a misguided effort to help the child. You're responsible for what you discuss with the school, since you will not have control over how the information is disseminated or incorporated into the child's record. If the school shares information with you, be sure to ask whether the information has also been shared with the family. If not, discuss how the information will be shared with them. A number of therapists mentioned that they had inadvertently passed along information that the teacher had not shared with the family directly, unnecessarily creating hard feelings on the parents' part.

Questions might be asked about you at the outset, or it may be that you'll ask the school representatives if they have any questions about you or the work you do, especially about your area(s) of expertise. When such questions arise, answer them as succinctly as possible. Avoid using this as an opportunity to advertise your work. At the end of the call, make it clear that further questions about you and your work are welcome: "Is there anything else I can fill you in on at this point?" By doing so, you've demonstrated your openness to questions that may arise in the future.

Bringing It All Together: A Case Example

Everyone knew 10-year-old Camilla in the small, urban parochial school she attended, not only because she had gone there for over five years, but because whenever there was a flurry of activity in the music room or voices were raised at recess, Camilla was in the middle of it. Teachers in the school found her either enchanting, exhausting, or both; inevitably boisterous; and often perplexing. Comments were made such as, "Camilla doesn't think that the rules apply to her" or "Maybe this isn't the right school for Camilla." Yet these weren't the characteristics that brought things to a head for Camilla, but rather the fact that she'd recently become less animated, "shut down," as one teacher remarked. Her mother, a single parent who had recently separated from Camilla's father, was invited to come to the school. Speaking with the teacher and school counselor, Camilla's mother was certain that Camilla was grappling emotionally with the recent separation, and homework and sleep had suffered as a result. When the counselor recommended outpatient therapy at the nearby clinic, the mother concurred.

The therapist initially met with Camilla, her mother, and Camilla's younger brother, and discussed the family situation in some detail. However, Camilla claimed that she was not upset about things at home; she just didn't like school anymore because it was "boring." It became evident that, though Camilla had never been an exemplary student, she had known how to get by. The therapist hypothesized that whatever Camilla had been doing to stay afloat at school was no longer working. Camilla and her mother agreed to let the therapist contact her teacher and the school counselor.

Once the therapist introduced himself on the phone to Camilla's teacher, the therapist stated that Camilla was unhappy at school and possibly at home, too. In turn, he asked about how Camilla was doing at school, what recent changes in her mood and behavior the teacher might have noticed, whether Camilla had shared any of her thoughts and feelings with the teacher, and what the teacher thought might be going on to explain the problem.

In conversation, the teacher indicated that she had wondered whether Camilla might be responding to something going on at home and said that her daily irritations with Camilla had turned to worries. At the same time, the teacher was not surprised to hear that Camilla told the therapist she was bored at school, given how frustrated and unfocused she had been recently. Notably, the teacher encouraged the therapist to have the long view of the problem since Camilla had been a concern way before this most recent change in her behavior. She also described how sad Camilla's mother was when they last spoke, and speculated about what supports Camilla's mother might need, too. With some humor, the teacher exclaimed, "You know, I worry less when Camilla is driving me crazy."

In Camilla's situation, the teacher not only had an important set of observations to share, but also thoughts about what might explain her difficulties, which substantiated the therapist's hypotheses. When the therapist asked whether Camilla was looking similarly withdrawn and defeated in other settings at school—in the lunchroom, at recess, in art or music classes—the teacher offered to talk with her colleagues who could observe Camilla in those settings. The therapist, in turn, agreed to review Camilla's homework with Camilla and her mother and read through past report cards to further examine the roots of Camilla's struggles. Might Camilla be struggling with an as-yet-unidentified learning disability? At the close of the conversation, they agreed to talk again at a predetermined time (in a couple weeks) and on a means of communicating (phone call).

The therapist also kept a written record of the conversation, including what was agreed upon and the preferred means of communicating. He also expressed appreciation to the teacher, a small courtesy but an important one.

Notice that the therapist and teacher agreed on a time to talk again. Also notice that both had jobs to do that represented pieces of the puzzle and allowed for a strong alliance. Remember how we looked at therapist's fears about not having the time to work with schools? Here's where doing a fair-minded appraisal of your own scheduling limitations pays off. The importance of this dimension of the work cannot be overstated, since a common complaint made on both sides of the therapist–school aisle is the failure to follow up. As prosaic as it may sound, being reliable is the foundational ingredient in establishing and maintaining collaborative relationships. Without this, you may quickly become known as "the therapist who never gets back to us," as one school psychologist said about someone who works with children in his school.

REVIEWING THE BASICS

The first conversations with the school can play out in many ways, and there is no way to fully prepare for what happens when someone picks up the phone. However, with enough planning and a genuine desire to collaborate, you'll establish an important connection that will widen the circle of care around a particular child.

- Remember that, first and foremost, you must get consent from the family and older child before initiating contact with the school.

- Be sure to obtain the proper release of information forms, and keep them up to date as needed.

- When communicating with the school, be mindful of what you put in writing. Ask yourself, "Would I feel okay if anyone read this?" Email communication can be a helpful follow-up tool after establishing initial contact over the phone.

▪ Follow the recommendation of the parent or older child when deciding whom to contact. In the absence of their direction, use the presenting problem and circumstances as a guide; if the child has an established relationship with a counselor or support staff member, for example, perhaps start there.

▪ Be clear about the exact information you want to gather and the overall purpose of the call before picking up the phone; even a small bit of preparation can keep the conversation from going in an unproductive direction.

▪ Overall, keep the collaborative framework in mind; no matter whom you speak with, be sure to try and establish a shared understanding of the problem, and always discuss a plan for following up.

CHAPTER 6

Observing Kids at School

One of the best ways to assess a child's school problems is to visit the school itself and observe the child going about his or her day. School psychologists and other school personnel regularly observe students as part of formal or informal assessments; it's one of the critical tools available to them when kids are having a hard time. Though therapists who work outside the school must get permission from parents and school personnel to observe children, it's one of the critical tools available to us, too. This chapter will look at reasons why observing children can be helpful, as well as how to plan and structure a successful observation.

Reasons to Observe Kids at School

There are certain kinds of school-based or clinical problems that can be better assessed by a school observation. Take the case of Ted, who was just starting fourth grade at a new independent school. Not only was he experiencing conflict with his peers, but he could also be oppositional with his parents and the teacher. Sometimes, he broke down crying at home about not having any friends. One day at school when he yelled at a classmate, the school counselor got involved. She recommended professional help because the problems Ted had in his previous school seemed to have followed him to this one. Though gifted in the language arts, especially poetry, Ted couldn't find a way to connect with his peers. His efforts left others confused and on guard.

Ted entered the therapist's office with, as his mother described, "an attitude." During therapy sessions, Ted said that he liked this new school much better than the one he'd attended previously, but felt worse because he'd thought changing schools would make it easier for him to form friendships, given his greater comfort with the new academic program. Despite the occasional outburst in the session, a true reflection of his unhappiness and frustration, Ted agreed to work with the therapist to figure out what was going on and also agreed to let the therapist come to the school to observe him in his classroom.

In this case, Ted had long-standing problems with peer relationships that spanned two schools. Furthermore, he had only a nominal understanding of what might be going on to explain these difficulties. The therapist decided that, by observing Ted in the classroom (specifically interacting with his peers), she could get real-time information that would guide and strengthen her hypotheses and therapeutic interventions. Ideally, she could spark a collaborative team effort among Ted's teacher, his mom, and other school support staff.

Presenting problems that may lead to school-based observations include anxiety, school refusal, autism spectrum disorders, problems with anger management, selective mutism, suspected learning or attention problems, and issues with social skills such as Ted displayed, to name just a handful. By no means exclusive, these are common problems that bring kids to therapy and alert us to the value of getting eyes on the ground through classroom observation. There are several reasons why observing kids who struggle with these or other problems can be helpful in the course of their therapy. It is a way of comparing the child to their peers and identifying their strengths and connecting more deeply with them. It also builds relationships among the teacher, the school, and parents, potentially helping to determine the appropriateness of a classroom or school.

Sometimes, it's important just to see kids in their natural environments, even if they don't have a school-related problem. Therapists can observe children who are doing well in school to better understand how they operate in the world more generally—their relationships with classmates and adults, ordinary struggles, and successes. If they are doing well at school, perhaps the skills they use there can be applied to other more problematic settings.

Opportunity to compare the child to peers

A big reason for observing a child is to see the child in relation to other same-age children. As one therapist said, "You want to see if the child you're observing is answering the 3rd math question when all the other kids are answering the 23rd question." The logic of this can be applied to any presenting problem, of course. If you find a math-impaired child in a room full of kids struggling in a math class, it means something quite different from seeing the child struggling alone.

Opportunity to identify the child's strengths

By observing a child at school, you not only have a chance to see evidence of the presenting problem, but also the absence of the problem, as well as his or her strengths. It's highly unusual for a child to be struggling all the time, so you'll have the opportunity to see what's going on when the child is doing well, or at least doing better than in the defined areas of difficulty. Take Ted's case. In English class, the therapist was able to observe that when Ted reached out to kids in the context of a group project, he did so effectively, first drawing attention to the part he was working on, and then showing interest in what other children were doing. The latter gestures evoked a friendly reaction from his peers, and the therapist could see Ted soften and smile in response. She, in turn, could bring this observation back to Ted and his family in the next therapy session, as well as collaborate with Ted's teacher about ways to structure his projects in ways that foster the kind of positive interaction she observed.

Help us connect to the kids we see

After observing a child, you can deepen your therapeutic connection with her by discussing your experience of being at her school. You might say something like, "You know, I was in your classroom the other day. It was great because I got to meet your teacher." Saying something positive about the classroom or what you liked about the school can help the child see that you identify with the child's world. The simple act of saying, "Do you remember that day I visited your classroom?" can give the child who is sitting in your office a real sense that you've been there, too.

With older kids, including teenagers, you might mention something specific that you noticed that connects with their experience. Immersing yourself in child's school for even a brief amount of time allows you to ask older kids more targeted questions linked to the concerns they've presented in your office.

Opportunity to build fruitful relationships with the teacher and school

By going to the school, you'll most likely meet the child's teacher and may also get to meet others who know and work with the child. They'll have the chance to get to know you, too, further strengthening relationships that can be crucial to supporting the vulnerable kids you see in therapy. It's possible that you'll meet a teacher who begins the relationship from a default "distrust" position, as one therapist described, a position that you can possibly begin to dismantle by being in the classroom and extending yourself to the teacher and the child. Whether for testing purposes or as part of the initial phase of therapy, some therapists go to schools routinely to observe their clients. Yet even a brief, single visit can help foster productive relationships with school personnel. As one psychologist claimed, "There's value if you spend even a half hour in a classroom and the teacher knows you're watching a particular kid."

By visiting the classroom, you and the teacher will subsequently have a shared experience of the child. How might that make a difference? Observing the child at the same time in the same space gives each of you a common frame of reference for the child's behavior, provides insight into how you each perceive the problem, and, it is hoped, establishes a level of mutual trust. In addition to witnessing your commitment to solving the child's problem, your ability to reference a situation that the teacher has also experienced enhances your credibility the next time you explore possible school-based interventions, since you'll be drawing from the same well of experience.

In Ted's case, for example, the therapist was able to say to the teacher, "Remember when I was in your classroom and Ted kept interrupting the other children when they were trying to talk? I could see how that made it hard for everyone to get the most out of the lesson, including Ted. That's probably one of the things he does that puts the kids off. I have an idea I'd like to run by you and see what you think. I wonder if you could meet with Ted just before a class discussion and encourage him to think of something he wants to contribute, and remind him to listen to others when they're speaking. I'll prepare Ted for this in the next session by letting him know that you and I are working together to help him have a better year. I'll talk with him about how to make sure his good ideas are heard in class discussions and coach him on ways to listen to others when they're speaking. I think Ted doesn't really see the impact of his behavior on the other kids, so his parents and I are trying to bring certain behaviors to his attention—like interrupting—in a way that isn't demoralizing. We can all work on finding ways to motivate Ted to behave in more socially acceptable ways so that he can make friends this year."

When a therapist is able to say something like, "I can see how Ted's constant interruptions slow things down for everyone," the teacher witnesses that the therapist is on her side, working to solve the same problem even if seated in an office across town. This demonstration of empathy and good faith can lead to better solutions for the presenting problem—ideas you and the school will fashion together with the resources the school can bring to bear on the situation. Collaboration of this sort makes it easier to self-correct, handle setbacks, try out new ideas, give and receive feedback, and work your way toward solutions that set the child on a better course.

Help bridge the gap between the parents and the school

Sometimes, the parents and the school see the child quite differently or are at odds in some way. For example, take the parents who are concerned that their daughter is being actively rejected by her peers, given her complaints at home. When you talk with the teacher, she reports that the child is removing herself from group activities rather than being actively excluded, making it hard for kids to get to know her. In this case, both the parents and teacher have, on one level, a similar understanding of the child—she is not fully participating in ordinary interactions with her classmates. However, they have a divergent explanation of how and why. Here's where a therapist can step in to help sort out the nuanced interactions between the child and her peers, since social isolation of this sort is often a complex result of all parties involved. After gaining a clearer picture of the problem, the therapist can work with the parents, teacher, and child to develop strategies that support her socially. Thus, the therapist's observations can become the foundation for establishing or restoring common ground between the family and school, and for intervening effectively.

Another case in which bridging the gap between home and school was essential involved a child who suffered from severe anxiety, including periodic bouts of school refusal. The child was adept, as many anxious kids are, at masking her anxiety at school. Yet at home, she spoke about how she would rather die than go to school the next day. Both realities were true. At school, this girl worked hard to appear confident and comfortable. At home, she would let down her guard and express intense fear and discouragement. After observing the child in the classroom, the therapist was able to educate those at the school about the nature of anxiety and how it was manifesting in this particular child, and develop plans to better support her in that setting.

By visiting the classroom, the therapist may also be able to help dispel or confirm negative views the parent has of the teacher. Negative views of teachers derive from many sources, including what the child reports when he or she returns home each day. Sometimes, the reports are accurate representations of problems a teacher is having, problems that may well include negative patterns of relating to the kids in the classroom. Other times, the child's problems at school inadvertently produce an unfavorable view of the teacher that can eventually turn into anger and blaming. When you witness the teacher trying to help the child who is struggling, or see how the child's problems undermine the teacher's efforts to instruct all the children in the classroom, you gain invaluable information to share with the parents. After you deepen their understanding of the situation, the parents can be coached to reach out to the teacher with a bigger picture in mind and from a less adversarial stance. What the teacher struggles with at school is often the same problem the parents and child struggle with at home, and this fact can become another strong point of connection.

Help parents determine the appropriateness of a classroom or school setting

Sometimes, families enlist therapists to help determine if a school or classroom placement is appropriate for their child. This is a tricky area. Obviously, therapists are not in a position to professionally evaluate the child's teacher, curriculum, or school. Only school personnel can assume that function. At the same time, parents may need help determining whether their child should remain in a particular educational setting due to concerns about safety, the quality of teaching, or the child's ability to succeed in that setting.

In these instances, it's important to think hard about how to contribute. You want to accurately reflect what you think and observe, yet don't want to "add fuel to the fire," as one therapist said. In one case, a therapist observed a classroom in which the teacher, attempting to manage a rambunctious group of students, repeatedly yelled at them. The child, Xavier, whom the therapist was observing, was not part of the rowdy group; he came into therapy because he returns home each day "stressed out," as his mother reports. During the observation, Xavier visibly withered in the classroom when the teacher yelled, glancing the therapist's way for validation and encouragement. By being in the classroom and sharing this experience, the therapist had a good sense of the discomfort Xavier feels each day and why.

Afterward, it becomes the therapist's job to report back to the parents in a way that is constructive and leads to a productive dialogue. In this case, you might speak of a *mismatch* between the child and the teacher. Using this term, when appropriate, makes it clear that the situation is not working well for the child without placing undue blame on the teacher or school. Generally, it's important to discuss the observation in a way that doesn't unnecessarily increase the parent's anger or frustration. In the case above, the therapist said that he could see the teacher trying to manage a group of very challenging kids, and this dynamic can be especially hard for a child who tends to be shy and sensitive. In short, think carefully about how to describe a given situation. And remember to be thoughtful about the language you use if you're writing up a summary of the observations.

When the child has an unhappy experience in a classroom for whatever reason and your observations confirm the child's reports, consider the options parents have to address the situation. Perhaps the current classroom or school placement is truly unworkable for the child. The problem may have gone on too long to be remedied, or there may be something onerous for the child in that setting (Schultz, 2011). Even if you conclude that the situation is untenable, it's important to convey your assessment respectfully. In the majority of cases, it's best to assume that the teacher is operating with good intentions. If you happen to encounter a situation in which you think the child is unsafe or being seriously harmed, then you need to bring this to the attention of the parents right away and determine steps to take with them and the school—luckily, not a common occurrence. Helping parents become advocates for their child will be addressed more fully in Chapter 11, along with how to work with public school special education systems in Chapter 12.

However, most of the time, there are strategies you can suggest that will support the child yet allow the child to remain—and sometimes even thrive—in less-than-ideal situations. In fact, one of the biggest contributions you can make in such scenarios is helping parents and kids come up with realistic plans and expectations after the family and you have deduced that the situation is workable, even if challenging. There is much that a child can learn from a mismatch between a child and the child's environment. Our work can sometimes focus on managing this mismatch rather than trying to fix what's perceived as wrong with the teacher. One therapist spoke about how she engages the teacher around the idea that "this is a child who needs to learn how to adapt in such circumstances," reducing judgments on the part of the therapist and defensiveness on the part of the teacher. Classroom observation becomes one of the ways that joint conceptualization of a problem can evolve. The parents, child, and therapist can also work together to focus on the things that are going right at school, which may include finding additional resources, activities, mentors, or counseling support. By acknowledging the challenging situation, you can work with the child to cultivate the resources and interpersonal skills that will serve the child well throughout life, reinforcing the child's resilience and ability to manage other challenging relationships.

Methods of Observation

For whatever reasons you might be observing a child at school, there are two ways to approach observations in a school setting. First, there are *formal observational tools* that are available for clinicians to use in their practice (such as the BOSS or BASC 2, reviewed briefly in Appendix D). The upside of using these more structured methods is that your observations are less subject to the bias that's inherent in the enterprise. These methods allow for a systematic description of the child's behavior and answer questions such as how often a particular target behavior is occurring or whether a child's specific behavior of concern is happening more or less than is true for other children. All of this can be very helpful in structuring an observation. These tools provide timed intervals for recording the behavior of the identified child in comparison to other children and are often used in psychoeducational evaluations. It's important to add, however, that one of the inherent problems associated with using formal observational tools is that many clinicians simply don't seem to use them very often or are not adequately trained in how to use them. As a result, they are often used in ways that aren't accurate or effective (Nock & Kurtz, 2005).

Second, children can be observed *naturalistically*, a common method that therapists choose (Hintz, Volpe, & Shapiro, 2002). There are multiple ways to observe children qualitatively that are also used in more structured observational processes, including: anecdotally, Antecedent-Behavior-Consequence (A-B-C) recording, using systematic direct observations (SDO), event recording, duration recording, latency recording, various time sampling procedures, observation of comparison students, and analogue observation (Dombrowski, 2015). Whatever system you use, there are several clinical and logistical issues to consider. Practically speaking, regardless of your observational method, be sure to come prepared with what you need to document your observations (including something hard to write on, for example). As you take notes on paper or on your computer or tablet, be sure that the child's name is not visible and that you're discreet about the information you gather. Kids will sometimes sidle up to the newcomer in the room and peek over your shoulder to see what you're writing. To maintain confidentiality, be sure that no one is in a position to discover the information you are collecting about a particular child. If you're asked a question or feel the need to say something, respond simply and discreetly. Formulate in advance what you might say if you are asked to introduce yourself to the kids: something like, "I'm here today to learn about your classroom" or "I'm interested in seeing how things work in your school." It's best to keep things simple so that the children are minimally influenced by your presence. Be sure to also consider factors of discretion when you're offered a place to sit or stand; perhaps move to a different spot, if needed.

The more observations you do, the better you'll become at understanding, documenting, and reviewing what you saw and experienced. You'll also learn the best times to observe, ways to connect with teachers, and more about your own biases. You may want to experiment with different methods of observing, as mentioned above, and discuss these methods with your colleagues. It is often helpful to engage in some combination of different types of observation—some more structured observations to get a sense of how frequently specific problems are occurring, for example, and broader, naturalistic observations to get a sense of people and context.

Steps Toward a Successful Observation

There are a number of steps to consider in planning and doing an observation of a child at school—from determining whether to observe the child before meeting him, to planning the observation with parents and teachers and providing feedback once the observation is complete. These steps will be explored as follows.

Determine whether to observe the child before you meet

One of the first decisions clinicians make is whether to observe a child before seeing him for an initial appointment, a decision that rests partly on the child's age and stage of development. For example, some therapists make it their practice to meet with parents initially and then observe the young child at school before meeting him, to minimize the impact of their presence at school. This is often done when doing psychoeducational evaluations in order to avoid what's called the Hawthorne Effect, when individuals behave differently (often more positively) as a result of being observed (Adair, 1984; Dombrowski, 2015). If you haven't met the child previously, it's possible that your presence in the classroom may go unnoticed by the child; in many schools and preschools, adults often walk in and out of the classrooms over the course of the day.

With older children, it's a different matter. Therapists will need to think hard about whether to observe an older child or teenager before they meet. Sometimes, therapists decide to observe anonymously as part of the process for determining the need for special education placement, wraparound services, or other types of interventions. Older children who are observed before meeting the therapist with whom they'll be working might feel that they've been deceived by their parent or therapist, which can interfere with the therapeutic relationship. If this happens, at the first opportunity the therapist, in conjunction with the parents and school, can offer an honest explanation for why this decision was made and answer any questions the child might have.

Plan with the parent and child

Before observing a child at school who is aware that you will be coming in, inform the parents and child about how you'll conduct the observation and why it will be helpful. Make a point of discussing the questions they or you might have that an observation can address, and what you're hoping to see and why. This will increase the value of the observation, since the more input and buy-in everyone has, the greater the chance of success. Parents can help determine whom to contact when setting up the observation, and some of the necessary logistics. As with your initial contact with the school, encourage the parents to inform the appropriate school representative that they are giving you permission to observe.

For most older children (and some younger), it's important to discuss the idea at least once in therapy before visiting the school (unless you've decided to observe the child before meeting). This way, certain decisions can be made jointly, such as whether the child would like to acknowledge your presence (a wave of the hand or quick hello) or not. Children vary in how they feel about being observed; some kids will say they are excited to show you their cubby or classroom, and others may be uneasy about the prospect. If you plan to inform the child that you will be doing an observation, explain something about how it works and why. Keep in mind that kids may say one thing in the session with you and do something different once you're in the classroom, so take your cues from them and use your clinical judgment in determining how best to respond when you're at the school.

Plan with the child's teacher

Before observing a child, make every effort to talk with the child's teacher (or another person at the school) to determine the logistics of the observation, that is, how the teacher prefers to incorporate therapists into the classroom. Let your clinical questions and hypotheses about the child guide your decision making regarding where and when to observe, as well as what to look for. For example, if a child is struggling with peer problems, you will want to observe the child during both structured and unstructured time. If the primary concern is that the child is not paying attention in class, you'll want to observe the child in different class settings: teacher directed, group activities, and independent work. With a child who can't seem to grasp math concepts, you'll want to time your visit to correspond with a math class. If possible, try to observe at least two activities or classrooms so that you can see how the child behaves during at least one transition. Remember that it also helps to observe how the child is faring in situations that go well, so that you can see the conditions under which the child is more productive and capable.

If you have a chance to talk with the teacher before you make the observation, ask where to sit or stand and if you can move around the room, if the nature of the instructional situation permits. If you haven't already met the child, make sure that he or she is identified before the observation begins. As mentioned earlier, come prepared with a phrase or two that you can say if you're asked to introduce yourself to the class such as "I'm here to learn about your classroom." Also, check to see if you can talk with the teacher afterward and, if not, set up a time for a follow-up conversation.

In one case, given his strong academic record over the years, Hector's parents were surprised when a poor report card arrived. His third grade teacher was worried about the sudden drop in his grades and growing tension with his peers; the teacher recommended to Hector's parents that they seek professional help. After several sessions, the therapist hypothesized that Hector might be struggling with an undiagnosed learning problem or autistic spectrum disorder, given the behaviors she observed in sessions: failure to make eye contact, responding to questions monosyllabically, and inability to engage in the ordinary give-and-take of conversation.

As part of the assessment process, the therapist decided to visit the school to observe Hector with these hypotheses in mind. She contacted the teacher to discuss her concerns and what settings might afford the most useful information. Together, they agreed that the therapist would observe in the classroom, at lunch, and during the transition to PE class in an adjoining building, each setting creating somewhat different social demands.

Based on her observations, the therapist could see that Hector simply didn't engage in back-and-forth interactions with his classmates or show any real interest in what they were doing. Sharing the observations with the teacher gave the therapist the opportunity to confirm that this was typical behavior on Hector's part, further validating her own observations.

Begin the observation before you enter the school

Blocks or even miles away from the school, make every effort to notice your surroundings and what they say about the community in which the school is located. Are there crowded, colorful storefronts with people gathered on the adjoining sidewalks? Is the school in a hollowed-out part of the city surrounded by fenced-in, broken-up concrete yards? Do you notice well-mown lawns adjoining large suburban housing lots? Though you may already know the school you're visiting, pay attention to what the environment and locale tell you about the school and its constituents. Not only can this lead you to better understand the child, but also the world in which the child lives.

Likewise, when you enter the school, make note of the ease with which you're able to enter the building, the greeting you receive (or don't), and the general atmosphere that's established for visitors. Many schools will require you to sign in and wait for someone to escort you to the classroom. Security guards may be present. Some smaller public or independent schools may permit you to enter at will and make your way to the established meeting place. These are observations that you can incorporate into the ideas and plans that are discussed in sessions with the child and family and possibly with the teacher or other school representative. This experience will also give you points of reference when talking to the child in later therapy sessions, as you communicate your own sense of walking down the same school corridors that the child experiences every day.

Debrief with the teacher after you observe the child

Teachers may be nervous about how they'll be judged or evaluated by you when you come to observe their classroom, so keep this in mind when discussing the observation. Whether you meet directly afterward or set up a time to talk in the future, be sure to let the teacher know the positive things you saw—ways that the teacher guided and supported the students, the way the classroom was set up, or some other feature of what you observed. Of course, inherent in the act of offering a positive comment is a judgment of sorts, but recognizing good work and stating so in a matter-of-fact way can be a favorable starting point, professional to professional.

As mentioned earlier, confirm with the teacher whether it was a typical day for the child, class, and school. If not, find out what was different and what the teacher thinks about the difference. For example: "You said that Aisha had a better day than usual. Can you tell me how it might have gone differently if I'd been here yesterday?" or "I understand that the kids have just returned after a long weekend. Is there any way things were different as a result?" Include questions about how the child's behavior, performance, or attitude compare to other children in the classroom, or others whom the teacher has taught in past years. This can be complicated, since teachers are often reluctant to compare children. Even so, such a comparison can aid in your understanding of the child's problem and what interventions might be most effective.

The therapist can also ask whether the teacher has had a student with similar problems before and what worked in those instances. Even if teachers have not solved this problem before, they may have ideas they've considered and interventions they or others have tried. A conversation with you might reveal ideas that seem more promising in light of the observations you've just made. As one teacher said, "We're thinking all the time about what to do with our students." Sometimes, this conversation can be the thing that sparks teachers to tap into their experiences and memories and move things along more productively. Also, be sure to agree on the best way to stay in touch. Prevent a trial-and-error effort of phoning or emailing that is frustrating to therapists and teachers alike.

Sometimes, in an effort to better instruct a child, teachers will ask for feedback about how they are handling a situation. Giving feedback isn't always easy, especially if the problem relates to the teacher. In the case mentioned earlier of the child who was stressed by the teacher's yelling, the therapist might say, "I noticed that there was a group of kids who needed a firm response from you and during this time I could see that Xavier hasn't learned not to take that in. I'll work with him on that, but I thought it would be good for us to talk again about his experience in the classroom since, for now, I don't think he'll let you know about this." In other words, when possible, make every effort to work with the teacher to help solve the problem, respecting the dilemmas they face in teaching a range of children with different needs.

Connect with the child and family after a school observation

As mentioned earlier, it's important to discuss elements of your observation with the child and family in subsequent therapy sessions, as one of the benefits of this activity is the opportunity to connect with a child on a deeper level. Whether you've met the child before the observation or not, it's important to acknowledge having seen the child at school when you next meet. Say something about the visit: "If I look familiar to you it's because I had a chance to see your classroom last week." This gives you and the child the opportunity to discuss what you saw in the classroom—pictures of Martin Luther King on the wall, colored blocks that were used for building towers, or a science experiment being conducted. One psychologist in a small group practice said that she begins to talk about her visit to the school while walking with the child from the waiting room into her office, a literal bridge from life at school to the upcoming session. By identifying what you observed at school and particularly what the child was doing that day, you can have a more natural conversation about the child's school experience, a reassuring prospect. All of a sudden you are someone who was there with her *that* day in *her* school.

With preschool kids you see for the first time at school, you might begin with, "Do you remember me? I was in your classroom and now I get to meet you and that's great!" Sometimes, there are funny, even disarming moments with kids regarding your having seen them at school. One therapist reported a child exclaiming, "I remember YOU! I thought you were watching me!" Such comments open the door to further conversations about the child's experience at school that day. Other times, a child won't even know that you were in the classroom or might register some discomfort at the prospect. This is relevant information, too.

Together, you and the child can reflect on how the child's experiences in school that day compared to other days, including what it was like to have you present and how it might have impacted the child's behavior. Inherent in listening to the child's perspective is the opportunity to understand the child's school life more fully and compassionately, in itself a good therapeutic exercise.

Potential Problems That May Arise

Occasionally, problems will arise when doing observations, though usually these are small ones. For instance, you may walk into a classroom and discover that a substitute teacher has replaced the regular teacher, who is out sick with the flu. Perhaps more likely, the schedule will have changed that day and the activity you'd hoped to observe occurred the hour before. In one instance, a therapist bemusedly said that when she went, as planned, to meet with a teacher after an observation, the principal suddenly appeared at the classroom door and ushered her out.

Therapists who conduct frequent school-based observations might walk into a classroom and unsuspectingly run into another child they know, a more likely prospect if they've already worked with children in that school. The child might even offer a greeting: "Hey, I know you!" Similarly, therapists may find that they will be observing a new client in the same classroom as a former or current client. In such instances, it's important to use good clinical judgment in determining how to proceed.

People who work with schools know from experience how often things don't go as planned. Being prepared for the unexpected affords us a chance to respond patiently rather than with irritation. It might help to see these unexpected disruptions as opportunities to share in the experience of those who work in schools, whose days vary constantly according to the complex needs and expectations of children, faculty, and staff. It might also give you a chance to see how the child handles unexpected disruptions or changes in the school routine.

Documentation and Billing for School Observations

Therapists need to discuss with the family how they will bill for the time spent observing the child in order to avoid any misunderstandings about what is being paid for and by whom. Travel time is another issue, since insurance does not generally cover the observation or the time going to and from the school and, in fact, may not cover any activities outside the therapist's office. There is no single legal or ethical determination about whether to charge for observations or travel time, so therapists need to use their best clinical judgment and negotiate this aspect of their work with the family. In other words, there is no prohibition or requirement to charge for observations or travel time—use your own good judgment. Finally, keep a record of the observation in your files as you would for a session, even if you haven't billed for the school observation.

Deciding Whether to Observe Kids at School

There are legitimate questions to be raised about the validity and reliability of school-based observations. Educators and mental health professionals recognize that children and school personnel may alter their behavior because they are being observed, and this poses a problem for the therapist in determining what to make of the data collected (Dombrowski, 2015). Despite efforts to examine our biases, as discussed in Chapter 1, therapists, like any observers, have biases we carry with us when we walk into the classroom on any given day, biases that affect how and what we observe as well as our interpretation of those observations (Pellegrini, Symons, & Hoch, 2012).

You must also consider the relative value of doing school observations, given the other demands of your work. School visits require the therapist to take a sizable chunk of time out of what may already be a busy schedule, factoring in transportation time and costs in addition to the time spent observing the child and talking with the teacher. In order to decide whether such an investment is worthwhile, there are a handful of questions to ask oneself, as shown below.

Questions to ask yourself when considering whether to do a school-based observation

1. What do you hope to learn about the child from observing the child at school?

2. Is the problem better understood through direct observation?

3. Would observing the child's performance or behavior in comparison to other children be useful?

4. Would there be value in connecting with the teacher and seeing the school or classroom for yourself?

5. Are there discrepancies among the different sources of information: parents, the child, teachers, assessments, and others? If so, might your own direct observations help resolve or explain those discrepancies?

6. Might a school observation strengthen your relationship with the child or family? Would it strengthen the relationship among the child, family, and school?

7. Might a school visit increase that child's vulnerability among the child's peers or with teachers? If so, are there other ways to gather information that would be better suited to the situation?

If You Aren't Able to Observe Kids at School

If you find yourself unable to observe a child at school but think an observation would still be helpful, you might ask whether there is someone at the school who does observations and would be willing to work with you. As one experienced psychologist stated, "With the schools I know well, I trust their eyes on the ground." Together, you and the teacher or school representative (most likely someone from the student support team) could determine the questions you have about the child's functioning, which they might also share.

In one group practice, the therapists sometimes ask one another to observe a child when they want to minimize the impact of an observer on the child's classroom behavior or when a therapist is unable to go to the school. This can be a good arrangement for the child, the family, and you, as it adds another therapist's expertise and perspective to the mix while helping mitigate observation bias. If you choose this route, you'll want to review the questions you have and secure permission from the parents and possibly the child. In these instances, it's best if the therapist doing the observation either writes up a summary of the observations or presents the data in a joint session with you and the parents (and sometimes also with the child).

While conducting school observations can be difficult, they're one of the most meaningful ways we can deepen our understanding of the child's world. They require time, energy, and commitment on everyone's part, but can yield invaluable information and strengthen important relationships in support of the child.

REVIEWING THE BASICS

Certain problems are best assessed by observing kids in school. These include but are not limited to: social and behavioral issues, problems with anger management, anxiety, autism spectrum disorders, and learning problems. Because observations are one of the critical tools available to us, there are several key points to keep in mind to ensure yours are collaborative and productive:

- Observations can help you see a child's problems and strengths unfolding in real time. Only in a classroom setting can you directly compare clients to their similar-aged peers and witness their relationships with other students and teachers.

- Observing kids in school can also help you build fruitful relationships with the school personnel that can in turn help the family and school deepen their own relationship.

- Observations can help you identify the appropriateness of a classroom setting for a particular child and assist the family with navigating a mismatch, if present. This can include promoting coping skills in the child (and family) or helping them consider different educational options or services.

- There are various methods of observation, including those that are more formal and analytic (see Appendix D) and more naturalistic ones. Different methods can help you gather different types of data and should be used depending on the circumstance and presenting problem.

- Plan the timing and other logistics of the observation carefully with the parents, child, and school. You should figure out, among other things, the activity you hope to observe, whether you will try to observe anonymously or not, and how to be an unobtrusive presence in the classroom.

- At the same time, try to remain flexible and prepare for the fact that the day might not go exactly as planned. School days are hectic and busy, and variables can change unexpectedly.

- Keep in mind the importance of following up. Make sure to connect with the teacher and family after the observation to debrief about what went on.

- You might be unable to observe a child for any number of reasons, or deem it clinically unnecessary. Some therapists arrange for others in their practice to help them with observations, or learn to trust the observations of certain teachers and schools with whom they work.

CHAPTER 7

Homework, Report Cards, and Testing: Using Other Data to Help Assess Kids

W hile talking with a child's teacher or observing a day in the classroom can be essential aspects of your work with a particular child, there are other tools that can help supplement and guide your assessment. Reviewing past homework assignments and report cards, as well as incorporating behavioral rating scales and results from neuropsychological and psychoeducational testing can give you a wealth of information about the nuances of a child's particular issues to help you formalize a hypothesis or treatment plan. Furthermore, an important part of the therapist's role when working with schools is helping the family and school come to a shared understanding about any problems such assessments may bring to light. This chapter will review other methods that you can use to glean data and information about a child's school problems.

Homework: A Link Between the Family and School

Homework is the most ubiquitous, tangible link between home and school. It's one of the most common activities that parents engage in to support their child's schooling. It is also one of the main facets of school life that therapists can use to both assess and intervene with a child. Ask any parent to talk about their child's homework and they'll surely say something revealing with respect to what they may think about the school, their expectations for their child, possible tensions at home including around management of their child's social media and online activities (Steiner-Adair, 2013), the child's ease or struggle with learning, or their faith in the whole educational enterprise. Common statements a therapist might hear are: "The school gives way too much homework, which keeps our daughter up late at night," or the alternative, "I never see her doing any homework and wonder whether the teachers just don't assign enough because they don't want to do the grading." Then there is the ever-present, "I can't tell whether she's studying or just on social media with her friends."

The value, type, and amount of homework varies from school to school. Perhaps the most significant difference is that which can be seen between a large public school and a small public or independent school. With students numbering in the hundreds in large public high schools, for example, teachers are necessarily constrained in the time they have to review long homework assignments. Contrast that to some private or smaller public schools where homework assignments can often result in lengthy documents or research papers. Another important variable is the school's expectations about parental involvement in homework. Parents will often ask something like, "If the school advises us to let our child do homework unassisted, what exactly does that mean?" Many parents feel ill-equipped to offer assistance other than supportive comments or rules for what they expect regarding time spent on homework and the extent to which it's done well. Some parents are simply not involved in their children's homework at all. This may be due to time constraints, low literacy levels, or lack of knowledge about a subject, the particular homework assignment or the Internet. They might know little or nothing about their child's nightly homework experience. There are also parents who need clarification about their child's homework lest they offer too much help. And then there are issues of parental anxiety and possible competitiveness with other parents that play out through a child's homework. Yet, we know that children whose parents actively support their learning have fewer homework problems and complete their homework at higher rates (Hill & Tyson, 2009; Sheridan, Knoche, Edwards, Bovaird, & Kupzyk, 2010).

Feelings about homework can be strong and may quickly tap into a family dynamic that is important to register when evaluating what's going on. There may be one parent who is more involved in helping with homework and another parent or family member who disagrees with that level of involvement. Or expectations for what is sufficient may vary for the child in question compared with other the children in the family. Given the importance of homework as a link between the family and school, the following questions are offered to help explore this issue.

?

HOMEWORK: Questions for PARENTS

1. What do you think about the amount of homework your child receives? How has your child's homework changed over the years?

2. In what ways are you involved in your child's homework (e.g., creating space in the house for doing homework, reviewing assignments, long-term planning, checking to see if the work is complete, setting limits regarding screen time and other activities, helping your child study for a test or prepare for a presentation, contacting the teacher with questions, providing emotional support, punishing or rewarding your child, managing time, organizing meals and family activities around homework)?

3. What problems arise surrounding homework, if any?

4. What are your memories of doing homework as a child? What happens when your ideas regarding how to do homework clash with your child's?

5. How are homework assignments recorded? If homework assignments are posted online, can you access this information? How often does this occur?

6. If you have Internet access at home, how much does your child depend on it for doing homework assignments? How much of a distraction is it? How have you tried to monitor the use of social media and non-schoolwork-related Internet use, and how is that working? What would a typical disagreement be like between you and your child about screen time? If you don't have Internet access at home, what resources are available for your child to get access? How is that working for your child? For you?

7. When your child struggles with doing homework, what typically happens? What solutions have you found?

8. What rules or strategies have been put in place about doing homework? How effective are these rules and strategies?

9. Do you ever limit the amount of homework your child does? Under what circumstances? How does that work out?

10. Have you collaborated with your child's teacher about homework? How has that worked?

11. What guidelines, if any, does the school provide about homework?

12. Could you bring in some of your child's homework to review?

Kids will have feelings about homework, too. For kids who have an easy time with homework or find it educationally fulfilling (and some do!), there may be little to discuss. Some kids put too much time into their homework, leaving them sapped of energy the next day and feeling burned out. Some kids do a minimal amount or no homework each night, falling short of the teacher's expectations and therefore experiencing the negative consequences in terms of their learning, grades, and overall progress. Many kids struggle with the pull of social media and online activities while doing homework. And most kids would likely say that, given the choice, they would prefer little or no homework at all. But for those kids who struggle with homework, either routinely or periodically, it's an area worth exploring.

Responses to questions about homework may provide information about:

- children's relationships with their teacher and the school
- their sense of themselves as students
- their ability to sustain their concentration after a long day
- their curiosity (either enhanced or diminished by a given homework assignment)
- their expectations for school achievement
- the school's expectations of them
- their perceptions of what their parents want from them
- family entanglements.

It's important to note that kids with learning and attention issues often have serious problems doing homework. Such problems can adversely impact academic achievement and leave them vulnerable to anxiety and depression, as well as contribute to family tensions (Power, Karustis, & Habboushe, 2001). To explore these issues with the kids you see in therapy, consider asking the following questions.

HOMEWORK: Questions for KIDS

1. Tell me about your homework. What's it like for you? What's hard and what's easy? Where and when do you do your homework? How do you organize and prioritize your homework?

2. How has your homework changed over the years?

3. Do you think you're doing the right amount? Too much? Too little? How about the type of homework? Does it seem fair?

4. What kinds of problems have you had with your homework recently, if any? How have you tried to solve them? How well has that worked?

5. When might you need your parents' help? A sibling? A tutor? The teacher? What happens when you ask for help?

6. How do you manage social media or other online activities when doing homework? What would your parents say about this?

7. What do your parents expect from you regarding your homework assignments? Have there been arguments between them and you about homework? How do these get resolved?

8. What do your teachers expect from you regarding your homework assignments?

9. How important is your homework to how well you perform in school?

10. Would you be willing to bring in some of your homework so that we could look at it together? What kind of homework would be most helpful in figuring out what is going on?

The quantity and type of homework varies developmentally. Young children typically receive less homework than do middle and high school students, and there may be big jumps in what's expected between elementary, middle, and high school. As such, most kids don't view homework as a uniform experience over time. One student might find the homework doable in third grade but consider fourth grade homework impossible. Another student may derive satisfaction from conjugating Spanish verbs but fly off the handle when writing a social studies paper. A high school senior claimed, "Until this year, I could finish my math homework during my free period, but not now. I just can't seem to do the problems until I'm at home."

Similarly, variation occurs in terms of whether and how kids can study at all at home. Many children say that they have no privacy or free time at home given the need to take care of siblings, prepare dinner, or simply exist in a household filled with disruption and noise. One parent of a middle school student recently said, "My daughter can't do her homework at home because there's too much yelling between me and my husband. This didn't used to be a problem because, in elementary school, what little homework she had she finished at school." Then there are kids who are active in sports or other afterschool activities. For these kids, homework has to be squeezed in, often at the expense of sleep, family time, and simply being able to hang out or decompress.

The national debate regarding the merits of homework is in full view in the media. Long-standing views hold that homework reinforces the learning that takes place at school, allows students to dig deeper into a subject, strengthens study skills and self-discipline, improves test scores in high school, and helps the child move ahead on the college track of choice (Joseph, Wargelin, & Ayoub, 2016; Reinhardt, Theodore, Bray, & Kehle, 2009). However, Kohn (2007), in his book *The Homework Myth*, popularized the alternative view that there is simply no evidence to support the notion that homework advances academic success. This argument has reached the eyes and ears of educators and families alike, along with research confirming that homework can lead to boredom, academic burnout, lack of sleep, less family time, and increased stress kids experience as a result of homework demands (Cooper, Robinson, & Patall, 2006).

You may find parents and children who have strong beliefs on either side of this debate, beliefs that either support or conflict with the school's own homework policies. And you may find that your own views align more with one side of the argument or the other. In those circumstances, pay attention to your bias while remaining open to seeing the situation from another perspective. Whatever the particular alignments and misalignments, make sure the parents know the school's homework policy. Request a copy for yourself. Knowing school policies makes it easier to assess the child's homework situation in light of the school's expectations and can create a more workable, viable path to take with the family and the school.

Reviewing Homework with Kids and Families

If a child is struggling with homework, ask the child or family to bring in a graded assignment to review with you, especially if you're trying to sort out whether the child has undiagnosed learning or attention problems. This will allow you to see what's working and what's not, as well as to ascertain the teacher's view of what was produced. In particular, take a look at the teacher's comments, and try to review homework that will shed light on the presenting problem. It's very helpful to let children tell you what they've done, how they've done it, and what might be hard for them. If the child is young or is uncomfortable discussing this, look over the homework yourself and say what you think might be going on. Be sure to positively recognize the work that was done and reinforce any success the child may be having, however small. Also, consider having the child and family discuss how homework gets done at home. Ask who is involved, what they do to support the child, what tensions arise around homework, and the way homework-laden evenings play out for the family. Sometimes, it's important for the therapist to identify possible strategies to help kids manage their homework more effectively (Olympia, Jenson, & Hepworth-Neville, 1996; Power et al., 2001).

Alex, referred to as a "superstar" student in the beginning of fifth grade at her suburban public school, developed behavioral problems as the school year progressed. She struggled with following directions, developed a "negative attitude," according to her teacher, and became silly and aggressive with her peers. Even when engaged in schoolwork, she did poorly. She hit a true roadblock when it came to homework, crying each night and complaining to her mother about how hard it was. Her mother sought help from a local therapist, who could immediately see that, though Alex was bright and engaging, she was also really struggling. The therapist thought Alex might benefit from being tested by the school psychologist for special education services, but she wanted to try several interventions first that, if successful, might increase Alex's skills and confidence. If they were unsuccessful, the therapist reasoned that she would gain valuable knowledge about Alex's ability to adjust to the increased demands of fifth grade and better assess the possibility of testing.

One of the interventions she proposed to Alex and her mother was setting up a homework plan that included finding a specific place and time to work each afternoon. Though apprehensive, with the therapist and her mother's support,

Alex was able to say that she preferred to work in the kitchen with her mom present. She also indicated that, if she knew "something fun would happen" when she was done, it would help her sit down and do the work. She and her mother considered several options before deciding on a television show that she could watch as a reward. The therapist also introduced the idea of doing homework in a limited amount of time—for 15-minute intervals. The teacher agreed to prioritize what was expected of Alex so that, if she didn't complete all of her homework, she could keep up with the class the next day. Over several weeks, the therapist worked with Alex and her mother, during which time she also stayed in contact with Alex's teacher. Together, they determined that, while the strategies significantly improved Alex's homework stamina, her continued problems with focusing and impulsivity indicated that testing was an important next step.

There are a number of practical strategies parents can engage in to support their children's homework challenges, including the following:

- Learn about the school's homework policies and practices.
- Engage in conversation with the child about their homework—what's hard, what comes easy, what help the child needs, etc.
- Establish a place to do homework, preferably with the child, and see that it's equipped with the necessary materials.
- Help the child set up a regular homework schedule.
- Encourage the child to become increasingly independent in managing homework, relative to age, needs, and other demands on time and energy.
- Take a problem-solving approach when concerns arise.
- Collaborate with the child's teacher when homework difficulties emerge.
- When appropriate, establish rewards based on agreed-upon goals.
- Seek help from the school's learning support team geared toward the child's particular homework difficulties.

Reviewing Report Cards

In addition, it is often helpful to request copies of the child's report cards in an effort to learn whether there have been any trends or variations in overall performance. You might be looking to confirm whether the child's problem is situational—a one-time event related to something particular such as a move, recent trauma, change in the family, or unusual circumstance at school. Alternatively, by reviewing report cards, you may learn that the problem has been evident over a stretch of time. A child who is being described as unmotivated, for example, might have a trail of teacher comments documenting this lack of motivation going back several years. Or the report cards might not reflect any concerns about this at all. Either way, report cards can be valuable information to have when attempting to form a hypothesis, another important data point in understanding a child's life at school.

Not all parents keep school report cards or, if they do, may not be able to locate them. If this is the case, ask the parents and child about what they remember about previous report cards, including any narrative comments that have been made over the years. Also, you can encourage parents to ask the school for copies of past years' report cards and, by doing so, give the parents a chance to see that the school will most likely honor their request. Finally, some schools use checklists and include few if any narrative comments about the child. For example, parents might wonder why their son received a "Satisfactory" in reading while being two years below grade level. When there are discrepancies between parents' expectations and their child's report cards, take the time to look for teacher comments that might be illuminating, such as an end-of-the-year report card comment that reads something like "I hope you have a great summer. Don't forget to practice your multiplication tables."

Incorporating Standard Behavioral Rating Scales

Along with reviewing homework and report cards, there are a number of standard behavioral rating scales designed specifically to evaluate how children are functioning at home and school (see Appendix E for some examples). They are relatively brief, have no imposed time limits, and are used widely. They are often part of the battery of tests that clinicians use when they conduct psychoeducational, neuropsychological, or other testing in their practice. Here we'll discuss the use of such assessments as an element of the more informal screening you can do to further understand a child's problem. They may serve the same or different purposes if they are being used for a comprehensive psychological, psychoeducational, or neuropsychological evaluation, discussed more fully in the next section. Generally speaking, these scales can be helpful in clarifying the problem the child is facing and creating common language with which to discuss it.

Assessing a problem using normative data

Behavioral scales that differentiate among emotional and behavioral issues can highlight what might be going on for a child who is struggling at school. For instance, therapists might use them to identify the subtle differences between anxiety and inattention or between inattention and depression. They also make it possible to see how the child functions in different settings (at home, in school, and within different classes) and according to different points of view, be it the parents', teachers', or self-reports from the child. The results may not be sufficient to yield a diagnosis or create precisely coordinated interventions. However, when combined with the clinical work you're doing and collaborative work with the school, they can help direct the design and implementation of interventions. Such information can also be useful in determining when to make a referral to another professional, such as a psychologist who tests children or a pediatrician, neurologist, or occupational therapist.

Additionally, certain problems are less observable in conventional ways. For example, anxious kids can be overlooked in schools because they are often compliant and do well academically. Their experience of barely keeping it together may be masked by their good grades and agreeable demeanor. Teachers are often genuinely surprised to learn that the student who's seated so conscientiously in the front row is experiencing extreme worries or fears that may or may not be related to what's happening at school. Behavioral assessments, along with clinical interviews, can make the invisible visible and ground hypotheses in what the child is experiencing.

Creating a common language

There are times when parents may not value or believe what the teachers are reporting about their child, especially if the family–school relationship is rocky or the child behaves differently at home. Behavioral assessments can unite people around a common language and, ideally, a common understanding of the problem, positioning them to create more workable solutions. Though not diagnostically definitive in themselves, the *language* of behavioral assessments can help furnish a level of objectivity and a platform for action.

Consider the case of 10-year-old Romilla, who had years of report cards that detailed her behavioral difficulties: "Romilla can't seem to sit still" and "We constantly have to remind her to focus on her work." However, Romilla's parents were disgruntled with the school and said that their daughter was bright, active, and perhaps a little anxious, but not the misbehaving child that the teachers described.

With the parents' permission, the therapist contacted Romilla's teacher and got an earful about Romilla's disruptive behavior, and the teacher's frustration with the girl's parents for not listening to what she and previous teachers had reported. Seeing the gap in understanding and the parents' reluctance to recognize the nature of their daughter's struggles at school, the therapist recommended to Romilla's parents they evaluate the situation further by asking the teacher to fill out a behavioral rating scale. Once completed, the therapist met with the parents to review the findings, which revealed high scores on the hyperactivity and oppositional scales. What Romilla's teachers had reported was now documented by an assessment that the parents saw as more objective. In this case, it was the more formal, standardized approach that persuaded Romilla's parents that her problems were ones to take seriously.

Using behavioral rating scales at school

When using a behavioral rating scale, there are a number of steps to take, beginning with discussing the idea with the parent and the older child (see the steps listed below). Make sure to provide information up front so that its use and purpose is fully understood by those involved. Most teachers will have experience receiving assessment forms from therapists or from their own school psychologist; thus, they will have some knowledge of how to complete them. If you learn that teachers in the school are not experienced in filling out such forms, offer to talk directly with the teachers or inquire whether there is someone knowledgeable and available at the school to answer questions about the questionnaire itself or the purpose it serves. For example, teachers might wonder who will see their responses apart from the therapist, and how their responses will be used. Teachers might say, "These questions don't accurately reflect what I think about the child" or "The questions are too black and white." It's important that either you or someone skilled in the use of these assessments is available to respond and offer guidance.

Although teachers may be more open and honest in their answers if they know that the results will go directly to the therapist rather than the child or family, it is important to keep in mind that parents are always within their rights to see any of their child's records, including results of behavioral rating scales (Jacob et al., 2016). Whatever your practice is regarding sharing the results with parents, inform the teacher(s) and parents. If you can, ask for input from more than one teacher to provide a broader basis for assessing how the child is doing at school. When reporting the findings, depending on the situation, you can provide general feedback such as, "The teachers indicated that Henry struggles to stay focused" and feedback that is related to specific teachers or classes, such as, "In math, Henry clearly is able to stay focused, in contrast to social studies and language arts, where he is distracted and fidgety."

Steps to take when using behavioral rating scales

1. Provide the parent or child with information about the assessment and the purpose it serves, and respond to any questions that are

raised by the family or school. Help parents understand that "Normal" in a test result has a more limited meaning than in everyday usage.

2. With the child and family, determine whom to contact at the school. If they are unsure, have the parent or you yourself reach out to the teacher or someone from the student support team (e.g., school psychologist or learning specialist) to seek advice about moving forward.

3. With the school representative, find out how such screening assessments are administered. Make a plan regarding to whom they will be sent and how they will be returned to the therapist.

4. Once the assessments are completed and returned, review the findings with the parents and child and discuss how information might be useful at home or at school.

The Therapist's Role in Psychological, Psychoeducational, or Neuropsychological Testing

Psychological, psychoeducational, and neuropsychological testing conducted in clinics, hospitals, psychologist's offices (or your own), or through the school system can be a significant source of information about the children with whom you work. Most commonly, testing is conducted for the purpose of understanding an individual's strengths and weaknesses or determining a diagnosis (in non-school settings) that, in turn, guides a set of interventions that can better support the child. Often, tests are conducted because of difficulties the child encounters at school—with learning, performance, skill development, emotions, behavior, or relationships. Thus, recommendations for testing often come from the school, and recommendations for what to do afterward are often implemented in the school setting (see Chapter 12 regarding testing issues related to IEPs and 504 Plans).

Sometimes, children have been tested before you see them in therapy. In these cases, you can ask to review the testing to help determine whether the problems identified and interventions recommended relate to the child's current struggles at school. As mentioned above, kids who receive special education services, for instance, will have had testing done that may be vital to your work. If your education and training did not include the study of psychoeducational testing, seek consultation (or additional training) in how to read and interpret test results. For any number of reasons, some children who were tested did not receive feedback about it or, if they did, have little recollection of it. Therefore, check with parents to determine how to best utilize what you glean from previous testing and how to bring the child into the conversation, if indicated. Finally, you may discover that the testing is not up to date, in which case the parents and you may decide that further testing is needed, either through the school system or via another route.

Whatever the circumstances surrounding the decision to have a child tested, therapists can and often do play a vital part in the process, either as the professional doing the testing, the catalyst for the decision, or someone who helps implement the suggested interventions. The therapist might also play a role in resurrecting an evaluation that is buried in a file. Teachers may not have read the evaluation, may have decided not to read it in order to form their own unbiased opinion about the child, or may not even know that it exists. If testing was done at the school, the therapist can also recommend that the parent reach out to someone knowledgeable there who could review the testing with the child.

There are at least three areas in which therapists can play a role with children, families, and schools regarding testing: assessing the need to test, preparing the child and family for testing, and following up after testing is completed. In each area the emphasis is placed on working with the school the child attends.

Working with the family and school to assess the need for testing a child

Part of the work you'll do with kids and families involves assessing whether to have the child you are seeing be tested by a psychologist, neuropsychologist, or another professional. The impetus to test may arise from the nature of the school problem or a referral. Or parents might enter your office already wanting to have their child tested for issues related to learning, behavior, or socioemotional functioning. Sometimes, testing is the first idea seized upon when a child is struggling with school problems. More often than not, exploring the idea of testing follows from a child's failure to respond to interventions that have been tried at home or school, failure for which there is no clear explanation

In working with children and families when testing is being considered, there are a number of questions to keep in mind to help make this determination, especially as it relates to your work with the school. You'll want to consider relevant information about the child—such as your own clinical assessment, report cards, previous standardized assessments, parent and teacher concerns, as well as observations at school and in your office. The questions identified below include the need for the exchange of information and collaboration with the child's school.

Questions to consider regarding testing

1. What interventions have already been tried at home or school, for how long, and with what impact?

2. What questions remain about the child that may be best answered by testing?

3. What is the child's and family's view of testing?

4. What do the child's teacher, student support staff, or others think about having the child tested?

5. Are there alternative ways of assessing the problem—behavioral screening, referral to a pediatrician, or further clinical evaluation? If so, what is the best way to pursue them?

6. Is testing needed to determine whether the child would benefit from receiving special education services?

In one case, the mother of 11-year-old Rob contacted a therapist because she was distressed by the constant stream of complaints from Rob's teachers. She knew Rob had problems paying attention at school, but she claimed that the school's way of responding was making things worse. The therapist and mother agreed that he would go to the school to observe Rob in the classroom. What he found was Rob playing with his pencil, interrupting classmates, and waving his hand to receive help regarding directions that others had quickly grasped. In short, he consumed a disproportionate amount of the teacher's time with his disruptions. The disjunction between Rob and the majority of his classmates' ability to get their work done was considerable, and that, combined with the teacher's exasperation and the therapist's observations, made testing a reasonable option. When Rob's mother heard the report from the therapist's observation, she was more open and willing to accept the validity of the teachers' concerns. This led to having Rob tested to see if he was struggling with problems associated with ADHD, an undiagnosed learning problem, or other contributing factors.

Helping the child and family prepare for and process the need for testing

As one learning specialist said, "Testing can be a huge thing for a child's process of self understanding . . . being tested one-on-one with a skilled professional can motivate a student to become curious, affirmed, and energized." After testing, kids can realize that they aren't "crazy," "lazy," or "stupid" (Kelly & Ramundo,

2006) but are instead struggling with problems like dyslexia or ADHD. By learning more about how they learn, kids can face their school problems more confidently, especially when appropriate supports are put in place. Some kids will say that they feel understood, validated, and even deeply reassured by the testing process and results.

However, sometimes a recommendation for testing is not received well by the child or family. The idea may be frightening to the child, possibly highlighting a problem that the child hopes will just go away. Some kids feel scared to find out what's really wrong with them or have already determined that it will be a waste of time because no one can tell them something about themselves that they don't already know. Some kids (and parents) worry about the child being labeled and looked down upon by their teachers or others who will review the findings. Kids also worry that they will have to leave the school. Even kids who are open to the idea of being tested are still often nervous and uncomfortable about the prospect. Be sure to take any such concerns seriously and discuss them thoroughly with whomever is involved. If you believe that it's in the child's best interest to follow up on a recommendation for testing, or if you've made the recommendation yourself, be sure to clearly state the reasons why. It's the responsibility of both you and the school to help the child or family understand the testing process and why it might be useful.

To help quell these anxieties, you can work with the family, child, and school to determine the questions that they're hoping the testing will answer. These questions—from the teacher, parent, school psychologist, you, or others—can be raised directly with the person doing the evaluation or passed along by the parent or school representative. Most children (including some younger children) will benefit greatly from having a say in what they're hoping to learn from the evaluation (Finn, 2007). Involving children will not only help shape the questions but give them more of a stake in the testing, and that investment can lead to a greater buy-in for whatever follows.

Therapists can describe what will likely happen during the testing. You might say that the person doing the testing is there to find out what the child does well and what may be hard for the child. You or the parent might also prepare the child by saying that some of what they do will be interesting, though it will be different from playing games or just having fun. For older children, you can do much the same but also appeal to what they have to learn from the experience about themselves and how testing works more generally. If the testing is being done at school, you can also collaborate with a person at school who can describe the testing to the child and offer an encouraging word. Hearing from the school psychologist, counselor, social worker, or a trusted teacher can help children feel supported and reduce their overall anxiety. In short, whenever possible, involve key people in the testing process, including the child and family as the most active participants.

Therapists can also be helpful to parents in exploring their expectations for what they want to learn from having their child tested and finding out from the person doing the testing when, where, and how the child will be tested. This gives them the opportunity to let their child know that testing will happen on a given day and send the child off to school with that knowledge as well as whatever extra support is needed. The more parents are aware of the timing and setting of the testing, the better they will be at preparing their child.

Following up on the testing

Once testing is completed, therapists are often in a position to review the written evaluation or talk with the person who did the testing to discuss the findings and recommendations. This is done in an effort to help coordinate services. If the testing takes place at the child's school, the tester, usually a school psychologist, will meet with the parents, child, and perhaps others at the school to review the findings and recommendations. If testing is being conducted to seek special education services, there are additional considerations (see Chapter 12). If the testing took place outside the school, and the family chooses to share the evaluation with the school, the clinician doing the testing may come to the school to meet with the appropriate members of the student's support team. In each of these cases, consider attending this meeting in order to help the child and family follow up on recommendations in a coordinated and collaborative way.

There may be differences of opinion about the results or recommendations or about what occurred during the testing process itself. For example, a child who is diagnosed with a learning disability and depression might receive a number of recommendations meant to help several distinct areas of difficulty that require prioritization. Perhaps the problem that is most challenging for the teacher is when the child goes into what he calls "shutdown" mode. The child, on the other hand, fervently complains about the assignments—she just "can't understand them!" Or the parents want to find ways to support their child without using special education services, but others at school see special education as the only good option. Here's where the therapist has a crucial role to play. You can help tease out and elucidate the different data and priorities and also help create a picture of the child that is, more often than not, complex but not cripplingly so. As information is gathered, therapists and others working with the child can continually fine-tune this portrait. In this follow-up process, the overarching goal is to establish common ground among those involved so that interventions can be carried out that maximize the energy and resources that are available to support the child.

Generally, the psychologist doing the evaluation will provide useful recommendations that can be implemented at home, school, and in your office. Sometimes, however, recommendations are made that, even if clinically appropriate, don't quite fit the school, classroom, or home environments in which the child lives and studies. This is one of the key places where you can be helpful. When there is a discrepancy between the recommendations and what can realistically be carried out in the child's environment, you can bring your perspective into the mix by working with others to modify or selectively choose what will work best, including collaborating further with the testing psychologist. In the case of IEP meetings that follow from testing, you might play an active role in collaborating with the parents and the school's student support team to help implement the recommendations, especially those that, by extension, apply to the child's life at home. (For more information about your role in the IEP process, see Chapter 12.)

In the case of a high school student, Mateo, the therapist, family, and school were struggling to comprehend why he was receiving poor grades in the second semester of his sophomore year. He'd been working with a therapist for a couple of months who suspected underlying learning problems in addition to his evident difficulties with severe anxiety. In order to figure out what was impacting what, testing seemed like a natural next step. The family hired a psychologist in private practice to do the testing, and he was able to discern that Mateo's symptoms of OCD and anxiety largely explained his academic problems. His learning profile was uneven, but not significantly so.

Prior to the testing, many supports had been put in place for Mateo, such as extra time on quizzes and exams, a system for being able to exit the classroom when his anxiety intensified, a reduction in homework assignments, and the ability to enlist steady emotional support from the school counselor and his teachers. But as a result of the testing, it became clear that, to effectively tackle the OCD and anxiety, certain school supports would need to be reduced or eliminated because they allowed him to avoid anything that caused him stress, prohibiting him from developing reasonable coping mechanisms. In a family–school meeting, the clinician who did the testing made a strong case for this, indicating that some tactics only increased Mateo's anxiety by allowing him to evade assignments or classes that made him uncomfortable. Here's where Mateo's therapist stepped in.

Together, the psychologist who did the testing, the school's psychologist, and Mateo's therapist devised a strategy for how Mateo could gradually tolerate the discomfort of remaining in class when he was very anxious. A plan was made for him to text the therapist during scheduled breaks in the school day. In addition, the therapist helped Mateo's teachers learn more about how anxiety impacts kids at school so that the teachers could uphold their regular expectations while encouraging him to hang in there. The therapist's aim was to work with the teachers, family, and Mateo to not only understand his anxiety and OCD symptoms more fully but also to ally with him in his effort to manage what had greatly interfered with his success in the classroom. Teachers were advised to say, "I see this is hard for you, so let's figure out how to work on this together," rather than offer reassurances that only exacerbated his problems.

As a result, Mateo was able to find new ways to cope with what had vexed and paralyzed him previously. In time, he was able to meet academic expectations in most of his courses, even with occasional setbacks. With the therapist coordinating the team's efforts, testing helped to clarify the nature of Mateo's problem and shifted the conversation to a new set of plans that made a real difference.

One key dimension of this case was the family–school meeting that took place shortly after the testing was complete. By bringing the key people together, it was possible to establish new parameters for what Mateo needed, something that might have taken weeks if not months to accomplish with phone calls or emails. Each person in the room, including Mateo, had the opportunity to hear from the testing psychologist what mattered most in addressing his school problems. This galvanized attention and energy to creating and implementing effective interventions.

REVIEWING THE BASICS

- Homework is an important link between the family and school. It can often illuminate the complex dynamics between the child and parents or the parents and the school.

- Feelings and expectations about homework often reveal underlying feelings about the child's education as a whole, and about the child's presenting problem.

- Reviewing homework assignments and report cards is a valuable way to assess patterns and problems in a child's learning that have just cropped up or that have emerged slowly over time.

- Incorporating behavioral rating scales into your assessment of a child provides a set of normative data that can help create a shared language and understanding of a child's problem. Sometimes, these more formal, objective assessments can help break through a tense, ongoing, or distrustful dynamic between the family and school.

- Psychological testing can also be an important way to gather information about a child, especially if you suspect the child may be struggling with an undiagnosed learning or emotional problem and could benefit from special education services.

- You can work with the family and child not only to determine the need for testing, but also to help them express their desires, fears, and expectations around the testing process. Keep in mind that it can be a tense and emotional experience for all involved.

- In the aftermath of testing, therapists familiar with testing may be well positioned to help sort through all of the given data about a child. In collaboration with the school, family, and testing professional, therapists can assist in developing a coherent vision of the child in question.

- With input from all of these sources in a child's life, you can continually fine-tune your perception of the child's problem and work to maximize the energy and resources that are available to support them.

CHAPTER 8

Family–School Meetings

Nowhere in the family–school–child triad is there more hope, pathos, and anxiety on display than in family–school meetings. These meetings are fundamental to our work with schools, and they show how the people and systems in a child's world fit together, for better or for worse. Until you attend one, the sense of belonging to a team, however impermanent, may not be something you experience directly. But by sitting around a table with all the stakeholders in a child's life, you can begin to understand the complex dynamics at play and how you fit in. Only in such meetings, for example, can you observe the subtle shift in the chair or raised eyebrow that exposes the underlying support, tension, or other emotion that's essential to understanding the situation.

Meetings with families of children who need special education services in public schools (IEP or 504 Plan meetings) are often a therapist's first entry point into family–school meetings. However, this chapter is designed to help you understand the part you can play in meetings at the child's school when the child is not necessarily a recipient of special education services. (See Chapter 12 for further guidance on working with the special education system.)

Preparing for a Family–School Meeting

Family–school meetings can be created for any number of reasons and can be initiated by the school, the family, or the therapist. For instance, there may be a crisis at school or in the family, and someone will decide that the best (or only) option is to meet in order to solve the problem. Some schools simply make it their practice to meet regularly with families to solve problems large and small (Minke & Jensen, 2014). Common reasons for initiating family–school meetings (other than those that are required as part of IEP regulations) are reviewed as follows.

Common reasons for family–school meetings

- The child's problem is serious and needs urgent attention.
- The child's problem is significant and not being addressed successfully in any other way.
- Family–school meetings are part of the school's regular practice.
- The family and school appear to have conflicting views of the child, and multiple perspectives are needed to determine how best to help.
- The child is transitioning to a new school or new division.
- Communication between the family and school has broken down.
- The family–school relationship needs strengthening.
- Momentum is required to push through a problem.

Often, therapists are in a position to help prepare the child and family to make the most of family–school meetings. When there is lead time, as in the case of an annual IEP meeting or a regular meeting to assess ongoing academic problems, preparation can happen over several sessions, evolving naturally out of the therapeutic work. At other times, family–school meetings occur as the result of an urgent problem, and preparations might occur on the fly, or in a brief few minutes before the meeting. In one case, a therapist was called in suddenly to a meeting at a local high school to address an incident that involved his 10th grade client, Larry, who was suspended for a physical altercation. Even though little prep time was available, the therapist was able to squeeze in a session with Larry and his parents to review what occurred, the questions they had about the incident, the school's rules, and what supports were available for Larry, presuming he was allowed to return to school. Regardless of the time you have, there are several elements to consider before attending family–school meetings, reviewed below.

Family-school meeting preparation checklist

- ☐ Clarify the issues with the child and family to address, and establish goals for the meeting.
- ☐ Establish what, if anything, should remain confidential.
- ☐ Determine if the child should be present.

- [ ] Figure out whom from the family or school should be present.
- [ ] Clarify roles.
- [ ] Determine where to meet.
- [ ] Agree on billing.

Clarify the issues and establish goals

As a first step, review issues that will be discussed in the meeting, and ask questions that elicit and clarify information about the presenting problem. Based on the questions you raise, goals for the meeting often emerge organically. Therapists operate with varying degrees of formality with regard to goal setting, so determining goals for the meeting should be similar to other goal-setting you already do. Either way, it's your job to help shape the client's and family's wishes and hopes into goals that are realistic, constructive, and commonly shared by as many family members as possible. Questions you ask can help clarify the goals for the meeting, such as those reviewed below.

FAMILY–SCHOOL MEETINGS:
Questions to raise with children and families when preparing for family-school meetings

1. What issues are important to discuss?

2. What issues might the school wish to discuss?

3. How has the school handled the problem so far?

4. What concerns and expectations do the family and child have about the meeting?

5. How can the therapist be helpful to the family and child?

6. What are the goals for the meeting?

Determining goals is partly related to what's at stake. If the child is in crisis, it's important to stay focused on the immediate concerns and what can be done to stabilize the situation. Goals, in these instances, might address very specific needs, such as safety. Whatever the goals, make every effort to include the child in the process. If the child is motivated and has buy-in, this is often the cornerstone of what works in a meeting. Some of the broader, more common goals of family–school meetings include the following:

Common goals for family–school meetings

- Learn how the child is doing at school generally.
- Obtain a clearer picture of the child's problem at school as seen by the school representatives.
- Review interventions that have been tried, and revise or change them as needed.
- Explore new ideas for how to deal with a particular problem.
- Forge or strengthen relationships with the child's teacher, counselor, administrator, etc.
- Establish a means for the parents and school to communicate.
- Identify school resources that can be mobilized.
- Seek guidance regarding how parents can support their child at home.

Let's again consider the case of Larry. Small in stature, Larry had been taunted by a group of boys for weeks. He couldn't recall exactly what had happened that day in the hallway, only that he was furious and deeply frustrated. He was even fearful that the boys would continue to take advantage of him once he returned to school. His parents had been unaware of their son's predicament until they received a call from the assistant principal, asking them to bring him home the day of the fight. They were, understandably, confused, upset, and unsure of how to support their son.

After hearing what happened from Larry's and his parents' perspective, the therapist needed to explore what they all thought about the school, and what they expected from the upcoming family–school meeting based on their past experiences. Larry's parents' expectations of the school were dismally low—the father's past injurious school experience caused him to believe that his son was being treated unfairly. If Larry didn't defend himself, he maintained, there would be no end to the torment he'd suffer at the hands of those who were bullying him, much as the father himself had suffered when he was a student. Larry, in turn, felt that when he'd reached out to his teacher about the problem, his concerns were minimized and he was "shoved along" to the school counselor. Fearing that exposing the group of boys would cause them to retaliate further, Larry became overwhelmed and couldn't bring himself to knock on the counselor's door. In short, the father was apprehensive, Larry was frightened and discouraged, and both parents were doubtful that much could be done.

During the lead-up to the family–school meeting, the following questions were identified by Larry, his parents, and the therapist as ones they would bring up during the conversation:

- What is the school's policy regarding fighting? Bullying?

- How do these particular circumstances—being provoked, teased, and bullied by peers—impact the outcome or consequence?

- Did anyone know about the problem before the incident, and what had been done about it?

- What supports and practices were in place for students—the bullied and the bully—in these circumstances?

- What can the parents and therapist do to be helpful?

- Providing Larry is able to return to school, how can everyone support his reentry?

- How is Larry doing at school in general and are there other areas of concern?

- What supports are available for Larry in general?

From the outgrowth of these questions, Larry's parents established three goals for the meeting, modest in scope: to speak up for their son effectively, to get answers to questions about the school's rules and resources, and to see how Larry could return to school safely. Initially, Larry's main goal was to make the bullying stop, nothing more. With the help of his parents, the therapist, and eventually the school, he was able to see how he could ask for more than simply the absence of fear, and he sought to learn what could be done for him to feel not only safe, but also comfortable at school.

Sometimes, when situations are tense, goal-setting can be a way to recognize and incorporate parents' worries and fears: "I can see how unhappy you are about what happened to your child at school. How about taking a few minutes to talk about what you would like to get out of the meeting, especially if it doesn't go as we hope?" By exploring what the family is hoping to accomplish, how they think school personnel view them, and what could possibly hinder your collective efforts, therapists can make sure the goals for the meeting remain realistic.

Being able to remain calm and collaborative, for example, can become a goal—even a central goal—of the meeting.

Establish what should remain confidential

Given the at times exploratory nature of family–school meetings and the open, conversational exchange of ideas that occurs, it's important to consult with older children and family members about the limits of what you are free to discuss—what remains confidential and what does not. Concerns about confidentiality can emerge in a meeting, for example, when parents are in the process of separating but don't want the school to know. Similarly, the family may be dealing with the loss of a loved one, a recently identified addiction problem, a serious illness, a financial crisis, incarceration of a family member, or plans to move or change schools. It helps to discuss such issues with the family before the meeting. Anticipating what might come up clarifies what the family wants to keep private as well as giving them an opportunity to reflect on the plusses and minuses of sharing information.

The therapist can also examine whether certain privacies might be inhibiting the child's progress and, if so, how to handle the situation. For example, as mentioned above, perhaps a mother is struggling with a recent cancer diagnosis but hasn't informed the child or others. Those at school might not need to know the exact nature of the problem, but knowing that there *is* a problem at home might help teachers adjust their expectations and level of support for the child.

It's possible that you may be asked to keep something confidential that makes it hard, if not impossible, for you to attend the meeting. For instance, parents may have decided to seek legal recourse regarding their grievance with the school. It will be up to you to determine whether you can attend a family–school meeting with integrity, given the seriousness of a situation that they are not disclosing to the school.

A final note: when you arrive at the school, you'll likely introduce yourself to whoever is in charge at the proverbial front desk and state the reason you're there. This can be an important relationship to establish and maintain over time, since people in front desk positions are often the gatekeepers to the school's administration and faculty. Such ties can be vital to your ongoing work with the school, but if a conversation occurs—a nice thing in itself—remember to be discreet with the information you have about the child and family. Though the administrative staff at the front desk may know the child and family, they are outside the range of people with whom to share information. This can sometimes be a delicate exchange, lest you appear unfriendly or dismissive.

Determine if the child should be present

A contribution of the Ackerman Institute's work (as discussed in the Introduction) was to promote the inclusion of children in family–school meetings. With the child present, they argued, the conversation becomes more grounded and honest, since the principal subject is in the room speaking for himself or herself rather than being spoken for. Having the child present is an essential component of IEP meetings in public schools (see Chapter 12).

There are a number of ways that family–school meetings are enriched by the presence of the child. For one, when discussing different facets of the child's life, the confusing "he said, she said" aspect of the conversation is minimized, since anyone can turn to the child and talk to them directly. Second, the adults may be less likely to become openly hostile with the child in the room. In my experience, people just tend to sit up a little taller when the child is present. Third, by speaking for himself or herself, the child's ability to self-advocate is strengthened considerably, a lifelong skill that increases resiliency and self-esteem. Fourth, family ties can be enhanced as the parents help their child speak up, or witness their child speaking up independently. Fifth, the child is able to offer opinions or tweaks to the specific interventions that are suggested, thereby maximizing the potential for the child's own engagement and follow-through. Sixth, the child often provides essential, sometimes surprising information about his or her experience at school that can open the family–school dialogue in new and important ways. Lastly, by being present, the child may develop greater trust in the people sitting around the table, strengthening the sense that everyone there belongs to the child's team.

When deciding whether to include the child, first consider the child's age and maturity level. The older the child, the more important it is for the child to be at the table, representing his or her point of view. Second, take into account the level of dysfunction within the family or between the family and school. There are some situations when having the child present could be detrimental. Examples are when tensions between the family and school are very high, the parents are at odds with one another, some type of litigation is pending, or there is concern about the possibility of violence in the home. In those instances, a family member or the therapist should represent the child's point of view. After the meeting, you can then have a follow-up discussion with the child in an age-appropriate way.

In some instances, the child might be too vulnerable to cope with a room full of adults talking about him and therefore shouldn't be present. For example, a child who is severely depressed or anxious may not be able to manage such a gathering. With preparation, however, a vulnerable child may be able to participate in some limited way. Kids who grow up in chaotic families can struggle with this dynamic as well. They may also fear repercussions from such a meeting: "My parents will be furious when they hear what my teacher has to say" or "Boy, am I going to get it when I get home." This may be true whether the child is present or not. As a therapist, be sure to make every effort to discuss the child's worries and fears, as well as what his parents are thinking, to ensure that the meeting will be constructive and there are plans in place if conflict arises. For example, try having the child sit next to someone considered a safe person, or create a signal she can use if she feels a need to leave the meeting.

The family–school meeting can also happen in stages. For instance, the child might be included for part of the meeting, either at the beginning or the end, or with different combinations of people in the room. It is essential for the child to hear someone talk about what they are doing well despite their struggles or hear their parents and teachers working together and speaking with a common voice.

Figure out who else should be present

Though therapists usually don't make the final decision about which school personnel participate in a family–school meeting, they can raise questions about whom to include that will expand and strengthen the therapeutic relationship. Even the conversation with the family and child about this topic can add value to the therapy by bringing focus to available resources. In addition, the therapist will learn who in the school is available to support the child or family or clarify who will do what going forward.

Ask the parent and child whom they would ideally like to have present from the school. There may be a trusted student support person who would be able to help in such a meeting. Or there may be someone else at the school who is less involved with the child but whom the parents think would be a positive influence or whose presence might be reassuring. Of course, teachers are often in such meetings, and their direct experience with the child is likely to be the richest source of information. Administrators are often present as well and can have important institutional knowledge to share, including what worked best in similar situations. Since Larry's problem, for example, was a disciplinary one (at least initially), it was important to have someone from the administration present who could clarify the school's rules and had the authority to examine the situation in light of the school's history of such incidents. Explore these options with the child and family, with full recognition that those whom you'd like to be present may not be available. Prepare the family for that exigency.

You might also consider including extended family members, caregivers, or someone who knows or works with the child outside the school. Children might have a tutor, for example, or an involved older sibling who helps with homework, who may have helpful insights to share. Additional people can also complicate the situation, too, especially when they are at odds with one another or with the school. If you do decide to include a grandparent, sibling, occupational therapist or others, include them in the planning or have the parents inform them of the goals of the meeting.

One experienced clinician made an important, final point: if the school is handling a problem reasonably well and the parents have a good relationship with the school, the therapist doesn't necessarily need to attend such meetings. Perhaps you played a hand in helping the child and family become effective partners with the school, or they might have come into your office with those skills under their belt. If the latter is true, you have something to learn from them, so listen to how they approach the problem their child is having and how they work with people at the school.

Clarify roles

Once you have a good idea of who will be at the meeting, it's important to try to clarify everyone's role. Beginning with the child, you can help her decide what she would like to contribute and how active she wants to be. Every considered initiative that comes from the child is generally a good initiative. The older the child, the more important it is for them to speak and act for themselves.

Similarly, ask the parents if they have ideas about who should say what during the meeting. Some of this preparation may unfold naturally or may be obvious from what the family has already told you about their relationship with the school. For example, Larry's father openly stated that he feared he'd become angry in the meeting and that this would make things worse. His wife, in turn, worried about her ability to remain comfortably levelheaded and whether her husband might erupt in exasperation, setting everything back. In this case, the family and therapist decided that Larry's mother should be the primary spokesperson, especially if Larry's father became distressed. Deciding who is going to do what matters most when conflict is anticipated or someone worries about his or her own ability to remain open-minded and constructive. You can also coach the parents and child in how to handle difficult situations if they arise, be that extra set of eyes and ears during the meeting, and provide valuable feedback when debriefing the conversation. Communicating effectively is often one of the express goals of family–school meetings.

Then, there's your role in the meeting: how active or passive you'll be and under what circumstances you'll step in to reinforce someone's point of view, redirect the conversation, introduce and assist in developing specific interventions, or even help facilitate the meeting (or all of the above). Much of what you do in the meeting stems from the goals that have been established, even those constructed hastily. For example, if parents decide that they want to voice disagreement with a decision coming from the school, you could agree to support them in this effort by helping to explain and document why they feel the way they do. Or you could decide that if the meeting takes a wrong turn, you'll step in to try to reorient the conversation. Whatever the situation, it's important to establish what you would like to say about the child, and also what might be better expressed by the child or family directly.

When you assemble around the table, if it seems as though no one has been assigned the job of starting or running the meeting, or if there's confusion about your participation, feel free to speak up. At the meeting's start, you can directly ask who is facilitating. You can also take a minute and say something about why you're there. It's usually best if you don't facilitate the meeting yourself but if, for some unanticipated reason, the job falls on you, here are some ideas about the type of introduction you might make:

- I understand that we're all looking for ways to support Jin and I am glad to join you in this effort.

- I've been working with Jin and his family for the past several weeks and hope to learn more about how he's doing at school so that we can find ways to support his learning at home.

- Jin's parents and I have some questions and concerns we'd like to discuss with you and thought that meeting together and hearing everyone's perspective would be helpful.

- (If Jin is present) We're all here to see how to make things better for you at school.

If you find yourself taking a more central role than you'd planned, see if you can share the responsibility with someone from the school and keep the parents and child actively involved. Again, this is not commonplace, but also not a problem should the occasion arise—as long as you are prepared.

Determine where to meet

Schools are busy places, and synchronizing the schedules of various participants can be challenging. Some schools designate times of day when family–school meetings can be scheduled (just before school, right after, or during a lunch period, for example). Other schools have more varying schedules. Remember that even though schools have much in common, they are unique institutions, and visiting gives you the opportunity to become more familiar with the culture, student population, strengths, and limitations—a real advantage for your clients as you translate that knowledge into finding ways to support the child.

Working parents, those who are disabled or severely dysfunctional, or those whose lives are limited by poor transportation options may struggle to get to family–school meetings at any time of day. Similarly, for some therapists, a lack of time, geographic issues, or the nature of their practice makes meeting at school untenable. If faced with such logistical difficulties, consider having one or multiple parties conference in by phone or video. Though being a disembodied voice or screen presence in the room can be challenging, it's still possible to conduct fruitful meetings utilizing these technologies (using HIPAA guidelines for videoconferencing).

In one family–school meeting, both the father and the child's therapist participated through a conference call, since neither could attend in person. In this instance, the therapist, who had prepared for the meeting with the family in advance, asked whether certain accommodations could be made for the child (e.g., reducing the homework load and dropping a class or sports requirement). Though none of the accommodations could be established at the time, those at the meeting were visibly (and audibly) pleased that the therapist was so intimately acquainted with the problem. Despite the therapist and parent failing to achieve their stated goal, the mood during the meeting remained positive. The goodwill that was generated caused everyone to work that much harder to find a workable solution for this particular child. Thus, with two key members of the team physically absent but there by phone, the groundwork was laid for finding other solutions that later were implemented.

In another meeting, an enterprising therapist who couldn't attend a family–school meeting joined the team by using a secure video platform (Centers for Disease Control and Prevention, 2003). During the meeting, in real time, she created a Google doc of all the work that the student had to catch up on as relayed in the meeting. While sitting around the table, the parents, student, teachers, and administrator were also able to log in to the document and see the missing work, discuss what supports were needed, and make a plan—in this case converting free periods into study halls. The document bolstered one of the goals of the meeting, which was to prevent the student from feeling overwhelmed by the work that had to get done.

When using Google docs (or the equivalent shared materials), you will need to be clear about the purpose of sharing information and what will be shared. Interventions need to be specific—this should not be an opportunity for complaining. Using such an information-sharing system can help in situations when the child says everything is fine, but you can see from the documents that the child is not fine.

Agree on billing

As discussed in Chapter 6, therapists need to talk with the family about how they bill for time spent at the school and travel time, in this case attending family–school meetings. Again, no legal or ethical determination for billing for these activities exists, so therapists should use their best judgment in negotiating this aspect of their work with the family.

The Core of the Meeting: Follow the Collaborative Framework

Since family–school meetings can evolve in various directions throughout the course of the conversation, try to keep the collaborative framework in mind as outlined in Chapter 4. This will help orient you during the meeting, especially if things become sidetracked or conflict-laden. To accomplish this, here again are seven key principles to keep in mind, with explanations of how they apply in this particular setting:

1. Stay focused on the child and established goals.
2. Empower the child.
3. Empower the family.
4. Make sure everyone gets heard.
5. Search for good ideas and resources.
6. Maintain a nonblaming stance and reframe the problem.
7. Pay attention to seating arrangement.

Stay focused on the child and established goals

As the conversation begins, pay close attention to what is said (or not said). Sometimes, either you or someone from the family may need to add a clarification, if what was stated seems different or misses a key element of what you expected to address. Comments such as, "We're here to find ways to work together to make sure that Mason has a good year in school" can be followed up with more specific ideas or questions, such as, "We were also hoping to discuss Mason's courses for next year and whether he can participate in one of the social skills groups." Stating the goals of the meeting at the outset may help to reduce anxiety and streamline the discussion.

If the conversation runs into headwinds, the first thing to ask yourself is whether you are focused on the child and the issues at hand. With many people in the room who may be anxious or unsettled, conversations can drift, or someone's side issue can become a real distraction. Even though you probably won't be facilitating the meeting, you can step in to redirect the discussion or raise a question that clarifies why a seemingly unrelated topic is being discussed (respectfully, of course). That's not to say that there aren't situations in which the conversation shouldn't turn to a topic other than the child, say the parents' frustration with the school's homework policy. However, it's important to make sure such conversations still somehow revolve around the child's presenting problem. For example, you might say something like, "It's clear that the school's homework policies are important to understand and discuss, yet I wonder whether we could first figure out what Sam needs in order to complete his homework in the next week or so. As we all know, he's been struggling to keep up." If the child is present, you might find a way to bring him into the discussion to refocus the conversation on his needs rather than the school's policies or some other issue that, while relevant, is not directly related to understanding and solving the problem. A simple and direct question to the child can often return the conversation to more reliable underpinnings.

Empower the child

As mentioned earlier, family–school meetings are a place where children can be empowered to speak for themselves. In one case, a therapist joined Judy, a high school freshman with significant depression, and her parents for a family–school meeting that included the school counselor, learning specialist, and advisor. Judy's depression had made it nearly impossible for her to participate in class discussions, and her grades were dropping as a result. The therapist met with Judy and her parents to prepare for the meeting, determining goals and coaching Judy to represent her own view of the situation.

Early in the conversation, the therapist turned to Judy and asked what she was hoping to accomplish in the meeting. Judy's halting and shaky delivery triggered her mother's anxiety, who jumped in and started speaking for her. Respectfully and somewhat playfully, the therapist interrupted and asked the mother to give Judy a chance to speak for herself. Eventually, Judy was able to explain how hard it was for her to talk in front of her classmates and how unhappy she was generally. A plan was subsequently made for Judy to talk with her English and Spanish teachers to see if they would collaborate with her. The therapist agreed to figure out steps Judy could take to speak up in class. And Judy willingly agreed to receive additional support from the school counselor who would serve as the contact person for Judy's parents, the teachers and the therapist.

Make every effort to notice the child's part in the meeting as it progresses. Even when children have established that they'll advocate for themselves, sometimes parents rush in and do it for them. Alternatively, some parents, especially those who are frustrated or angry with their child, might leave them stranded in a sea of equally frustrated school personnel. In these instances, consider stepping in to head off avoidable tension among family members and needless embarrassment for the child. In this case, the therapist interrupted the mother in order to support and empower Judy, an intervention that was helpful at many levels, including showing the school representatives that Judy was motivated to express her own ideas and that Judy's mother was open to friendly feedback.

Empower the family

Parents can be taught how to represent their own viewpoints in family–school meetings as well. This might involve helping the parents prepare for a meeting in which you will be present or for one that they attend without you. In a subsequent family–school meeting, Judy's parents met with her Spanish teacher, the school counselor, the learning specialist, and Judy to follow up on the plans that were made in the previous family–school meeting. The therapist had met with Judy and her parents beforehand to brainstorm ways that they could respectfully encourage her Spanish teacher to maintain her commitment to meeting with Judy on a regular basis, since the teacher had missed a number of their scheduled meetings. They also came prepared to step back if the conversation turned contentious, given Judy's mom's worry that she might become anxious and testy with the teacher. As much as possible, encourage parents to find ways to manage the situation—exploring the "what ifs" before the meeting—and be sure to check with them when you intervene so you convey your respect for their central role in their child's life.

Make sure everyone gets heard

It doesn't take training in psychotherapy to understand the rising volume that can emanate from the person sitting silently at the table. Here's another way that your clinical skills add value to a family–school meeting. You may be able to help direct the conversation when you see that someone, especially someone in the family, isn't speaking up. When preparing for the meeting, you may have anticipated that one parent may be less likely to say what's on his or her mind and thought about how to support the parent in this effort. Use your clinical skills to bring that person into the conversation without putting the parent on the spot unnecessarily, thereby affirming the parent's role and value in the meeting. As a clinician, you know that the quality of the conversation naturally improves when everyone's voice is heard, including school personnel as well.

Some voices may be too loud or dominant in these meetings. If those voices are those of the parents or child, you may be able to help guide the conversation—respectfully interrupting, asking others to speak, signaling to the voluble person, or using other gestures to redirect and make more space for others. These are skills you use every day as a clinician, and they can be very useful in family–school meetings as you help foster a productive environment.

Search for good ideas and resources

A unique thing happens when people come together in family–school meetings. Discussing the problem with so many stakeholders causes ideas to bubble up that normally wouldn't. Resources materialize because something is said that jogs a memory, or an open disagreement might result in modifying an intervention that's stopped working. Information and dynamics that may have been submerged become visible. You might observe, for instance, that whenever the learning specialist speaks even slightly critically about the student, the student's advisor jumps in to make a more positive counterclaim. Or the principal might ask whether anyone has recommended the school's midmorning teacher–facilitated study halls. Until then, perhaps you and the family weren't aware of this valuable resource or didn't know that the advisor was such a steady source of support. Additionally, the general climate of care and concern often renews and reaffirms everyone's commitment to helping the child.

Family–school meetings are also times when you might become aware of a school's limitations in terms of what it can do to support a particular child. Therapists who can accept and adjust to such limitations are better equipped to maintain goodwill and find other solutions that better fit the school culture. You might hear a science teacher say, for example, that she can't meet with the student after school because she's also the baseball coach and has to be with her team, or that the behavioral chart that you want the first grade teacher to fill out each day is too burdensome given the number of kids in her class. Keep an eye out for the realities of the school culture, the demands placed on teachers and kids, and other exigencies that might make your recommendation untenable. Taking into account the energy and time it takes for someone to implement recommendations is an essential task of the meeting and something you should address directly.

Maintain a nonblaming stance and reframe the problem

Attending a family–school meeting can generate anxiety within all participants, including the therapist—especially meetings in which disagreement or conflict is anticipated. One of the common by-products of these intense emotions is blaming (see Chapter 9). Preparing for the fact that blaming might occur will help you find ways to redirect the conversation more productively. In rockier moments, it can be very helpful to restate the established purpose and goals, thereby focusing the conversation along a more constructive path.

In the case of 14-year-old Viktor, for example, a family–school meeting did not run smoothly. A standoff had developed between him and his history teacher, so the family, school, and therapist agreed to meet to see what could be done to untangle this tense relationship. With some coaching, Viktor and his therapist agreed that he would make a brief appearance at the beginning of the meeting in order to say that he thought his teacher treated him unfairly because of his deficiencies in spoken English. Prior to the meeting, in the safety of the therapist's office, he'd also wondered whether the teacher was biased against him as a recent Russian immigrant.

Indeed, in the meeting attended by Viktor, his parents, his teacher, the school psychologist, and school principal, the conflict between Viktor and his teacher was palpable. The teacher clearly felt unjustly criticized, and Viktor experienced her behaving as she did with him in the classroom—not looking him in the eye, speaking to him in clipped sentences, and so forth. In turn, Viktor had little to say. With evident bitterness, each saw the other as the problem. Viktor's mother clearly shared her son's view that the teacher was at fault.

Since the therapist could see the mother straining to be patient and little guidance was coming from the school representatives, she inserted herself in the conversation by saying, "I can see how concerned everyone is about this situation, and maybe we could pause for a moment and sort out what to do next. I know that Viktor and his mom are worried about how Viktor can make progress in history, especially given his goal of attending a good university in a few years. I'm sure that everyone here wants the same thing for him. Does anyone have an idea about what we can do to move forward?"

By bringing the focus of the conversation back to the most pressing issue and reframing the problem as one that relates to Viktor's aspirations, the therapist turned everyone's attention to the goal of finding a way for him to succeed in his history class. The school psychologist recommended scheduling a series of meetings with himself, the history teacher, and Viktor to review Viktor's writing assignments and help him prepare for tests. The therapist, in turn, suggested meeting with Viktor and his mom to help him prepare for these meetings so that they could make the best use of the time. The principal said she would talk with others in the school about ways Viktor could practice his English through theater, clubs, or other activities, and thus broaden his experience with peers and other adults at the school. Given the frustration on Viktor's and his mother's part, and the clear breakdown in communication between Viktor and his teacher, the therapist suggested meeting again at the school to follow up on the plan. The family–school meeting ended uneasily, even with plans in place. But this was understandable, given the stressful nature of the problem and the fact that an unspoken accusation had been laid at the door of the teacher, regarding her prejudice against a particular group, an issue that Viktor's parents had firmly decided not to explore at the time.

The planned meetings with the teacher, school psychologist, and student turned out to be a useful way to identify problems that interfered with Viktor's understanding of both the teacher's expectations and the material, even though Viktor's feelings of discrimination were still not addressed directly with the school. Only later, when Viktor was making progress in his studies, did the therapist, Viktor and the family delve into the family's perceived sense of being discriminated against for their language and culture. Subsequently, a plan was made for the parents to discuss their perceptions and worries directly with the principal.

Let's review what steps were taken by the therapist to maximize the success of the meeting, given its tense nature:

1. Prior to the meeting, the therapist encouraged the student to come to the family–school meeting to talk about his concerns and helped him prepare what to say.

2. Tensions between the teacher and student, and between family and school were identified by the therapist as a problem that could be addressed at least in part through a family–school meeting. In planning for the meeting, the therapist supported the parents in their decision to defer addressing their particular concerns about the teacher until a later time.

3. The therapist assumed that everyone was there with the intention of finding ways to help and support the student, so that when the conversation broke down, the therapist sought to reframe the problem and find common ground. Everyone could agree that the goal was for the student to do as well as possible in his history class as a way to further his future goals.

4. The therapist remained focused on the student and what could be done to improve his situation at school.

5. Plans were made: regular, facilitated meetings with the teacher, helping the student become more involved in school activities that supported the student's adjustment, and continued therapy.

6. A follow-up meeting was scheduled.

Pay attention to seating arrangement

When you arrive at the meeting, make an effort to situate yourself in a way that allows you to connect easily with the child and parents. These are small gestures, but meaningful ones. You might notice, for example, that child sits next to the mother, leaving the father at an awkward distance. Might this reflect the structure of the family relationships (Minuchin & Fishman, 1981)? I remember one instance in which a teenager entered the room and assertively told her parents to sit on either side of her, clearly fearing that tension would mount if they sat next to each other.

If you notice that the conversation is somehow inhibited by where you, the parents or the child is sitting, consider speaking up to find a better position saying something like, "I'm having a hard time following the conversation from where I'm sitting, I wonder whether I could come to the other side of the table?" It may take practice to feel comfortable changing where you sit, but over time you will see that where you sit can affect your ability to contribute effectively and thus the quality of the meeting overall.

Wrapping Up

As family–school meetings conclude, the facilitator or another participant should summarize the key takeaways and review the shared understanding and plans that were developed. In the absence of a serious breakdown in communication, enough groundwork should be laid so that you can all affirm some kind of agreement. If the summary given by the facilitator or other representative doesn't align with your experience, step in with a question or comment, as needed. For example, you might add, "Yes, though it's not exactly clear why Devon is so stressed, we do know that she is not doing well in several of her classes, so perhaps we might gather more information from her teachers or others at the school and explore this further in another meeting." As always, ask the parents and child to express their points of view, as well.

It's common for meetings to come to an end with questions still to be answered, even when there is genuine agreement about what happened. In these cases, a clarifying statement can also be helpful: "It looks like we all agree that school is very stressful for Devon this year. Yet, several questions remain about what might be causing her writing difficulties in English." Again, build on whatever was jointly constructed by the participants in the meeting, and go from there. Try not to get flustered if common ground hasn't been found. It happens. Even though you are an active member of this team, you're not in control of what transpires at school (or at home, for that matter). You can try to figure out next steps when you see the family or child in therapy after the meeting.

Additionally, make sure to form some kind of plan for what comes next. Plans can be simple and discrete—a referral for testing or a medical checkup, a change in a class schedule or teaching tactic, and so on. Plans can also be quite complicated and involve many people and issues. In short, plans should fit the problem as presented and flow from the concerns that were expressed. Again, it is usually the facilitator's job to review the plan; it's best not done by the therapist, who carries no responsibility for what people at the school decide or are assigned to do. If no one steps in to review the plans that were made, you can ask if everyone could quickly say what their understanding is about next steps and who's responsible for what. Be sure to write down what was agreed upon, though someone from the school may put the plan in writing and distribute it.

The clearer everyone is about the nature of the student's problem and support offered, the more likely you'll be able to assess whether the planned interventions are working. You may have a chance to address this specifically as the meeting comes to a close. For example, you (or someone else) might ask, "Given that Devon is going to be meeting with the school psychologist and seeing me in therapy, what should we expect will happen next? How will we know if these interventions are working?"

Following the meeting, find time to talk with the parents or child about their understanding of what happened and the plans that were made. This might involve setting aside time in the next session or speaking by phone in the interim. Either way, it's essential that you listen to what family members have to say, comparing your experience with theirs. You might have feedback to offer them, and they, too, may have questions that arose as a result of the meeting. Be sure to ask whether they thought the goals that had been set were accomplished and, if not, why not. Check in with them about your role, too. Feedback about our work is always valuable, and this is a good opportunity to solicit it. Also, consider being in touch with someone from the school if an intervention is not working or to confirm that it is. Should the interventions fail immediately or the collaboration between the family and school deteriorate in the coming weeks, consider a follow-up meeting at the school.

When family–school meetings go well, everyone tends to become engaged, forward-thinking, spontaneous and increasingly relaxed. Inevitably, there is a palpable sense of relief in the room. The kids in question become more than simply an amalgam of their strengths and weaknesses. In meetings that work less well or go badly, there are still positive things to salvage. The child's support team has become visible and therefore more comprehensible. Perhaps you see the mother become furious with the learning specialist; you can address this in the next therapy session. Or you observe that the vice principal really is as punitive as you'd heard, and as a consequence you have to go back to the drawing board to figure out the next steps. In these cases, you come to understand problems that wouldn't otherwise be discernible. Ideally, with this information, you can begin to find ways to solve the problems or decide to work around them. What doesn't help in family school meetings is losing hope. However the meeting goes, it's important to maintain confidence that something can be changed to improve the child's life and, if possible, strengthen the family–school relationship in the process.

REVIEWING THE BASICS

- Make sure to prepare beforehand by discussing questions to ask, goals to achieve, roles, confidentiality, and logistics.

- Consider meeting virtually if you or someone else can't meet in person.

- Find a place to sit in the meeting room that allows you maximum ability to connect with the child and family.

- Pay close attention to what is said about the purpose of the meeting as it begins, and add clarification if necessary.

- If no one has been assigned the job of facilitating the meeting or the school assumes you are the facilitator, offer an introductory comment and try to find someone from the school who will take a facilitative role with you.

- Share observations about the child—details and facts rather than interpretations.

- Recognize areas of strength and success for the child.

- Encourage dialogue by making sure everyone is heard, even people who might not be in the room (a pediatrician, tutor, etc.).

- Recognize that anxiety, fear, and frustration are endemic to the conjoining of the family and school systems.

- When conflicts or stalemates emerge, stay focused on the child and continue to identify points of agreement, redirecting the conversation if blaming occurs.

- Empower the child to speak on their own behalf.

- Discuss what's been tried to support the child at home and school, and identify what's worked and what hasn't. Build on any successes.Make specific plans and determine who is going to do what following the meeting and how to know if the child is doing better.

- At the end of the meeting, make sure that someone summarizes whatever shared understanding has been achieved,.

- Debrief with the family and child after the meeting.

- Trust that everyone has the child's best interest at heart.

PART III

Challenges

CHAPTER 9

Common Challenges

Some of the common challenges that arise when you work with schools are also endemic to your work as a therapist—these challenges are the sea in which we swim. Though there's no precise formula for resolving every difficult situation, the purpose of this chapter is to review the broader issues you'll most likely encounter. Doing so allows us to step into rather than away from whatever challenges we meet, with eyes wide open and the skills to help.

As kids mature, bumps in the road are not only inevitable, they're also essential for them on the path to becoming healthy adults (Hallowell & Thompson, 1993; Duckworth, 2016). Take this situation: a history teacher proffers a new way of understanding a societal problem that his student hadn't considered before. Argument and debate ensue in the classroom, and the student goes home to talk with her parents about this alternate worldview. A second debate erupts as this teenager, momentarily adopting the teacher's position, tries to convince her parents to see things from her now-adopted perspective.

Somehow, in the course of these ordinary interactions, the student begins to think for herself and develop her own notions, until the next time a similar situation occurs and she has to reexamine her assumptions again. The teenager's parents will likely be impacted by this interaction as well, as they may feel threatened by the confrontation and distrustful of the teacher's intent. And the teacher, leaving school that day, may wonder whether he'll come home to an inbox filled with concerns or complaints registered from confused or disgruntled parents. All of these dynamics are the natural outcome of learning, a process that extends outward from children and families into schools and communities and back again (Lawrence-Lightfoot, 1978, 2003). These normal tensions, in part, relate to the concept of extrafamilial influences on children (in this case, the teacher and school). It makes for the animation of multiple normative factors at play, creating shifting ground onto which problems evolve, are understood, and sorted out. Sometimes, however, these normal tensions can become true discord, and kids, families, and schools suffer as a result. This is where therapists can step in to help keep the problems small and, it is hoped, tackle the bigger problems collectively and constructively.

This chapter explores some of the challenges that you may face as a therapist that arise out of the strong emotions that are generated when children have problems at school. Misunderstandings and complications also occur as a result of not following through on plans, getting off track, and not knowing or meeting our professional responsibilities.

Anxiety, Blaming, and Triangulation

Sara Lawrence-Lightfoot (1978) wrote eloquently about the intrinsic tensions that exist between families and schools in her landmark book, *Worlds Apart: Relationships Between Families and Schools*. She states that there is a "great irony that families and schools are engaged in a complementary sociocultural task and yet they find themselves in great conflict with one another." By this, she's referring to the dissonance and discontinuities that exist between these two primary child-raising institutions, some positive and some negative. On the positive side, children benefit from the inherent differences between families and schools by expanding their repertoire of behaviors and ways of experiencing the world. On the other hand, differences can become dissonant in disruptive and destructive ways, resulting in each side finding fault with the other. Given the fundamental and often aggravating strains, it is easy to understand why tension occurs.

In particular, there are three interrelated, very human, dynamics that come alive in family–school relationships: anxiety, blaming, and triangulation. Being aware of their existence can help therapists avoid becoming overly influenced by the way these dynamics can disrupt relationships and interfere with solving problems that kids have at school.

Anxiety

Regarding anxiety, Harriet Lerner (2009) writes, "Whatever your emotional vocabulary, no one signs up for anxiety, fear or shame, or for any difficult, uncomfortable emotion. But we can't avoid these feelings, either." Given their ubiquity, it's important to consider the sources of anxiety that can be aroused in parents and those who work in schools. Signs of anxiety can be apparent when people raise their voices in a meeting or fail to follow through on plans that were made; situations that can interrupt or even derail a child's treatment if not fully addressed. As Lerner went on to say, "I am convinced that the more we can look these uninvited guests in the eye, with patience and curiosity, and the more we learn to spot their wisdom as well as their mischief, the less grip they will have on us" (Lerner, 2009).

Some sources of anxiety are inherent in the job of raising and teaching children. It's important to consider potentially anxiety-producing situations for parents and teachers alike, lest we be thrown off by their appearance and respond in ways that interfere with the goals and process of our work (Thompson, 2009; Thompson & Mazzola, 2005). When parents send their child off to school in the fall—in addition to some enjoyable anticipation—typically there are some anxieties and worries as well, such as:

- Whether their child will be successful as a student and get along with his or her classmates

- Whether their child will be safe

- Whether their child's teacher(s) will treat the children fairly, including, if not especially, their child

- Whether they'll be able to discern how well their child is doing and identify problems when they arise

- Whether they will know how to engage with the school appropriately and constructively

- Whether they're spending too little or too much time supporting their child's work and life at school

- Whether they're to blame or will be blamed for the problems their child is having at school

- Whether the people at the school will respect their family's values and composition, as well as their ethnic, racial, and socioeconomic backgrounds

Similarly, teachers, student support teams, administrators, and staff begin the school year with hopes and desires. They also have anxieties that accompany the work they do. As therapists working with kids and families, we may not be aware of the challenges faced by those sitting around the table, especially given our natural alliance with the child and family. Therefore, it's worth reflecting on common sources of anxiety for teachers and others who work in schools:

- Whether they can keep children physically safe on a daily basis

- Whether they can find a way to teach and support all students, especially those who are not ready to learn due to lack of sleep, family or community stresses, illness, learning or emotional problems, and so on

- Whether they can form good relationships with parents, especially when receiving their requests and demands

- Whether they will be criticized or blamed for a child's difficulties and, if they are criticized or blamed, whether they can competently manage the situation

- Whether they can meet the regular curricular demands and conflicts about what and how to teach

- Whether they can meet the demands associated with standardized testing and how that fits with their own teaching style and interests

- Whether they can be a vital part of a school community, avoiding isolation and feelings of demoralization and developing good relationships with colleagues, staff, and administrators

- Whether they will be acknowledged or appreciated for the work they do inside the school and out

Taking time to consider commonplace sources of anxiety for parents and teachers may be sobering, but it can help us recognize when anxieties become heightened in the course of our work and give us the opportunity to step in constructively. In our offices, we can explore why parents are anxious or fearful and, by doing so, try to address the underlying issues. Sometimes, problems are immediate and resolvable—a mother is unable to secure a reduced-fare, public transportation pass for her son to get to school, for example, or a daughter's asthmatic cough warrants more medical attention than it's receiving. Efforts can also be made to address past experiences or current circumstances that leave parents (and kids) emotionally vulnerable or volatile. For example, a parent who was emotionally abused as a child may experience her son's teacher as threatening and untrustworthy when the teacher is critical of her son's work, or a father's panic disorder might be triggered when his daughter is caught cyberbullying, given that his history of incarceration leaves him fearful that the police will become involved.

Though we're not typically in a position to explore the experiences of teachers or school personnel in the same way, being aware of common triggers allows us to be more attuned to signs of anxiety when they appear, whether in meetings, classroom observations, phone conversations, or even through online communications such as email, texts, or school portals. There may be opportunities for you (or the parents) to directly address a teacher's anxious response by making a comment in a nonthreatening, nonpatronizing way: "If I were you, I'd also be concerned about how Steph's angry outbursts affect not just her but all the kids in your classroom. It can't be easy managing these situations when they happen." We should also be aware when anxious parents collide with anxious teachers or other school staff and use our clinical skills to help steer the conversation to a more productive place. As one educational consultant said when discussing what therapists can do to help in tricky situations, "Therapists are good communicators—they can get down to eye level and see what's going on, especially when the human connection gets lost in anxiety, fear, and frustration."

As a therapist working with kids, families, and their schools, you can be sure of one thing: at various points along the way, someone will do or say something that will make you anxious, too. Part of providing therapeutic services involves finding ways to manage these tense and difficult moments. We know that anxiety can cause us to react in ways that are less thoughtful and measured than we might intend or result in our withdrawing from a situation when further engagement would be more helpful. Being aware of our own anxiety triggers can help us develop ways to remain grounded, focused, and, perhaps most importantly, patient with ourselves when anxious moments arise.

Blaming

One problem that can result from anxiety is blaming (Lawrence-Lightfoot, 1978, 1983). Blaming is a piece of our psychological and interpersonal hardware, a means of quelling uncomfortable emotions like anxiety. When problems arise, schools often blame parents, parents blame schools, and therapists can get caught in the middle (described below in the section on triangulation). Yet, blaming itself deserves special attention since it's one of the most common problems therapists encounter.

Therapists, of course, are not immune from blaming others or being blamed themselves. We've all had the experience, especially under trying circumstances, of feeling the wave of blame toward someone and losing perspective. Likewise, we have all felt that particular discomfort and hurt when we are blamed for something unfairly. And when we feel blamed by someone, we're less likely to want to engage constructively. If we do the blaming, it's likely to elicit defensiveness rather than compassion or understanding. This natural tendency to blame can intrude on relationships, interfere with our ability to take appropriate levels of responsibility for what might be going wrong, and hinder the primary goal of helping the child, family, and school move forward productively (Dowling, 2018). Consider the child at dinner describing how his teacher embarrassed him in class by pointing out his failure to complete an assignment. His father feels uncomfortable because of his child's distress and becomes angry with the teacher; the father gets stuck there, rather than moving beyond that to also consider his child's failure to finish the assignment.

When systems develop a pattern of blaming, be it the family, school group or organization, it can leave people vulnerable to functioning inflexibly. This can deplete the energy and creativity needed to solve problems. It's more likely than not that, at some point in your life, you've stepped into one of these dysfunctional systems and experienced how rapidly one can slip into the pull of blaming others. Though it is multidetermined, the tendency to blame does seem to grow in an *us versus them* climate. It can be difficult to dislodge, partly because blaming doesn't bring out the best in anyone, and ultimately creates self-defeating cycles of behavior. In relationships or systems in which blaming is common, someone else is at fault for every problem, and people interact with a deficit of trust and safety. Over time, if one comes to know and understand a family or school well enough, it's possible to understand how this tendency to blame became part of the system's infrastructure. That insight can perhaps lead you to find a way to help reset the system dynamics.

We've all heard blaming statements such as the mother who derogatorily exclaims, "That teacher is terrible!"—hoping that you'll join her in attributing the child's problems to the teacher, or the teacher who says that the child you are treating is fully to blame for a range of problems in his classroom. Then there's the child who says that she would have made the team but the coach has his favorites. Of course, any of these statements could be true—there are many situations in which someone is genuinely at fault in small or catastrophic ways. But before you make a judgment, be sure to listen and understand so that whatever judgment you come to will be as valid as possible.

The therapist has a unique opportunity to be helpful when working with systems when blaming occurs. As comparative outsiders, we can observe, listen, and look for ways to interrupt the blaming by redirecting or reframing the conversation in a more productive way (Christenson & Sheridan, 2001; Minuchin & Fishman, 1981; Weiss & Edwards, 1992). Certainly, as therapists, we usually enter the scene where we identify with the child and family, but we are a step removed, and that step gives us the degree of freedom we need to see things a bit more objectively. That, coupled with a commitment to remain focused on the child, gives the therapist leverage that others may not have. The therapist can enter into a fraught dynamic with the goal of discussing what might work best rather than who's to blame for what isn't working.

Triangulation

As described earlier, we often work in and with triadic relationships—family-child-therapist, parent-parent-therapist, or family–school-therapist, for example. Triangulation, according to family systems theorists, is born when a third person enters into a relationship between two other people who have some sort of unresolved struggle or tension, and, by entering, reduces tensions in the system (Bowen, 1985; Erdem & Safi, 2018; Minuchin, 1974). Sometimes, that reduction in tension does not represent meaningful, sustainable change but rather is an artifact of the introduction of a third party. For example, parents who are fighting with each other about their acting-out teenager can become temporarily united around their shared anger at a teacher. The parental alliance might create an interim calm, but will likely not hold if the marital problems are serious.

A common form of triangulation that can occur among family, school, and therapist involves the therapist aligning with the family (and child) against the school, given the experience of hearing unfavorable descriptions from the parents (or child) about the school in therapy sessions. Similarly, if a child is referred to a particular therapist by the school itself, the therapist might side with the school against the parents if they hear about the family's contentious behavior toward a teacher. As these cases illustrate, you may find yourself triangulated in a situation that existed before you entered the picture. When stepping into a triangular dynamic, it's important to be mindful of your role and the various pulls for alliance in order to ensure that you're not just inducted into the system but are part of the solution.

It's also true that, as child and family therapists, we've learned how to build on triangular dynamics—to use triangulation as a therapeutic tool to aid in creating change and systemic reorganization. For example, a charged parent-adolescent dynamic can often benefit from the presence of a trained third party—the therapist—who strategically takes sides, alternating her support for each person in an effort to strengthen the overall balance and bond between the dyad as they sort through their difficulties. By stepping in, the therapist can interrupt a frozen dynamic between the two parties.

The therapist's understanding and use of triangulation as a strategy can ultimately benefit the child, even though the therapist is brought into a conflict that is deeply complicated or toxic. Though the therapist will likely feel the push and pull of a threesome in which they may feel precariously ensconced, understanding that there is a possible role in which the therapist can be helpful makes the situation workable.

One common triangle is the one formed by the family, school, and child when the family and school are at odds with each other and the child is stuck in the middle. Caught between the two systems, the child can become the "primary communicator" (Tucker & Dyson, 1976), a difficult, untenable position that can leave the child vulnerable to developing emotional or behavioral problems (Dowling, 2018). Children in this middle position can also intensify the family–school disconnect by adding negativity and misstatements to the mix, thereby dodging responsibility for their part in whatever is going on or maintaining a troubled family dynamic already in place. In these instances, therapists can become the primary communicator, placing themselves in the middle of the family–school conflict, thereby relieving the child of this burden. In this position, the therapist can begin to work with the family (and school) to understand and resolve the underlying tension.

Considering the pitfalls and opportunities of triangulation, the following guidelines are offered.

Guidelines for therapists regarding triangulation

1. Start with the expectation that everyone is doing their best to help the child.

2. Make every effort to understand all sides of the problem.

3. Take advantage of opportunities to work with all parties.

4. When possible, address the underlying anxiety or nature of the problem itself.

5. Be alert to being pulled into a system and triangulated inadvertently. Use triangulation as a therapeutic tool when indicated.

6. Take a position when needed.

Regarding the last guideline—taking a position when needed—there are times when we find ourselves in the middle of a triangle and we need to take a stand on one side of an issue or person or another. In fact, sometimes our expertise is solicited in order to do just this—give guidance or direction when there are different views represented. For example, in one case, a parent disagreed with the school's recommendation that her child be evaluated; the therapist sided with the school, supporting its recommendation by making the case for testing. In another instance, parents disagreed about whether to make a complaint to the school about their child's teacher, and the therapist sided with one parent over the other, arguing to go forward with the complaint given the seriousness of the problem and the parents' months-long efforts to try to improve the situation.

Take the case of the therapist who received a call from a principal with whom she'd worked over many years, asking if she would be willing to take the referral of a high school senior, Michael, who was suddenly doing poorly academically. Michael was adamant that his mother not know he was seeing a therapist, and the principal concurred. If the mother knew, the principal reported, she would likely "come down hard on him," given the pressures she was facing in her own life. The therapist, highly experienced in working with seriously dysfunctional families, felt that she was in a bind. Her natural preference was to reach out to the mother and try to enlist her support and involvement in the therapy with her son. At the same time, the therapist respected the principal from her past experience working with the school and wanted what was best for Michael. Together, the principal and therapist agreed that she would see Michael alone, something she could do given his age, and the principal agreed to work with the school social worker to find ways to reach out to his mother.

In collaboration with Michael and the therapist, the school social worker began to meet with Michael's mother to help connect her with social service agencies, including a job training resource. Eventually, with Michael's consent, the social worker was able to connect his mom with the therapist so they could work on problems in their relationship. In this case, the therapist had to weigh her options in determining which course to take. As it turned out, she was able to maximize her support of Michael by being aware of the nature of triangulation, seeing both sides of a problem, assuming that everyone was doing their best, and working at the nexus of three parts of the system—the child, parent, and school. The therapist was also able to focus on Michael's core strengths as he tried to get a foothold on his problems without initial support from his family.

In another case, a therapist decided to observe his client, Alicia, in her preschool classroom, since there had been multiple complaints about her behavior in that setting that had prompted her parents to seek help. Following the observation, the teacher took the therapist aside to complain about Alicia's father. The teacher thought that the parents' bitter separation was the cause of Alicia's problems in the classroom, especially singling out her father who, the teacher said, "was no help at all." The therapist wondered if by simply listening to the teacher, he was generating a false impression on the teacher's part that he was agreeing with her, thereby taking sides with her against the father. The therapist also wondered whether redirecting the conversation would cause the teacher to feel dismissed or to conclude that the therapist was on the father's side in the struggle. The therapist felt triangulated; he eventually was able to respond by validating the teacher's concern and then discussing next steps.

The therapist has a range of possible responses when put on the spot, as in the above case:

- "I hear your concern and am looking forward to getting to know [the child's] parents to see how I might be helpful."

- "It sounds as if things have been rough for [the child] and his family, and I wonder what you've found that's useful in your work with them."

- "I think both parents are worried about [the child]."

- "There's a lot going on with [the child], and I know the parents are trying to figure out how to best support her."

Each of these comments allows the therapist to respond to a push-pull situation without taking sides, being dismissive, or sounding condescending. Sometimes, it's as simple as respectfully acknowledging what is being said and adding that you really aren't able to comment about the situation, and why. As one therapist said, "Teachers don't usually ask further questions because they see your natural alignment with the family and that you're just trying to help."

Misunderstandings

Some problems or misunderstandings seem rooted in blaming or triangulation, yet others occur naturally as a result of working with numerous constituencies. For example, what can be more commonplace than having the ideas you've shared at one point in time reflected back to you at another point in ways that are barely recognizable? Therapists are drenched in this experience, as are all of us, given the complexity of our lives and our inevitable misspeaks, inaudible remarks, poorly articulated ideas, misunderstood digital communications, and limited attention spans. Usually, there's plenty of fault to go around when something we've said comes back altered and changed by someone else's outlook, memory, or interpretation. If we were really able to step back and enjoy more of life's absurdity, we might even find ourselves celebrating when mutual understanding has occurred.

With more people involved, misunderstandings can multiply. In one case, after talking with her anxious son's therapist, a parent called the school office to say, "My therapist says that my son cannot come to school today." While the therapist had discussed the issue with the parent, no recommendation was made about whether the child should stay home, only that the therapist would meet with him that afternoon. In another case, the therapist spoke on the phone with the school psychologist about a student who was exhibiting symptoms of ADHD, though the therapist had only indirectly raised the topic with the parents. The school psychologist relayed her own concerns about the child's behaviors at school—difficulty sitting still, not getting work done on time, distracting others—behaviors that fit the ADHD diagnostic profile. The conversation went well enough, yet in the next therapy session, the parents were miffed because the school psychologist had told them that the therapist said their child had ADHD. All of a sudden, the therapist needed to untangle a problem that hadn't previously existed.

Sometimes, perhaps often, you may not be able to sort out the source of such misunderstandings. They can emerge from the school, the family, the child, or you. Sometimes, it's worth the effort to figure out what happened with the child and family, as it turned out to be in the first case described above. But it may be difficult if not impossible to discern the cause of a misunderstanding that involves the school, unless you know the school representative well or can see that a constructive conversation is possible. Nevertheless, you should make every effort to speak clearly about the child and the recommendations you have. Keep notes of what you've said. When indicated, consider sending a quick follow-up email to the school representative in which the recommendations are faithfully restated.

Take for granted and with as much generosity of spirit as possible that what you say may be misremembered or misunderstood. This allows you to clarify things along the way and not be too hard on yourself when your own memory or perception inevitably falters.

It is possible, however, that you will run into someone in a school who may deliberately misrepresent your ideas for his or her own purposes. Fortunately, those situations are rare and akin to other difficult relationships you've encountered in your work and life. Should this occur, decide what to do based on the necessities of the case and your own professional standards of practice. In over 40 years of working with schools, I've encountered only a handful of people with whom it was impossible to work due to the confusion and disruption sown by our attempts to collaborate. The odds are that it won't happen often, if ever, to you.

Lack of Follow-Through

Another common challenge that occurs when working with schools is lack of follow through. Let's say that you've observed a child at school, met with the teacher, worked with the parents and, as a result, jointly crafted careful plans that everyone agrees to implement. Then, someone at the school fails to do what they said they would do or takes a different approach without further collaboration or consultation. Take, for instance, the school social worker who agreed to set up a meeting at the school, but after several weeks nothing has happened, and he is not returning your calls. Or the teacher who in a family–school meeting agreed to send home a list of incomplete homework with the child every Friday, but has not followed through. Like parents, therapists can become confused and irritated when calls aren't returned or plans aren't implemented. Unlike the child and family attending sessions, we don't see the teacher or school social worker to discuss whatever may have interfered with the plans that were made.

When plans are short-circuited for reasons that aren't clear, hang in there for a while longer and encourage the family to do the same. After you leave your third phone message with a teacher, for example, keep in mind the diffuse nature of her responsibilities as you determine what to do next. Parents can follow up with the teacher, and preteens and teenagers can be encouraged to contact the teacher themselves to streamline the process. The entire set of relationships takes an immediate upgrade when kids can reliably act on their own. It helps to assume that others are doing their best under the circumstances and to withhold judgment about what might be simple miscommunication as opposed to true uncooperativeness.

Sometimes, plans are short-circuited because the therapist's view of a problem and what to do about it conflicts with those who work at the school. This difference of opinion may be openly expressed or emerge more subtly. Several therapists spoke about these difficulties in their work with anxious kids in particular. If a teacher doesn't agree with a recommendation you make, doesn't follow through, or alters the recommended intervention, it's your job to figure out with the parents what to try next. Look first at whether you've invested sufficient time and energy in understanding the problem from the teacher's perspective. If not, find a time to talk with the teacher to think through her ideas and sense of what might work. One teacher candidly said, "You know, we never disagree with therapists' recommendations. We just don't always do them." The comment was not said with any cynicism or animosity, just with full awareness that therapists' recommendations don't always sit right with teachers, whether for reasons pedagogical, philosophical, or practical. As always, consider working with the family, child, and other student support staff to look for other ideas that might be more effective.

This is one of the best arguments for generating goals and interventions conjointly. In one interesting case, a therapist reported that after a frustrating stint of trying to work with a teacher who wasn't following through with her recommendations, she found out that the teacher simply didn't have a good method for keeping track of the child's behavior, given the intensity of her day. This is not unusual, given the demands on teacher's time, in the classroom and out. In one phone call, the therapist offered to instruct her how to use a computer app to record and share information, and in this case at least, the problem was solved.

Getting Off Track

Sometimes, in the process of working with schools, therapists can get diverted and lose focus on the child and situation at hand. For example, we might find ourselves talking with a school representative about issues that are peripheral to the reason we called in the first place. One therapist described how, in a discussion with a school psychologist about accommodations for a developmentally delayed student, she found herself slipping into an argument about her particular therapeutic approach, which was under scrutiny in the field. Only later did she recognize that her insecurity about the case had tripped her up.

Once, in my role as a school consultant, I remember talking with a therapist who was working with a student in the school and using a different therapeutic approach than what I thought would be most beneficial. I began to lay out an argument for working with the child's family using a family therapy approach. The silence that followed was a wake up call for me. Clearly, I was off track, no longer focused on the child and having to rewind the conversation. I remember feeling like something significant was lost in the process, and perhaps it was.

Several things can alert us to the fact that we've veered off course. When we find ourselves defending a point of view, going on at length to explain ourselves, or trying to justify our actions, we would do well to pause and consider what might underlie these behaviors. It's not that such behaviors aren't common, of course, but it's best to observe them as a sign that something may be amiss. By being more self-aware and relying on families and trusted colleagues for feedback, we can signal a need to return to a more purposeful path.

We also may be thrown off track as a result of the isolation we feel as therapists or by being too busy to do what we said we would. Other times, progress may not have been made according to our or other's expectations. Naturally, we want to make sure that we're doing the right thing. It's understandable that we may want others to know how hard we're working, even how frustrated or worried we are about a case. But when we find ourselves focusing on ourselves or defending our therapy, take stock. This may be a result of pressure we're feeling from others or our own internal expectations or insecurities.

Years ago, a learning specialist said something simple—when in doubt, just stay focused on the child. It's one of those truisms that sound too obvious to actually matter. But in an unsettling or unproductive conversation with a school representative, ask yourself if you're talking about the child or about something else (including you). If so, reorient the conversation around the child—her challenges, strengths, and possible interventions—and see if momentum and good energy can be restored. Usually, it can.

Unclear Boundaries and Scope of Responsibility

Sometimes, therapists are in situations where the scope of their responsibility is unclear. For example, when working with one child, sometimes we're alerted to problems that another child is having in the school. These problems usually run the ordinary spectrum of age-appropriate misbehavior or social awkwardness, but sometimes your client will mention a peer or friend who is seriously at risk.

One parent recently asked a therapist whether she should call her daughter's high school advisor about a situation going on at her daughter's school. She'd heard from her daughter that one of her classmates was physically threatening another student on the playing fields. The parent contacted the therapist because she wasn't sure what to do with this information. She worried that, by contacting the school, it might emerge that her daughter passed along the information and some sort of retaliation would follow from the student making the threats. The therapist advised the mother to call the school psychologist to see whether such information could be shared confidentially. Eventually, the mother, daughter, and school psychologist decided to meet to figure out how best to proceed.

Perhaps a child comes in to ask your advice about a friend whom they fear may be suicidal. What is your responsibility in this situation, and what guidelines should you follow? In instances in which a serious concern about another under-age child is brought to your attention and you've assessed the situation with the child (or family), there are several ways to respond:

Encourage the child to talk with his parents. One option is to encourage the child to discuss the situation with his parents, who may be willing to call the parents of the child in question or contact someone at the school who will be able to help.

Encourage the child to talk with her classmate or friend. Depending on the severity of the problem, with older kids especially, you might suggest that they talk directly with their classmate or friend to encourage them to seek help. Under such circumstances, be sure to follow up with the child given the level of responsibility they may feel toward their peer or friend.

Encourage the child to talk with a trusted teacher, someone from the student support team or another school representative. Some kids may be willing to talk with someone from the school and inform them of the situation and seek their involvement and counsel.

If your client's concern does not involve danger to the person in question or others, it's important to address this issue as you would other clinical issues—that is, in terms of what's in the best interest of your client: should she talk with her friend about her concerns? Might she be overly involved in her friend's problems and need to take a step back in the relationship? Would it be helpful to bring her parents into the conversation so that they can offer their support and guidance? All of these examples fit into the category of ordinary issues that arise in working with kids and will reflect your own orientation and ways of working.

Make special note of the fact that if you hear anything about possible abuse of a child (your client or someone the child knows), it is your obligation to be familiar with your state's laws on child abuse and act accordingly. You are legally mandated to follow the guidelines of the state in which you work, including knowing the definition of abuse and mandatory reporting requirements (Kalichman, 1993).

In yet another example, a therapist came to a school to meet with the student support team about an elementary school student he was treating. As the meeting concluded and everyone was walking out of the room, the school counselor took the therapist aside and expressed concern about another student in the school. The concern happened to be of a serious nature and the therapist wasn't certain whether or how to become involved. In this case, the therapist diplomatically asked the school counselor if she had spoken about the problem with someone else on the school's student support team. It quickly became clear that the tensions among the team members the therapist had seen surface in the meeting were symptomatic of ongoing intrateam problems. Given the severity of the child's problem, the therapist agreed to discuss possible referral sources with the counselor by phone later that day.

There are no definitive guidelines for what to do in such situations, but your clinical judgment and general concern for the welfare of children and the school should guide you in your decision-making process. Sometimes, it's as simple as respectfully acknowledging what is being said and asking a few questions so that the person can think through the next steps he or she can take. It's possible to direct the person to a particular resource or professional, including those that exist in the school. At other times, you can step aside and find a way to tactfully return to discussing your client or return to a previous conversation.

REVIEWING THE BASICS

- Therapists face common challenges that often become activated when working with a child-family–school triad: anxiety, blaming, and triangulation.

- Parents, teachers, school personnel, and even therapists can become anxious during the course of a child's therapy. Take some time to reflect on common sources and signs of anxiety for each group (including yourself) so that you can be better prepared to face them when they inevitably crop up.

- Blaming is a problem that often springs from anxiety. Therapists are uniquely positioned to help reframe and redirect blaming tendencies, since we are relative outsiders and thus have greater objectivity.

- Triangulation is another common facet of working with multiple stakeholders in a child's life, and often you will find yourself in the push-pull of one of these complex dynamics. Make every effort to understand all sides of the problem, address the underlying issues, and take a position when needed.

- Misunderstandings are commonplace; they only multiply as more people become involved. Assume that your words might sometimes be misrepresented. In order to mitigate this situation as much as possible, try to articulate your ideas clearly, make note of what was said, and perhaps reiterate important statements in your follow-up communications.

- Sometimes, a teacher or family member won't follow through on plans that you've jointly created. If this happens, try to figure out what the root of the issue might be, and if necessary, consider exploring other options that rely on different resources or actions.

- It can be easy to get off track given the complexities and difficulties of working with so many people in a child's life. If you find yourself speaking about yourself or defending your interventions at length, take stock and refocus on the child.

- At times, you may be asked by a client or someone at the school to involve yourself in a situation that goes beyond the scope of a child's therapy. Use your clinical judgment to figure out the best way to intervene in these scenarios. You can offer to refer the person in question to another clinician or just help the person think through the issue on his or her own.

CHAPTER 10

Navigating Complexity and Crises

I n addition to the more common challenges that are part and parcel of our work as therapists, it's important to learn about the complex situations that can arise from kids' multifaceted identities and how they intersect with your own multi-faceted identities. Unfortunately, we also must prepare for the (rarer, thankfully) emergencies that sometimes occur when we work with kids and schools—natural and other disasters, deaths in the school community, crises with the children we see in therapy, instances of violence in schools, and the more common occur-rences of ostracism and bullying. This chapter will explore the ways therapists can engage more effectively with these difficult situations so that they can help as broad a population as possible, and step in when they might be needed most.

Navigating Complexity Arising from Race, Class, Ethnic, Religious, and Gender Differences

The biographical details of our lives—where we live, our race and gender identities, as well as ethnic, religious, cultural, socioeconomic, and political backgrounds—all converge to determine in some measure who we are, the opportunities we're afforded, how we operate in the world, and how we are perceived by others. Cer-tain groups of people are more vulnerable, while others are more privileged. And a person may be vulnerable in some ways and privileged in others, an intersec-tion of identities that can be complex for the therapist to parse.

It's clear that racial, religious and ethnic minorities, and LGBTQ individuals often face discrimination that is endemic to their everyday lives, including their lives at school. We also know that children who grow up in poverty, whose parent suffers from mental illness, who have physical handicaps and other disabilities, and who experience violence in their home or community are vulnerable to a whole range of problems, including those that manifest in school (Conger, Conger, & Martin, 2010; Werner, 2013). Parents raising children with significant behavioral difficulties experience high levels of stress and problems as well (Gupta, 2007). Acknowledging that these profound differences exist and shape the lives of children we see in therapy is crucial to our ability to assess, collaborate, and intervene in ways that are empathic and effective (Robinson-Wood, 2016). Two dimensions of how we responsibly acknowledge and work with our differences will be discussed.

Understanding multiple layers of identity

We all possess multiple layers of identity, at the individual and group level. Recognizing that people and families contain multiple layers of identity allows us to consider various motivations for their actions, including those that aren't immediately apparent. Depending on the community in which we practice, we may work with children and families whose backgrounds resemble our own or who differ from us in significant ways. Failing to reflect on your own identity in relation to a particular child may cause you to form a judgment that misses the bigger picture or even interferes with therapeutic goals. For instance, you might find yourself reacting strongly to the way a parent from a different cultural background disciplines their child, thinking the parent is needlessly strict. Yet, some families may have a heightened sense of concern for their child's safety and monitor their behavior and activities rigorously. For them, obedience and respect for authority are a means of protection in an unsafe world (Kotchick & Forehand, 2002). Behavior that has survival value for a certain family may seem overly controlling to you until you are familiar with their day-to-day lives. Conversely, your background might lead you to perceive some families as being unduly lenient or permissive, granting their children a level of control over their lives that leaves you concerned about their child's safety and well-being. While it is imperative to understand differences in cultural backgrounds, it is also true that just because something is a cultural norm doesn't mean that it promotes healthy development (Montalvo & Gutierrez, 1983). Being open to exploring the family's specific circumstances and culture widens the lens and thereby increases your ability to help the child.

Likewise, some therapists work with children and families with similar backgrounds, and this presents a different set of challenges. It's important to recognize that your similar background doesn't mean you will understand the child, family, or school any better. More familiarity with a family's culture may be informative and useful, but it also may be accompanied by complicated feelings, assumptions, and biases that are inextricably linked to experiences you've had as a member of that same group. By assuming that people and families contain multiple layers of identity, we can consider various motivations for their actions, including those that aren't immediately apparent to us.

Understanding the structural and systemic barriers to a child's well-being based on the child's life circumstances can have implications for how you work with the child, family, and school (Entwisle, 2018). For some kids, school is a safe haven; safer than their lives at home. For those whose family life is filled with conflict, taking on an afterschool activity or school sport that shortens their evening hours at home can be beneficial, especially if some kind of concurrent support can also be found for the family. As a therapist, you may be in a position to help find resources (such as afterschool programs, school-based health care services, activities provided by religious or other community organizations, school-community liaisons, school-based trauma-informed services, and educational advocates) connecting the child to people and activities that can provide caring environments and needed services.

In contrast, kids coming from more privileged backgrounds can and do suffer from a range of problems associated with their privilege, such as intense pressure (internal or parental) to achieve, stress from involvement in too many activities, anxiety, depression, substance abuse, and more. Your work with kids from more privileged families may involve helping them reduce their afterschool activities or explore the pressures they feel to perform and achieve, and counsel them and their families accordingly. Nonetheless, kids coming from privileged circumstances are more likely to have access to outside resources that are unavailable to many children. This contrast is immediately apparent when, say, you are able to recommend tutoring for a child from a family of means but are unable to do the same for a family with more limited resources. Or a family may be able to afford a therapist's fee, but not therapy and a tutor. It's important for the therapist not to make assumptions and, equally important, not be afraid to ask what's feasible.

Confronting tensions with compassion and humility

However near or far you are from the life experiences of those with whom you work, missteps and misunderstandings can arise. Take, for example, a recently immigrated Korean mother who panicked when she was asked to attend a meeting at her child's new school, thinking that any such meeting signified a serious problem with her son. Meanwhile, the principal and school counselor simply hoped that by inviting the mother to come to the school and familiarize herself with its personnel, she'd be more comfortable and thus better able to help ease her son into his new school environment.

When we see well-intentioned professionals, in this case the school counselor and the principal, do their best to reach out across a cultural divide yet still create tensions and misunderstandings, we realize how complicated this process can be (Hill, 2010). This example doesn't address discrimination or bigotry that are covertly or overtly expressed, which also occurs at the nexus of many family–school relationships.

Regarding discrimination and its impact on kids, according to Stevenson (2014), schools replicate the broader world and as such are places where racial discrimination inevitably occurs. He and others note that there has been a widespread failure in our society to have meaningful conversations about race. In his research, he explores how "racial stereotypes haunt . . . American education and the quality of relationships in schools"; these stereotypes are "powerful elephants in the classroom." Yet, facing racism and its effects, according to Stevenson, causes tension and stress on the part of educators, families, and kids (and undoubtedly therapists as well). Nonetheless, he cogently argues:

> *If educational leaders, teachers and parents could see the racial conflicts, then perhaps they could be resolved. If educators could admit to their fears, then perhaps students could feel safe to admit their fears. If fears were acknowledged, then perhaps school climates would improve and schools could become safer places to speak outwardly on diversity of racial and nonracial matters.* (Stevenson, 2014)

Recognizing problems that occur as a result of difference can cause discomfort––we may notice the pit in our stomach or that flush of embarrassment and not know whether to speak up. We may not know what to say or wonder whether we have the skills to address the problem. We may be so preoccupied with appearing a certain way—as someone without prejudice—that we choose to disregard difficult encounters or fail to see our part in them. Notably, we may think that by speaking up, we could inadvertently make the situation worse by saying the wrong thing and offending someone unintentionally. Nonetheless, part of our job is to be aware that differences among people and groups sometimes create misunderstandings, confusion, and hurt, and to take responsibility for our part in these complex situations, beginning with noticing when they occur (Webb, 2001).

Take, for example, a case of a young African American student, Lamar, who was suspended for missing morning classes at his urban high school. His therapist was familiar with research that showed that black students are suspended nearly four times more often than white students, often for the same infractions (Bottiani, Bradshaw, & Mendelson, 2017; Wallace, Goodkind, Wallace, & Bachman, 2008). She also knew that this disparity helped explain the disproportionate number of minority students entering into the criminal justice system (Okonofua & Eberhardt, 2015; Wald & Losen, 2003). The therapist worried that the decision to suspend Lamar from school might give him yet another reason to become disillusioned with the school community as well as alienate his mother in the process.

Prior to meeting at the school, the therapist met with Lamar and his mother to assess the reasons he was frequently late to school. It was important to discuss what supports he might need moving forward, as well as how they all might find common ground with the school. With the latter goal in mind, everyone agreed that, by missing school, Lamar suffered academically and socially.

Together the therapist and mother began the family–school meeting by joining with the school in their concern: "We all know how important it is for Lamar to be in school." This made it possible for the school social worker to feel comfortable asking Lamar about what made it difficult for him to get to school on time and to review how Lamar was doing overall. When the conversation turned to the decision to suspend Lamar, the therapist decided to address the situation head on. She spoke openly about the problems related to suspending African American students and asked for information about the school's suspension policies, including possible alternatives to Lamar staying out of school. In the meeting, the vice principal reviewed the policies and said she understood the risks associated with the decision to suspend Lamar. The school social worker then spoke up about other students of color who had been able to return to school successfully following a suspension. Lamar's mother and the school representatives agreed that the social worker could ask one such student to reach out to Lamar to discuss strategies for reintegrating into the school. In addition, the therapist and mother set up a reward system for Lamar to help motivate him to get up in the morning. Once he returned to school, Lamar agreed to meet with a learning specialist from the student support team to better prepare for quizzes and exams. Though the suspension remained in place, the therapist worked with the family and school to build a support structure that could, possibly, mitigate the negative impact of the suspension. Perhaps as important, the disparity between how African American kids and white kids are treated was openly discussed.

While it is difficult to offer a detailed set of guidelines that are generalizable for all situations in which difference is a factor, one overarching guideline that all therapists should follow is to seek opportunities to engage in diversity training when possible. We all have biases, but it's what we do about those biases that matter. As one public school administrator said, "Very few educators are consciously racist. They want to believe that they are treating all kids fairly. They are unaware of the implicit biases that exist in their expectations that may be impacting kids." In recent decades, mental health professionals (and educators) have devoted considerable attention to establishing diversity guidelines and training, making it central to best practices in every field (Lopez & Byrsztyn, 2013; Ratts, Singh, Nassar-McMillan, Butler, & McCullough, 2016). The goal of such efforts is to educate mental health professionals about their potential biases and beliefs concerning race, class, religious, ethnic, cultural, and gender differences, as well as to gain knowledge about other cultures.

Those who are in positions of relative power—the privileged—have an additional obligation to find opportunities to broaden their knowledge through continued education and consultation with colleagues, thereby remaining open to seeing the world from another person's perspective. Yet, even with eyes wide open, things are said or left unsaid that cause visible or invisible strain on relationships. If we accept that these fault lines exist, we can work toward developing the kind of openness and honesty required to resolve existing or newly created problems. Though professional standards have been set and groundwork has been laid, increasing cross-cultural competency should be a lifelong enterprise (Jacob et al., 2016; Miranda, 2014).

Discovering Problems with a Teacher or a School

At some point, you might hear about or observe something at a school that's perplexing, disheartening, or alarming. In one example, a therapist observed a teacher yelling harshly at his students in an effort to manage an unruly classroom. When that failed, he asked the therapist to step in and help quiet them down, which she wisely declined. In this instance, the therapist was concerned that she would be overstepping a professional boundary or, as she jokingly said, "make the situation even worse" through her unskilled efforts to assist the teacher in classroom management. Several therapists spoke about encountering such awkward situations and ways they responded when they were there to observe kids in the classroom. One therapist said that she makes general statements such as, "I can see you're working hard here" or "You have such a challenging class." Another therapist said that she tries to lighten things up by saying something funny that lowers the tension and redirects the focus to the child she is observing and what the teacher can do to help.

Some problems you discover might be best handled by the student and family directly. In one case where a student repeatedly complained about a teacher who came to class unprepared, a therapist said that she helped the student and parent craft an email to the principal to address the problem. However, it's also possible that you'll encounter someone who presents a serious problem to students that goes beyond the "not a good teacher-student fit" scenario (though it may initially be presented to you as such). It's possible, for instance, that you will observe a teacher who treats a child or certain groups of children unfairly or cruelly based on their race, religious background, gender or other difference. Also, you may find problems with the school itself—excessive fighting among the students, spaces that seem structurally unsafe, classrooms in which children are not adequately supervised, and more. These problems may be a function of poor management, inadequately trained personnel, or a lack of essential resources. Sometimes, things just go wrong and it happens to be at a time when you're at the school. There are also situations where schools fail children profoundly, such as in cases of sexual abuse by school personnel (Smith & Freyd, 2014). Remember that it is not necessarily your job to resolve the problems, but it is your job to make note of the impact that these problematic people or conditions have on the child and his classroom. In serious cases, it is important to speak with parents directly about your observations in addition to seeking guidance from other trusted professionals, including a representative from a professional organization with which you are affiliated.

If you observe something that concerns you, first check your own biases. It's possible that you are missing a broader picture or making assumptions that have impacted your observation in a particular way. Make sure, for example, that it's not just that you don't like time-outs as a disciplinary measure, but rather that something bigger is at stake. Remember that there are cultural differences in families and communities that may manifest in school. You could also momentarily lose perspective by being too aligned with the child. If your concern remains, it's important to act promptly and effectively.

Consider discussing your concerns with a trusted colleague, especially one who might know the school and can offer an informed perspective on the situation. A close colleague can provide feedback on potential biases you may have and whether or not your experience stands out in any way. Also, consider talking with the parent or older child about your concerns, being careful to discuss what you observed in a way that doesn't further inflame the situation or undermine the teacher unnecessarily. You might begin by asking the child about how the class in question typically goes or if there was something unusual about the day you observed. Another possibility is to speak more directly about your observation by saying, for example, "I noticed that the teacher seemed to consistently call on a certain group of kids" or "The teacher seemed to be having a hard day and taking out her frustration on certain kids in the classroom. Does that happen often?" or "I noticed that some students were intimidating others in the hallway" or "The classrooms lacked sufficient heat." If the child confirms what you've observed, or if the situation seems severe or truly disturbing, it's essential that you talk with the parent about what you've observed and strategize about next steps.

Dealing with Aggression and Violence in (and Out of) School

Nearly all schools must, at some point, deal with instances of violence or threats of violence and bullying, especially middle schools, where the rate of violence is highest (National Center for Education Statistics, 2017). There's also violence in which schools are the target, making it necessary for those who work in the schools to be prepared and to prepare students for such a destructive event; this brings with it fear and anxiety for everyone involved. Acts of aggression can be physical, verbal, or sexual; can be perpetrated by individuals, groups, or gangs; and can occur in person or online.

Online bullying (including ostracism), often called *cyber-bullying*, has become a potent and potentially devastating experience for kids, given the potential for anonymity and the viral, 24/7 nature of information flow. Therapists can learn about a child's potential for cyber victimization by asking about the child's social media and digital communication habits (Underwood & Ehrenreich, 2017; Williams, 2009). Discussing social media with parents can be helpful since parents can and often do play an active role in helping kids reduce risk by monitoring their Internet usage and trying to keep up with the latest trends in technology (Perren et al., 2012). In addition, therapists can encourage parents and older children to seek information about policies schools have to address cyber-bullying specifically (Felix, Green, & Sharkey, 2014).

Whatever form it takes, violence or threats of violence and bullying leave everyone feeling less safe and less able to focus on teaching and learning (Bazelon, 2013; Green, Felix, Sharkey, Furlong, & Kras, 2013; Larson & Mark, 2014). There are several ways that your work with kids and families may directly intersect with bullying, aggressive behavior, ostracism, or threats of violence at school. In some cases, you may be working with kids who are violent or have made threats of violence. In others, you may work with kids who have been bullied or experienced violence themselves, either directly or indirectly.

Some kids may be referred to you because of their aggressive behavior or because the school is concerned about their potential for violence. Part of the work therapists do is to try to determine whether children are a risk to themselves or others and, when there is the potential for danger, to assess what's going on and try to protect and support all parties involved. Today, the number of children referred to therapists for *risk-for-violence* assessments has increased as a result of the tragic deaths of children and teachers from school shootings and other forms of school violence, even though the vast majority of those referred don't end up posing a danger to others (Halikias, 2013).

Assessing the potential for violence is a complicated process that requires not only knowledge of research in this area, but also familiarity with schools and their policies surrounding such issues. Certain members of a school's student support team may be trained and experienced in assessing possible danger and will work with you, the child, and the family to evaluate the risk. Even so, there is no sure and effective way to predict whether someone will engage in violent behavior (Larson & Mark, 2014). Most schools have implemented some type of violence prevention and response practices. These may include training teachers and school personnel in conflict de-escalation, trauma-informed practices, establishing programs for threat assessment, and the design and staging of lockdown drills (Larson & Mark, 2014). While the public discourse surrounding this issue is evolving, we have not yet reached a meaningful consensus about how to address the problem; many school districts are actively seeking solutions, however disparate those may be.

You may be working with kids who engage in or are victimized by behavior that doesn't warrant such intense intervention or risk assessment, but nevertheless warrants serious attention. Bullying is one such example, impacting victims, perpetrators, and bystanders. Though there are many definitions of bullying, perhaps the one most widely used is from Olweus (1996), who described bullying as a type of peer victimization with an imbalance of power between the person perpetrating the bullying and the person being bullied. There is no doubt that bullying victimization, which is widespread (CDC, 2015), puts kids at risk for serious mental health problems that can last well into adulthood.

Since being either the victim or the perpetrator of any form of bullying is linked to mental health and behavior problems (Reijntjes, Kamphuis, Prinzie, & Telch, 2010; Sansone, Leung, & Wiederman, 2013), it's important for therapists to understand how bullying and peer aggression are handled in a given school when therapists encounter such problems. Try to learn about policies and resources that may be available, especially given the fact that how schools address bullying substantially affects kids' feelings of safety. Most states have created legislation to implement bullying prevention programs in schools, though the laws vary by state and may be at odds with current research on best practices (Felix et al., 2014). Many schools have programs and activities to help kids with anger management, socioemotional learning, restorative practices programs, cognitive-behavioral strategies, safe social media use, and other educational opportunities (Espelage, Low, Van Ryzin, & Polanin, 2015; Sulkowski & Lazarus, 2016). Many student support teams have members who are trained in bullying prevention. They, too, can be a source of information and support.

One group that is significantly at risk for bullying is LGBTQ students, especially transgender students, who are at higher risk for dropping out of school and suicide (Kosciw, Greytak, Giga, Villenas, & Danischewski, 2016). Sean, a ninth grader, new to his local midsized public high school, had transitioned from female to male over the summer, following a serious depression in middle school. It was during those early teenage years that he realized he could no longer "pretend to be something [he] was not." The female gender assigned to him at birth had never fit his experience of being in the world and when his mood plummeted, his mother sought help from an LGBTQ-friendly therapist who had been recommended by the school social worker. With help from the therapist and his supportive mother, Sean began the school year somewhat optimistic that he could start over. However, problems at school began early on when several students challenged Sean in the boys' restroom, insisting that he didn't belong there.

When Sean spoke with his advisor about the incident, they discussed Sean's life at school, including where and with whom he felt safe and where he felt less so. It turned out that Sean had established ties with several students who were also new to the school and that he generally felt comfortable, though the bathroom incident had shaken his confidence. At the end of the conversation, they called Sean's mother and his therapist, inviting them in for a meeting at school to discuss what had occurred. Sean's advisor also reached out to the school's behavioral support team and the vice principal to determine how to address the incident with the boys who had bullied Sean.

At the family–school meeting the following morning, a handful of key school representatives were present in addition to Sean, his mother, and the therapist. These representatives included the advisor, the high school principal, school psychologist, an advisor to the school's Gay-Straight Alliance club, and the school counselor. Based on the preparation Sean did in a session with the therapist the night before, Sean was encouraged to talk about his experience of being a student in the school generally, the incident, and his thoughts about going forward. Throughout the meeting, Sean and his mother felt supported by the school and spoke about their hope that Sean could continue on there while efforts were being made to prevent further bullying.

The school's antibullying policies were discussed and the principal agreed to send out a notice to the entire school community restating these policies. He also spoke of his plan to talk with the students who had intimidated Sean. At one point, the therapist recommended that the school provide training for all students, using a program with which she was familiar and had found effective in other school settings. In addition, Sean agreed to use the gender-neutral restroom temporarily, something he had hoped would not be necessary in his new school environment. Sean also decided to talk with his new friends about the incident and attend the next Gay-Straight Alliance meeting. Together, they decided that Sean would check in with his advisor on a daily basis and inform him immediately if any further threatening encounters occurred. The therapist also recommended that Sean's mother reach out to a local affiliate of PFLAG (formerly Parents, Families, and Friends of Lesbians and Gays), a national organization that provides resources for gender nonconforming kids.

The advisor suggested that everyone meet again in a couple of weeks to give the school time to address the problem with the students who had bullied Sean. Though there could be no guarantees, the principal strongly asserted the school's commitment to doing all they can to help create a safe environment and to work with him, his mother, and the therapist to achieve that end.

Working with the School During Crises

Working with kids does mean occasionally dealing with urgent or life-altering crises, and it can be difficult to know how best to collaborate with their schools when issues are high-stakes and time-sensitive. This section will explore guidelines for working with schools during times when your clients are suffering from extreme circumstances or recent trauma.

Resolving urgent problems with the kids you see in therapy

As one therapist remarked, "There are those calls you just hate to get." When you work with kids, it's not unlikely you'll receive a call because one of your clients is in crisis. Sometimes, the urgent situation or crisis occurs at school or relates to the child's life at school. In either instance, you may need to work closely with the school (in addition to the family, of course) to help solve the problem.

One therapist received a midday call from the school regarding his severely depressed teenage client, Amara. With apprehension, the therapist picked up the phone and spoke with the school psychologist, who said that Amara had gone missing. Amara's friends had last seen her at an assembly, but she had apparently not attended classes thereafter. The family had been contacted and the school psychologist, who had referred Amara for therapy, wanted the therapist to be informed, too, in case he had knowledge of Amara's whereabouts. She also wanted help determining what should be done if Amara returned to school. Over the phone, the therapist and school psychologist decided that, if Amara did return, the school psychologist would contact her parents and the therapist right away and then determine how to proceed. In the meantime, the therapist agreed to call Amara's parents to coordinate efforts with them.

In such cases, the therapist must make several quick decisions regarding how to respond to a time-sensitive and pressing situation. When an urgent problem with a child necessitates your collaboration with the school, consider the following guidelines:

- Assess the situation as you would any other urgent situation.

- Remember that the child and family are your clients, not the school. With that said, make every effort to collaborate with all parties.

- Seek information from the school about its crisis management plan or policies

- Identify a person in the school with whom to collaborate, if there isn't someone established in that role already. Check with that school representative about the person's availability, especially in the days immediately following a crisis.

- Since those at school may need specific input and recommendations from you, be sure to let the school representative know your availability, and be prompt in your response.

Determining when and how often to be in touch with the school following a crisis with your client depends partly on the severity of the problem. If the child's problem that precipitated the crisis developed fairly recently and is less serious, the parents may be the ones to collaborate with the school, and subsequent contact between the therapist and school may be minimal. In fact, with minor problems, a therapist would do well to help the parents work directly with the school themselves—gently leaning in to offer support as needed. Yet, when a child is seriously at risk and remains at risk, the therapist may need to be more involved with the school directly. In fact, it might take a hefty commitment and highly synchronized efforts on the part of everyone to ensure that the child is safe and sturdy enough to be in school. It's worth noting that many vulnerable kids do better by being in school rather than staying at home. Assessing whether a child can be in school safely is not an easy decision to make and should be based on your clinical judgment and collaboration with school personnel and other professionals who may be involved with the child.

Through experience, therapists learn to navigate this ebb and flow of working with a school to support a child during and after a crisis. As with an accordion expanding and contracting, intense collaboration with the family and school may be necessary immediately following a crisis and can ease up when serious problems begin to resolve (Eno, 1985). Whatever the phase of your involvement, be sure to let the school know that you can be called on, offering parameters for how and when you can be reached.

Responding to a death in a school community

In addition to religious and other local institutions, schools are one of the places that can help kids process the death of a loved one (Poland, Samuel-Barrett, & Waguespack, 2014). Given that between 4% and 7% of children will experience the death of a parent before the age of 18 (Social Security Administration, 2000), it's important to consider how you might work with a child's school following the death of a family member. For urban, low-income kids there is a horribly high percentage who are exposed to deaths (and violent assaults) of family members or others in their community, peers as well as adults. If you are working with a child and family who have lost someone they love, the following are nine recommendations to keep in mind, informed by the work of Sirrine (2014) and Poland and colleagues (2014).

1. **Learn what the school has to offer.** Most schools have a student support person or administrator available to help coordinate the support of a bereaved child and family. Some schools provide bereavement counseling, education about grief, and more (Poland et al., 2014).

2. **Work with the child's teacher(s).** Teachers can play a large role in helping a child adjust back to school. As Sirrine (2014) notes, teachers can be "safe people" from whom the child can seek and receive support. Teachers can also help assess the child's ability to work and concentrate, and they can help monitor the periods of grief that may follow from the original loss.

3. **Help the child return to school.** Depending on the age of the child, children may need help returning to school. First days back can be particularly challenging, so thinking through ways that make the process less stressful can be clarifying. Keep in mind that, for many kids, routines and familiar people and places can normalize the child's life and be a safe haven for kids following the death of a family member. For kids who are reluctant to return to school, teachers can help assess the situation and work with the family and you to determine ways to facilitate the child's reentry, much as you would do with a child struggling with school refusal.

4. **Treat the grieving child like a child with temporary special needs.** Kids who have suffered a loss may struggle academically. For example, they might need extra time on tests and quizzes as well other accommodations to help with their adjustment. The child's ability to do work at school and independently at home can be very different. This is where the teacher's observations are crucial and communication between the family and school may need to be more frequent.

5. **Incorporate your knowledge of child development to inform your decision making.** Trained in child development, therapists are aware that children's perceptions and understanding of death are tied to their age and stage of development in addition to their own particular circumstances. This is essential information for guiding your efforts to support the child (and family) who has suffered a serious loss.

6. **Have someone at the school inform others about the death— the coach, school social worker, and others who know and work with the school can play a role here.** It's possible that you will be asked to give advice about whom to contact and what to say, given your relationship with the child and family. Collaborate with the family and other school representatives as needed.

7. **Consider providing information about grief and grieving.** It's also possible that you will be asked to instruct members of the school community about grief and grieving and how it might impact that particular child's functioning. This can be a helpful contribution to make at a sad time in the child's and family's life.

8. **Help schools think about the rest of the school year.** An upcoming grandparent visitation day, Mother's Day, or Father's Day may prove difficult for the child who has lost a grandparent or parent. Preparing for such events can be very beneficial.

9. **Advocate for the child and family.** When the family's energy is low, and they need extra support, step in to advocate for them.

In one case, a therapist received a call from the mother of a preschooler, Roberta, saying that Roberta's father had died suddenly and she was seeking help for Roberta and the whole family. Since the therapist had worked with Roberta's school before, it was decided that the therapist would contact Roberta's teacher to get some background on Roberta and discuss how to facilitate her reentry into school. In the phone conversation with Roberta's teacher, the therapist learned that Roberta had been having a difficult time adjusting to her new classroom before her father died. As a result, her teachers were worried about how she would face this loss and how they might responsibly support her.

When the therapist met with Roberta and her family it was clear that they wanted Roberta back in school as soon as possible. As a result, the therapist and mother agreed to meet with Roberta's teachers and school director the next day so they could explore what supports the school offered and how to facilitate her first day back. During the family–school meeting, Roberta's teachers and principal received the family and therapist warmly and sympathetically. This reception and the meeting that followed paved the way for Roberta's mother, grandmother, and older half-brother to trust that the school would welcome Roberta with care and attention, too. The school's past experience assisting children in similar situations was evident in the recommendations they made: Roberta would come to school for only a couple of hours the next morning, with a backup plan if she was too unhappy to remain. They also decided that the teachers would reach out to the parents of Roberta's classmates, informing them of Roberta's father's death so they could tell their children at home that evening and later, in coordination with the parents' association, deliver meals to the family.

Responding to natural disasters and collective trauma

When natural or human-caused disasters occur—floods, fires, hurricanes, mass shootings, or other life-changing events—communities suffer trauma and damages from which it is difficult to recover, particularly if they do not receive sufficient support (Bonanno, Brewin, Kaniasty, & La Greca, 2010; Heath, 2014; Walsh, 2016). Children are particularly vulnerable to the immediate and long term effects of disasters or traumatic events because of their dependency on others (Dodgen et al., 2016). Their families may suffer from geographic displacement, job loss, fragmentation of needed services, high levels of stress, breakdown in routines, and so on. The scale of disasters or traumatic events in communities varies greatly, as do attendant supports and resources that are made available (Saul, 2013).

Following a disaster or traumatic event, therapists can be important resources for children and families who have been affected or traumatized. A growing body of research is available to guide therapists in disaster situations, although more practical, applied research is still needed (Grolnick et al., 2018). Should disasters occur, seek out the necessary education and training to be effective, including learning how to support parents who can provide stability and supervision for their children (Webb, 2003).

Therapists may also be in a position to support children and families outside their offices by working with local schools following a disaster or traumatic event since schools are one of the institutions that can help sustain communities. Schools may also need community support in return (Heath, 2014; Fu & Underwood, 2015). In fact, working with kids and families who are impacted by a disaster often takes place at local schools (Fu & Underwood, 2015; Brock et al., 2014; Fu & Underwood, 2015). As Grolnick and colleagues stated, "Schools are a 'natural,' low-stigma environment well known to children and their families, who are often familiar and comfortable with school-based services and wellness centers" (p. 223).

It's important to know that mental health services provided through schools can originate from school–mental health agency partnerships (Kataoka et al., 2009) or can be offered through a clinic or hospital where you work. For therapists working in private or group practices, ask around about existing partnerships in the area. Additionally, should a disaster occur, you might contact someone from a professional organization with which you are affiliated or a local mental health facility that provides such services. Finally, there may be opportunities for you to become involved directly due to your own relationship with a school, but don't presume this is the case.

If you've spent time in schools and they know and trust you, it's easier to volunteer if a disaster happens. Likewise, if you know the school in which community mental health services are being provided, you'll have something additional to offer. Over two and a half decades ago, there was a tragic midair plane and helicopter crash in which wreckage fell on the playground of a local elementary school in suburban Philadelphia. Two children died on the playground in addition to those in the plane and helicopter, including a U.S. Senator. Others were injured, too, from falling debris. Administrators from the elementary school immediately reached out to local mental health facilities and invited clinicians to come to the school and meet with kids, faculty, staff, and families over several days following the accident. Though there was little disaster-related mental health research at the time to guide us, a group of professionals gathered with school personnel in support of a community suffering from multiple losses. A truly collaborative and mutually supportive effort strengthened ties at a very difficult time.

Today, many if not most schools have programs and policies in place to prevent, mitigate, and respond to crises. These involve having emergency supplies on hand; having crisis-training through the Red Cross, FEMA, or other crisis-preparedness and trauma-informed services; and providing appropriate individual and systems-level interventions as needed (Heath, 2014). Securing resources and supporting the resilience of families and communities is the basis for interventions provided by such programs.

REVIEWING THE BASICS

When it comes to handling complexity and crises, there is no one-size-fits-all solution that therapists can employ in every situation. However, keeping the collaborative framework in mind, we can seek to broaden our understanding of our clients and the potential challenges they face and prepare ourselves as best we can to help them navigate rough waters. To be the most effective in challenging circumstances, it's best to:

- Seek out diversity training and other resources that can educate you about your clients' differences and related concerns that arise.

- Continue to interrogate your own biases, beliefs, and assumptions and how they inform your work both positively and negatively.

- Given the complexity of the issues, consult with experienced and knowledgeable colleagues to explore possible directions to take.

- Keep in mind that all of your clients will have multiple layers of identity that you must take into account in order to see the fullest picture of their life.

- Challenge yourself to confront with openness and compassion uncomfortable situations that arise from differences, as opposed to leaving them unacknowledged.

- If something in a client's school seems dysfunctional or dangerous, first make sure you understand how your biases might be impacting your assessment of the situation, and then intervene appropriately if need be (start by speaking with the child's parent, a trusted colleague, or a representative from a professional organization with which you are affiliated).

- All schools experience events on the spectrum of violence, and you can help intervene with victims or perpetrators of bullying as well as collaborating with the appropriate school representatives.

- While schools often have broad plans in place for dealing with emergencies and traumatic events, your therapeutic expertise can be a valuable resource that can help mitigate the negative effects of devastating occurrences. It's important to seek training in how to effectively respond to a disaster in your community. Try to connect with organizations (e.g., the Red Cross) or school-agency partnerships when reaching out in a crisis.

PART II

Parents as Advocates

CHAPTER 11

Parents as Advocates
for Kids

C an you remember a time in your school career when one of your parents intervened on your behalf and how cared for you felt as a result? Alternatively, might there have been a time when you hoped your parents would step in and they didn't? Equally unsettling, there may have been an incident when one of your parents became involved with your school in a way that left you embarrassed or angry, wishing they'd left things in your hands. Maybe you also remember one of your parents simply helping you with your homework during a rough patch, and how much, in retrospect, this activity supported your education.

An important part of our work with kids involves finding ways to support parents as advocates for their children. In the broadest sense, parental advocacy includes a whole range of activities—from everyday practices like checking in on homework and making sure bedtime rituals are maintained, to more serious measures like going to the school to speak with a teacher or principal. Kids need a lot of support to be successful at school, and most parents will have to advocate for their children in both large and small ways at some point in their lives, including helping their children learn the skills to advocate for themselves (Lythcott-Haims, 2015). This chapter will explore the many ways that parents can be advocates for their child, and how you can support them in their efforts.

Parenting Practices That Support Kids at School

Helping kids succeed in school requires all manner of parental and community support starting with the way parents are able to strengthen and structure kids' environments at home. No matter the presenting problem, sometimes helping parents support their child simply means helping them implement common parenting techniques that are known to enhance school success. Some of these practices are ones you studied in your clinical training and others have been brought to your attention by the families you've seen in therapy or how you parent or were parented yourself. Keep in mind that parenting practices are diverse—they evolve and vary by context (e.g., community and school resources) and culture (e.g., beliefs, values). Thus, there is no single "dominant family form" to which all practices can apply (Clauss-Ehlers, 2017). And, for many families, some of the practices listed below may be a luxury or irrelevant due to lack of time, energy, and resources. Nonetheless, it's worth reviewing some general parenting practices that can be learned and implemented:

Ways parents support kids at school

- Creating a warm home climate that encourages learning and values education
- Establishing and maintaining mealtimes, bedtimes, and bedtime rituals
- Establishing and maintaining age-appropriate rules for time spent on the computer or social media
- Creating a space and time for studying and help with time management strategies
- Supporting reading activities and providing materials that enhance learning
- Asking questions that encourage independent, age-appropriate thought and action
- Securing help from a parent, sibling, family member, friend, or paid professional when difficulties arise
- Providing opportunities to discuss school concerns
- Soliciting information about activities, whereabouts, interests, and friends more generally
- Finding appropriate rewards and consequences for school performance
- Identifying and seeking out extracurricular activities that complement and enhance school life
- Having the child tested for learning or other problems, if needed
- Getting to know your child's classmates by encouraging your child to invite classmates over for afterschool or weekend play dates
- Becoming involved with other parents in the school and school activities generally

- Fostering a collaborative relationship with the child's teacher and other school personnel
- Advocating directly on behalf of the child

Whatever the parents' mindset or familiarity with these or other strategies and activities, it's our job as therapists to explore and understand something of their parenting practices. Sometimes, these activities take the form of reading over homework late at night or limiting Internet access, or simply providing a shoulder to cry on when a child comes home upset about being excluded at recess. Sometimes, parents design behavioral charts or create calendars for long-term projects. Other parents will place a note in their child's lunch container reminding them to talk with their homeroom teacher about a missed assignment. It is also true that once you know how the parents parent, you may come to the conclusion that less is more. It's possible for parents to do too much, undermining their child's self-esteem, competence, and resilience, and adding to family resentments, tensions, and fatigue (Lythcott-Haims, 2015). You'll want to know at least something of what's been tried, how effective it's been, how the family and child feel about the efforts that have been made, and what further help they are seeking from you, (Christenson & Reschly, 2010). Once you have knowledge of how the parents parent, you'll have a better sense of what kinds of interventions to recommend, including turning to school- or community-based parent education activities and programs (Gordon & Siegel, 2009).

Helping Parents Advocate Using a Collaborative Approach with the School

Even with strong parenting practices in place, there are times when a parent's voice needs to be heard. Without it, a difficult situation can become prolonged or deteriorate further. As one school psychologist said, "It's not only okay for parents to advocate for their child, sometimes it's a necessity." Working at the intersection of the child, family, and school, therapists are in an optimal position to support parents as advocates. Sometimes, all it takes is for you to remind a parent that most teachers find it helpful to hear from them or that the school usually has the same goals for the child that they do. At other times, therapists can step in more decisively and help determine *how* parents can advocate for their child. For example, a mother might come in for a session to discuss how to reach out to a teacher about her son's learning problems and what to say if conflict arises. Looking over a draft email a parent composes or having the parent try out what he or she wants to say by role playing with you can be a productive experience.

Sometimes, parents are reluctant to speak up because they're reserved, have a desire for privacy or are fearful of negative consequences for their child. Again, the therapist is in a good position to help calibrate constructive involvement. As one therapist said, "There are parents you need to encourage to get involved, and other parents you pull off the ledge." You can review the history of the family's relationship with the school and provide a more objective opinion regarding their level of contact, assessing whether a call to the school might help or worsen the situation in question. Needless to say, the best way for some parents to support their child is to refrain from making another call to the teacher and instead figure out more measured ways to engage with the school. For example one therapist recommended saying to the parent, "I can see why you are unhappy with the situation, but remember that you see your child in relation to your family and people at the school are seeing your child in relation to other kids." Helping parents see things from the school's perspective and adopt more reasonable expectations can position parents to advocate more effectively.

Of course, there are times when parents don't step in due to circumstances that make them unable to advocate effectively. For example, parents might have poor English language fluency, undocumented status, or serious problems that prevent or inhibit them from communicating with the school. They may need basic support in the form of food, shelter, or safety. Parents' own lack of self-efficacy might impact their child's academic success (Ardelt & Eccles, 2001; Carless, Melvin, Tonge, & Newman, 2015). For many, the idea of engaging in the parenting activities mentioned above goes beyond what they are capable of at a given time. The consequences for kids living in such vulnerable situations are many, including disruptions in the ability to learn and develop age-appropriate social skills (Teti, Cole, Cabrera, Goodman, & McLoyd, 2017). Parenting practices like those mentioned above may be applied in some cases, but often the child's needs are so significant that attention must be given to the more immediate threat to the child's and family's integrity and functioning. When this is the case, sometimes the best way for therapists to help parents advocate for their kids involves helping them advocate for themselves, a topic that goes beyond the scope of this volume (Walsh, 2016). Other times, it will be your job to advocate for them (as discussed in more detail later in the chapter).

In one instance, a therapist worked with a family that was exceedingly deferential to institutions, including their daughter Emily school. They sought help because Emily, a bright and academically capable middle school student, behaved oddly and was at times provocative with her peers. Her teachers found her disagreeable and withdrawn when they spoke with her about her behavior. The therapist urged the parents to meet with Emily's teachers or someone from the school's student support team, but, due to fear of engaging with the school, they repeatedly declined. Eventually, they agreed that the therapist could contact Emily's homeroom advisor herself on their behalf.

When the therapist spoke with the advisor, it was clear that he knew Emily well, since teachers had brought her to his attention several times. Those at the school had wondered if Emily's behavior reflected a developmental disorder since she seemed unable to receive feedback and appeared disconnected at times, though she was doing well enough academically to put a recommendation for testing on hold. The therapist spoke with the advisor about how much the parents cared about their daughter, as demonstrated by them having sought help from the therapist, but explained that they felt uncomfortable coming to the school to meet and talk. The therapist and Emily's advisor reviewed what the school had tried in the past, what resources were generally available, and how to translate the work that the therapist was doing in her office with supports that could be put in place at school.

The therapist recommended that the family and Emily's teachers address the same behavioral problems at home and school, expanding on the work the therapist was doing in her office. They all agreed that they would insist that Emily make eye contact with adults and that Emily's teachers would begin conversations with something positive they'd noticed she was doing that day. With everyone's involvement and support, Emily made progress over several months. As a result, her parents could see the individual attention and care she was receiving from her teachers. The parents eventually agreed to attend a family–school meeting accompanied by the therapist. Over time, with encouragement and patience, they learned to speak up for their daughter.

Guidelines for parents advocating for kids

As Emily's case demonstrates, trust and good faith efforts are critical elements of the advocacy process. As one therapist said, "It's hard to advocate for your child if you don't trust the school." At the same time, one of the ways to build trust is for parents to advocate effectively. Developing trust on both sides is an important dimension of advocacy work, and it may take time and patience on everyone's part to get there. The following six guidelines can help make that happen (see Box 11.1).

Box 11.1: Guidelines for Parental Advocacy

1. Help parents collaborate.

2. Encourage parents to see that, with rare exceptions, schools are trying their best.

3. Remind parents that their child is one of many students.

4. Help parents learn about the rules and regulations that apply to their child's educational needs.

5. Help parents remember that if something goes wrong, first take a deep breath.

6. Determine when it's best for you to advocate directly for the child on behalf of the parents.

Guideline #1: **Help parents collaborate.** It can be difficult to approach problems with a cooperative, problem-solving spirit, especially when there are disagreements, disappointments, and anger in the mix. Nonetheless, chances are that a difficult situation will be steadied or even improved if parents are able to see their way to collaborate rather than confront. At times, parents might not grasp the importance of their own tone and way of speaking. By learning how they can present their views and describe problems in a nonblaming way, their conversations with school representatives can be significantly enhanced. Except in cases of real damage on the school's part that require a more forceful, if not confrontational approach, parents can learn to stay away from faultfinding and focus more on how the situation can be improved for their child.

Some of what parents learn about collaboration and teamwork will come from the way you talk with them about their child, the problem, and the school. It will also derive from the way that they see you interact with those at the school. I remember one family–school meeting in which the child's therapist spoke to the child's teacher condescendingly, even accusatorily, at times. The parents watched and listened (as did we all) and later spoke with a comparable level of antipathy toward the teacher, as well as the entire student support team. Interestingly, the meeting was nevertheless productive, since we were able to come up with a reasonable plan for the student. However, the relationships visibly declined, making it difficult to plan a follow-up meeting, which would have been useful. Pay attention to your own inclinations and feelings so that you can try to model ways of interacting that are respectful and generative, including intervening when the quality of the conversation deteriorates.

In summary, part of your job is to encourage parents to reach out to their child's teacher (or other school representative) with a problem-solving mindset. By reaching out in this way, school representatives will hear concerns without fearing that their "head will be bitten off," as one teacher said. It takes a certain level of trust to reach out, of course—trust in the therapist or the school. Inquire about past experiences and look for ways to strengthen the relationship with the school, keeping in mind that one way to build trust is to do something that is trustworthy—letting a teacher know that you see how hard he or she is working, inviting ideas and sharing experiences, making amends, or speaking clearly about goals and wishes.

Guideline #2: **Encourage parents to see that, with rare exceptions, schools are trying their best.** Though we're trained to try to understand the complex reasons why humans do what we do, we often don't know what motivates people's behavior. We hear from parents that their child wasn't able to retake an exam after being out sick for several days and we wonder, "Why would the teacher make such a seemingly punishing, shortsighted decision?" The parent complains about the teacher's failure to call on a child in class discussions and wonders whether there is racial discrimination woven in. We scratch our heads, and we form opinions and hypotheses, too. These depend on any number of considerations: biases and past experiences with the school, assumptions and knowledge we hold about the child and family, and perhaps our own experiences of felt injustice.

So why does it matter whether we enter into a situation with positive or even benign assumptions? By stepping into a conversation with the parent (or school) with the assumption that the teacher or school counselor is doing his or her best, we are more likely to create workable, less complicated, problem-solving relationships. Likewise, we're more likely to be able to support parents in creating positive responses and environments, too. By focusing on commonalities and making benign assumptions, parents can present their ideas in ways that teachers and other school representatives are more likely to absorb, as opposed to defensively reject.

Guideline #3: **Remind parents that their child is one of many students.** As therapists, we want parents to be advocates for their children, but also to be wise and thoughtful about the wider circle of people with whom their child interacts, both for their child's sake and the sake of the school community. It's important to note that sometimes parents aren't thinking about the teacher, classroom, or school apart from their child's particular needs. Again, therapists are in a unique position to widen the parents' lens and help them make good decisions for the child and, ideally, the child's community as well.

One teacher reported that she had not been told when a student's parents had their child discontinue his ADHD medication. The boy's sudden eruptions and fighting in the classroom were so alarming that the teacher called the parents to try to understand what was going on. In this not-so-unusual case, the parents said that they had wanted the teacher to be blind to the change so that they could evaluate the effectiveness of the medication. In this instance, the parents didn't take into consideration the impact of their son's behavior on the teacher and classroom activities. The teacher said that as a result, her opinion of the parents (and if she were completely honest, she said, the child also) was negatively affected. At a minimum, therapists can help parents think through the various pros and cons of a decision that might affect the teacher or the entire class. In this case, with the parents' permission, the therapist might have collaborated with the child's pediatrician, who was prescribing the medication and found another, less disruptive, way to evaluate medication efficacy.

There are times when conflict between a family and school arises because of the allocation of limited resources. The school system wants what's best for *every* child. The family wants what's best for *their* child. This is one of the inherent tensions that exist when families and schools come to the table. If therapists are aware of this tension, they may be able to help the parents' interests align with a more reasonable standard. Parents know their child best, yet there are other viewpoints to consider when problems arise; when parents keep this in mind, they will be better able to advocate effectively.

Guideline #4: **Help parents learn about the rules and regulations that apply to their child's educational needs.** Parents advocate for their children along a continuum, from minor problems—like requesting an extension on a homework assignment for their sick child—to more significant ones, like deciding to formally appeal a decision in order to have their child transferred to a school for kids with special needs. Given the breadth of possibilities, it's important to remember that parents need to know something about the school's regulations, services, and resources and, in the case of public schools, the laws and guidelines that are in place to support kids with special needs (Hiatt-Michael, 2004). This can be a daunting task, for you as well as them. It's possible that parents don't even know what questions to ask or even if it's okay to ask questions. From the start, it might be helpful to acknowledge to yourself that learning about this dimension of the child's school, and educational resources more generally, can seem overwhelming. Nonetheless, you (and others) can help parents learn what's needed to effectively advocate for their child. In some cases, you'll be learning with them, so be candid about the limits of your knowledge and experience. (Key elements of what therapists need to know in special education cases are reviewed in the following chapter.)

Guideline #5: **Help parents remember to first take a deep breath if something goes wrong.** Learning how to slow down is a one of the hallmarks of thoughtful and effective parental advocacy. When parents react quickly to a problem, especially with intense, negative emotions, a wake of complications may follow that can damage important relationships in ways that may be hard to undo. One of the first options you have is to help parents take a moment before engaging with the school when a problem arises. One educator recommended asking parents to weigh the seriousness of the situation on a scale of 1–10. Such an exercise could give them (and you) not only a sense of the intensity of their emotions, but also an indication of how much this situation matters and why; thus it helps determine how to move forward.

By taking a deliberate pause in the action, parents can process what is upsetting and try to think through various dimensions of the problem. You might discuss possible solutions with them, including how to find the best person (and next best person) at the school to contact and who should reach out. Asking parents to role-play what they would say to the school representative gives you a chance to help them find a constructive way to say it. For example, "I heard from my son that he was involved in an argument at school and someone got hurt, and I'd like to hear more about what happened" is the kind of statement a parent could make that would open the door to a conversation without implying that someone at the school is necessarily at fault.

Encourage parents not to email or text when they are still upset. However, you can encourage them to contact the school and say they'd like to find a time to talk. This gives both the parent and the person at school the opportunity to think through the problem. At the same time, for some parents, time to think equals time to stew or seethe. Keep this in mind, lest the interval between the incident and the conversation becomes the runway for more anger and stress. There are times, of course, when parents are angry because of a serious misstep by someone at the school. In such cases, make an effort to think through the most effective ways they can promptly present their justifiable complaint that may require a swift response.

Kids benefit tremendously when they see their parents working well with the school, another reason to help parents step back long enough to move forward as calmly as possible. Such collaboration demonstrates how to handle problems and potential conflict, protects kids from becoming triangulated in a conflict of loyalties, and gives them hope that something can be done to help with whatever isn't working in their school lives.

Guideline #6: **Determine when it's best for you to advocate directly for the child on behalf of the parents.** Therapists must take into account family strengths and limitations, circumstances, and resources when a child is doing poorly at school and needs parental advocacy and support. An important part of your role is determining when it might be necessary to step in and advocate directly on behalf of the parent and child. There are many parents so burdened by poverty, undocumented status, addiction, individual and family dysfunction, neighborhood violence, mental illness, incarceration, losses, or trauma that they are not able to provide the kind of support and advocacy their children might need. The parents themselves need an advocate in the form of a therapist who can support them in their parenting role and sometimes directly step in with their child's school. If the parents are significantly limited in what they are able to do, then you can work with them to determine how you can help represent their viewpoint. Perhaps you might all attend a meeting at the school, but determine beforehand that you'll take the most active role in the meeting. At other times, you might advocate directly with the school on behalf of the parents without them present. In addition, therapists are also in a good position to recommend that the family seek help from an educational lawyer or advocate, something that will be explored in the following chapter.

In one case, a psychiatrist spoke with a school administrator multiple times over several weeks to advocate for a child whose antidepression medication was being adjusted. The teenager was too depressed to come to school but hoped to return in a matter of weeks and didn't want to lose too much ground academically. Since the girl's mother was working two jobs and was often overwhelmed by her daughter's needs, the psychiatrist and the school social worker collaborated to create modified curricular expectations for the student. In addition, the social worker agreed to stay late one day in order to meet with the student and her mother in an effort to forge a tie that had not existed before.

REVIEWING THE BASICS

As one experienced therapist said, "I do more work helping parents become good advocates than doing advocacy myself." This is a clear reminder that, while we sometimes do have a role to play in being the child's or family's advocate, our first job is to find ways to support the child's parents taking on this responsibility. Some of the basics are as follows:

- Assume that most parents can and do learn how to advocate for their child in ways that are reasonable and constructive. Therapists can help parents develop the mindset and skills that make that possible.

- Try to learn about the parents' familiarity with common parenting techniques that can help support their child at school, and understand what's worked and what hasn't.

- As much as possible, help parents approach the school with a collaborative rather than combative mindset. Remind them that, except in rare exceptions, schools are trying their best.

- Help the child to self-advocate, especially older children who can benefit from being part of the collaborative process.

- Some parents might be unable to advocate for their children due to mental illness, language barriers, or other issues. In these instances, it's best to focus of the immediate problem and help the parents find the resources they need.

- Most problems that public school kids face are normative and can be solved before seeking special education services. However, if you are working with a child who has exhausted regular educational supports, then you're in a position to help the parents advocate for their child within the system that's designed for kids with special needs, a topic that will be explored in the next chapter.

CHAPTER 12

Helping Families Navigate Special Education Systems

Therapists who have worked with kids seeking special education services may have some knowledge of the systems in place that are designed to optimize each child's educational experience. Yet, unless you are trained as a school psychologist or school social worker (or are otherwise familiar with education laws and regulations), your knowledge may be limited. Because of the nature of our work with kids and families, we need to know some of the basics about education and civil rights laws and how they apply to the children we see in therapy. This chapter will explore the education and civil rights laws that determine special services public schools must provide, the therapist's potential role in the process, and educational advocacy services that are available to parents who need them.

Though there are broad rules that direct school policies, each school implements them differently. When discussing this issue, one school psychologist said, "The biggest piece to learn is how to adapt to the situation you're in." By that he was referring to the large differences among schools—class size, available resources, safety, curriculum, disciplinary rules, and so on. For instance, in some schools, the school psychologist has the last say in the decision-making process; in others, the principal makes most if not all of the decisions. Some schools are more collaborative than others, or collaborative in different ways. Certain schools may be able to mobilize a range of services in-house, while others are bare-bones operations with little to offer in that regard. As one therapist said, "The well-resourced districts bend over backward to support a kids that poorer districts can't." In short, there is no one-size-fits-all proposition when it comes to helping kids receive special education services, even though laws are in place to which school districts must make every effort to adhere.

As therapists, it is essential that we begin with the knowledge that public and charter schools (referred to as public schools throughout this chapter) must find appropriate educational settings for all of their students. In contrast, private schools are free to dismiss a student who has learning or emotional challenges beyond what they determine they're able to handle. Since public schools have an obligation to deliver educational services that meet the child's individualized needs, the public school system can, at times, be a more reliable place to find support if it's determined that a student needs a tutor, special services such as speech and language therapy, or learning and testing accommodations. That's not to say that the process in public schools won't be filled with bureaucratic obstacles (it often will be) or that the school will have the necessary resources in that setting. But it is to say that one significant difference between public and private schools is that public schools must provide special services by law. As a taxpayer, make note of the fact that every parent is entitled to some services (e.g., speech and hearing services, testing, etc.) within their school district, even if their child is attending a private school.

Understanding Special Education and Disability Laws That Apply to Public School Education

As one teacher said, "Public schools are nothing if not their acronyms." For therapists not trained as educators, school psychologists, or school social workers, sometimes those acronyms—IDEA, IEP, IST, MDT, FAPE, LRE, FERPA, RTI, and others like them—can seem daunting. Knowing the most relevant of these terms can help therapists better understand the legal backdrop for how children with educational disabilities receive the help they need. Some, if not all, of these components may be familiar to you already, but take time to think about how these regulations might apply to the kids you see in therapy. To review an expanded glossary of terms and regulations that focus on children's rights with regard to disabilities under IDEA, consult Appendix E. Again, private schools are not required to adhere to these regulations, though their policies are likely significantly influenced by them.

IDEA and IEP plans

The system for determining special education services for children in public schools was established in 1975 when Congress passed the Education for All Handicapped Children Act (EAHCA). This was later modified and improved in 1990 through the Individuals with Disabilities Act (IDEA), public law 94-142, which provides children with disabilities the same educational opportunities as students who don't have disabilities. Under IDEA, children with disabilities need specially designed instruction (SDI) that involves one of three considerations: the content (e.g., student is unable to learn math), method (e.g., student hasn't learned to read by the third grade), or delivery (e.g., student can learn but can't learn in large-group instruction). A school's special education services must be consistent with these federal standards in order to receive federal funding.

Under IDEA, children with disabilities are entitled to receive an Individualized Education Program (IEP). IEPs are designed to address a child's unique learning needs and include specific goals applicable to that child. They are also legally binding. IEP teams must be formed and include the child's parent(s), one special education teacher, one regular education teacher, an administrative representative, someone who explains and interprets the child's evaluation (a school psychologist or other designated representative), other school representatives considered relevant, and possibly the child with parental agreement (e.g., an older child should necessarily be involved in transition planning). Parents may bring anyone to the meeting, including a family member or friend, a therapist, or an educational advocate (who may or may not be an attorney). Importantly, parents and school staff are considered equal members of the team. The basics of IEP meetings and the role therapists can play in the process are discussed later in the chapter.

504 Plans

504 Plans are not the same as IEPs. In short, they are accommodations that are made available to children based on the federal civil rights law, Section 504 of the Rehabilitation Act of 1973. This act created the basis for 504 Plans, determining that children with disabilities that interfere with their ability to learn in a general education classroom should not be discriminated against. Therefore, children with disabilities must receive additional support and accommodations in school, allowing them to access education like other students. The 504 Plans include a broader definition of disability than that established by IEPs and also ensures the right to a free, appropriate public education (FAPE). For instance, kids with 504 Plans might be physically impaired and require specialized access to buildings due to mobility issues.

Therapists may not know that some children who qualify for services under a 504 Plan might not qualify for services according to IDEA, which requires an IEP. This occurs when access issues are easily resolved with minor accommodations such as using a ramp to get a student into a gym class. A student with learning issues who requires significant accommodations in the classroom or modifications to the curriculum will usually require an IEP. Furthermore, parents have fewer rights in 504 planning than in the IEP process. Though parents do not have the same safeguards, they can still play an important part in ensuring that their child receives the services they need. Not all schools create 504 Plans, however, and if they don't, they must have documentation on their 504 Plan policies.

Unlike students who have an IEP, there are no set rules for what a 504 Plan should look like. When they exist, they include accommodations that are designed to solve access issues. These might take the form of testing accommodations for kids with ADHD or anxiety, for example, or changes to the classroom environment (e.g., a specific seating arrangement). Typically, school counselors and classroom teachers monitor the student services established under the 504 Plan. (One confusing element of these designations is that there is no reason to have a 504 Plan and an IEP. If the child has an IEP then the child is automatically covered by the parameters of the 504 Plan.)

Identifying and Supporting Kids Needing Special Services

In order to receive services under an IEP, children must be formally evaluated by their school district. Districts must have a screening process in place to identify children who are struggling, as a way of beginning to evaluate whether special education services are needed. Institutionally, schools have a responsibility to identify children with disabilities, a duty that is termed *child find*. Each school must have a system for finding and screening all children living in the area, regardless of status (homeless children, those in the custody of child welfare services, or in independent schools, etc.). This typically occurs through the school's Instructional Support Team (IST) and includes a Response to Intervention (RTI) model of designing evidence-based interventions and evaluating their effectiveness.

If the school recommends that a child be evaluated to determine eligibility, parents must be informed and sign a Permission to Evaluate (PTE)-Consent Form to put the process in motion. Parents can also request that their child be evaluated for services by contacting the school's principal or designated staff person. If the parents request an evaluation, the school must provide a Permission to Evaluate (PTE)-Evaluation Request Form within 10 calendar days of the request. One thing worth noting is that the majority of psychoeducational evaluations are administered by school psychologists employed by schools (Dombrowski, 2015) rather than by outside professionals. An outside professional may be brought in to conduct an independent evaluation (IEE) if there is disagreement about the district's evaluation, something that will be reviewed later in the chapter.

Parents often ask whether schools can refuse to evaluate their child. The answer is yes, but they must follow a process in doing so. Based on their experience with a child, schools have a right to decide that testing isn't necessary, but must do so through a written notice to the parents called a Notice of Recommended Educational Placement (NOREP). Parents can disagree with the decision but will need to either ask for mediation or request a special education hearing to try to compel the district to reconsider the decision (discussed later in the chapter). When schools agree to do an evaluation, they must complete it within 60 days from the time the parents return the signed Permission to Evaluate-Consent Form to the district, no matter how many other children also need evaluations. Make note of the fact that schools are not allowed to place the child on a waiting list for an evaluation. Evaluations are free, including examinations related to physical impairments such as deficits in hearing, vision, and mobility. At the same time, schools are not permitted to evaluate a child for special education services without receiving written permission from the parent. Schools can request a special education hearing officer to order an evaluation for a child or a family court judge can authorize someone other than the birth parent to sign the permission form.

Children attending private schools are also entitled to request testing without cost from the public school district in which they reside, and district policies provide guidelines for how this is carried out. Therapists working with children in private schools whose parents are seeking testing for their child can refer them to their local school district. There they can make a formal request in writing, much as a parent of a public school student would do as described above. Following this action, the same rules and process applies to private schools as they do for public school kids.

Understanding Special Education Evaluations

Once all relevant parties have agreed that a child should be evaluated, a team of professionals at the school will design an evaluation tailored for that child. Usually, but not always, a certified school psychologist does the testing, aligning with the school district's policies and procedures for how testing is conducted. Regardless of who designs the evaluation, they must take into account all areas of difficulty for the individual child, including: (1) health, (2) vision, (3) hearing, (4) social skills and emotional needs including behavior support, (5) general intelligence, (6) academic performance, (7) speech and communication needs, and (8) motor skills. Relevant information can also be provided by former teachers, tutors, therapists, pediatricians, and others. The district should seek releases from the parents so this information can be freely shared. There are no specific tests or number of tests that must be administered. Importantly, testing must take into account language and cultural differences to avoid bias. In instances where children need a bilingual evaluation, the district is required to conduct one.

Parents also have a right to request that their child receive an Independent Educational Evaluation (IEE) at the school district's expense. An IEE may be sought when parents disagree with the school's evaluation and want a second opinion. If the school district agrees to that request from the parent, an IEE will be administered by someone outside the school district. In such cases, the school district pays for the evaluation from an independent practitioner, often someone who specializes in doing these types of evaluations.

Sometimes, parents seek an IEE in preparation for a due process hearing (discussed later in the chapter) and would like recommendations for a more appropriate educational program. In these instances, parents will most likely pay for the testing. Parents can ask the school for the names of independent evaluators who have the credentials to conduct IEEs, though parents are not required to choose a person on that list. Parents can also request information about the criteria that are used to conduct an independent evaluation. The school must consider the findings from an IEE but does not need to follow the recommendations.

If the school district does not agree to fund an IEE, it is required to initiate a due process hearing to defend its evaluation as being appropriate. If the school does not move forward with the hearing request, parents may want to consider various options to help resolve the situation (reviewed later in this chapter).

One important feature of testing conducted in schools is that the Diagnostic and Statistical Manual of Mental Disorders (DSM) or International Statistical Classification of Diseases and Related Health Problems (ICD) categories for diagnosing children are not used. Instead, schools use one of thirteen definitions of disability as defined by IDEA (see Box 12.1). This can be confusing for therapists and independent evaluators since their diagnoses are based on the above-mentioned medical diagnostic categorizations. For example, a pediatrician might diagnose a child with OCD, yet that doesn't mean the child will automatically qualify for special education services as a result. The school psychologist must make a determination that a child is eligible under one of the disability categories. Note that the disability categories are broad and usually encompass any diagnosis that affects a child's success at school. There is also a catchall category called Other Health Impairment (OHI). When children are found ineligible for special education services, the child may be eligible for extra supports under a 504 Plan, as discussed earlier.

Box 12.1:	Disability categories under IDEA

1. **Specific learning disability (SLD)** refers to a nonverbal learning disorder such as dyslexia, dysgraphia, auditory processing disorder, etc.

2. **Other health impairment (OHI)** includes problems that limit a child's strength, energy, or alertness, such as ADHD, anxiety, epilepsy, etc.

3. **Autism spectrum disorder (ASD)** covers a range of symptoms associated mainly with social and communication skills.

4. **Emotional disturbance** refers to problems such as significant anxiety, depression, bipolar disorder, schizophrenia, etc.

5. **Speech or language impairment** refers to a range of communication problems such as voice or language impairment, stuttering, impaired articulation, etc.

6. **Visual impairment, including blindness.** This is not covered if eyewear can correct the problem.

7. **Deafness** refers to those children who have a severe hearing impairment that interferes with their language processing.

8. **Hearing impairment** refers to those children whose hearing loss is not covered by the definition of deafness.

9. **Deaf-blindness** refers to those children who are both visually and hearing impaired and whose communication and other needs cannot be met by deaf and blindness programs.

10. **Orthopedic impairment** refers to any impairment to the body, regardless of the cause, such as cerebral palsy, etc.

11. **Intellectual disability** refers to children with below-average intellectual abilities, such as those with Down syndrome.

12. **Traumatic brain injury** refers to head injuries that are caused by some kind of physical force or accident.

13. **Multiple disabilities** refer to those children who have more than one of the above conditions (such as intellectual disability and deafness) that create severe educational needs.

Early Intervention and Gifted Services

It's important to note that children with special needs are eligible for services starting at birth. Federal law divides special education services into different age ranges: 0 to 3 years, 3 to 5 years, and then school-age services. Services provided before children reach school age are called early intervention services and states have different ways of delivering them. Medical providers are often the people who help coordinate services for children ages 0 to 3 years, and therapists with expertise in early childhood can be involved as well. Services for children ages 3 to 5 years can include a special needs preschool and the full spectrum of educational and related services such as speech, behavior, occupational, and physical therapy. A special education attorney or advocate can also help with securing preschool services for children ages 3 to 5 years, especially during the transition to kindergarten and the school-age services provided thereafter.

Many states provide services for children who qualify as gifted, even though education experts and states differ with regard to the definition of giftedness. Services for gifted children are governed by state law since the federal IDEA does not provide special education services for gifted children. However, there are students who are what we call twice exceptional—in states with gifted services, these children can be both gifted and eligible for special education services. For example, a child may be gifted and diagnosed with autism, dyslexia, or socioemotional problems that make the child eligible for special education services. In other words, the federal government recognizes that gifted students can be IDEA eligible; high IQ or high academic achievement does not disqualify a student needing special education services. When considering the needs of gifted children, therapists should familiarize themselves with state laws and their application in local schools.

Where Therapists Fit into the Testing Process

Therapists may be invited into the testing process at any point along the way. Some of the ways that therapists can be involved include:

- Helping parents explore whether testing would be useful
- Making a recommendation for testing
- Collaborating with the person doing the testing (whether at the school or not) to share observations of the child

- Helping to implement testing recommendations as they relate to the work the therapist is doing with the family and child

- Testing the child if this is part of your scope of practice

Sometimes, families ask therapists to review or redo previous testing in the hope that, as objective evaluators, they will come to a different conclusion (a process that is separate from an IEE). In the latter case, state regulations vary with regard to how much weight schools will give to such evaluations, so be sure to check out your state's regulations to better inform the parent of the limits of what you or an independent evaluator can offer based on educational qualifications. As one therapist with expertise in this area said, "Psychologists can make all the recommendations they want and the school can say, 'Yes, no problem.' Or they can choose not to. It's their decision."

Sometimes, families ask therapists to review or redo previous testing to either directly confirm or challenge the conclusions of the school district. In the latter case, state regulations vary with regard to how much weight schools will give to evaluations by outside providers. Nonetheless, outside opinions can be helpful to parents to confirm the district's conclusions or document what the district did not get right. Keep in mind that the school district is always responsible for providing a free and appropriate education (FAPE) for all children, so if the therapist reveals a need that the district has not addressed, the district ignores that conclusion at the risk that a hearing officer will later determine it should have taken the perspective into consideration. As one educational lawyer said, "It always helps to have an outside opinion that confirms a parent's concern. If it confirms the district's perspective, then at least the parent knows he or she can go with the district on that point."

At a minimum, therapists can avoid becoming involved counterproductively. Several school representatives spoke about therapists who recommended that the school test their students prematurely, from the school's perspective. With visible frustration, one school psychologist said that a therapist "jumped the gun" by recommending that a parent seek testing for her child without fully understanding the how, why, or when, of testing. Nor had the therapist sought information about interventions that might have been put in place and if so, whether they were effective, a minimal first step before requesting testing for special education services. The therapist had apparently listened to a parent's concerns and agreed that there was no harm in requesting an evaluation, yet the therapist agreed without acquiring sufficient information to come to this decision. The school psychologist said that their instructional support team would have preferred to proceed along a more incremental path, working with the family and therapist to assess the situation together and, perhaps, plan interventions accordingly before a request for testing was made. As it was, the mother was puzzled and unhappy when the request for testing was denied, since she'd expected that the request would be met in the affirmative.

When testing is being considered, therapists need to explore with children and families what interventions have already been implemented at school and the effectiveness of the interventions. As one school administrator said, "Supporting a parent's request for testing that is not supported by the school can lead to mistrust between the school and parents." She added, "Oftentimes, parents to do not realize that 'testing' can lead to special education and then are upset at the labels that testing leads to or the pull-out services that follow."

IEP Meetings: The Basics

Within 30 days of a child being found eligible for special education as a result of an evaluation, the parents and children ages 14 years and over must be invited to an IEP meeting for the purpose of establishing an educational program that best supports the child's needs. Prior to the IEP meeting, the school's multidisciplinary team (MDT) should have reviewed the evaluation results to approve or disapprove the conclusions or recommendations.

The school may create a draft IEP to review at the meeting, or the team will develop an IEP during the meeting that parents (and older children) can sign or take home to review and sign later, though it is advantageous for the school to have a draft prepared and reviewed in advance of the meeting. Throughout the IEP meeting, parents or anyone the parents bring to the meeting can raise questions as well as suggest changes to the draft IEP, since the purpose of the meeting is to produce the best possible plan for the child. It's important for parents to read and understand every page of the draft IEP and, if there are disagreements or confusion, ask for a second meeting or sign only those parts of the IEP with which they agree. However, keep in mind that, for a revised or new IEP, services can only begin once the parents give consent. In this regard, it helps if parents are able to decide as promptly as possible so they are not seen as unreasonably delaying services. IEP meeting fundamentals include the following:

- Specific goals and action plans must be established based on the testing, as well as a timely way of assessing progress.

- The meeting will be facilitated by an administrator and include the child's parent(s), one special education teacher, one regular education teacher, someone who explains and interprets the child's evaluation, other relevant school representatives and, with parental permission, the child (older children involved in transition planning should be present).

- Meetings have to be provided at a date and time that is convenient to the parent(s). Alternatively, parents can attend the meeting by phone, but being there in person is recommended.

- Parents can ask that specific people be present (e.g., if the child is being bullied in the gym class, the gym teacher might be invited).

- Parents and school staff are equal members of the team.

- Parents have the right to see the child's records.

- Parents must sign off on the plan for it to be implemented.

- Parents can ask for a meeting at any time (the same is true for 504 Plan meetings), and the school has to honor the request in a reasonable amount of time.

- There must be at least one IEP meeting each year.

- If the school has made reasonable efforts to include the parents and they refuse or can't attend, the school can conduct an IEP meeting without a parent present.

The Therapist's Role in IEP or 504 Plan Meetings

The school and legal representatives with whom I spoke all recommended that therapists attend IEP meetings whenever possible. One educational attorney enthusiastically said, "If [the therapist] can go to the meeting, that would be amazing." A school psychologist made an equally compelling comment when he said, "An ounce of prevention is worth a pound of therapy. Attending one IEP meeting can save you a boatload of meetings later." Since therapists working with kids and families may have the opportunity to participate in IEP or 504 Plan meetings, what is our role and how might we be most helpful?

Much of what applies to the therapist's role in family–school meetings outside the special education process (explored in Chapter 8) applies to IEP and 504 Plan meetings, yet with some additional features and expectations corresponding to the obligations associated with the kinds of services the child is receiving. By knowing what to expect, the therapist can better judge how to effectively participate as a member of the IEP or 504 Plan team.

Preparing for the meeting

Therapists can help parents prepare for a meeting by reviewing goals they have for their child and what might get in the way of achieving them. Reviewing what to expect can be accomplished through any number of therapeutic strategies including role playing; coaching; and identifying what might trigger anxiety, fear, or anger in the meeting—and what to do about it. Having reviewed goals and expectations, therapists can take that proverbial deep breath with the parents (and the child) before walking into the school that day. When helping to prepare families for IEP or 504 Plan meetings, therapists can:

- Review the child's records and encourage the parents to review them as well.

- Help the parents clarify and prioritize their concerns in sessions prior to the meeting.

- Discuss practical solutions with the parents before the meeting, solutions that fit within the IEP or 504 Plan frameworks.

- Explore any tensions or disagreements between the parents or the parents and child to maximize the effectiveness of the meeting.

- Consider reaching out to the school (with parental permission) before the meeting to seek or share relevant information.

- Help parents understand that sometimes the child's problems are significant and can't be resolved in one IEP or 504 Plan meeting. It may be necessary to meet more than once to determine an IEP.

- Accept that, as therapists, we are not expected to know all the ins and outs of the rules and regulations, but we may be able to help make the meeting a successful one.

Participating in the meeting

As in other family–school meetings, therapists can be helpful in a number of ways when participating in IEP and 504 Plan meetings:

Therapists can help serve as unofficial mediators between the parents and school, possibly salvaging a conversation that takes an unproductive turn. One therapist said that he helps support parents who are displaying signs of anger or anxiety by first acknowledging these feelings, saying "I can see you're feeling uncomfortable here" and then finding ways to help them reenter the conversation more productively. In an effort to bring the two sides together, he will do the same for the school, acknowledging what it is doing to support the child. As one therapist said, "Sometimes, I can connect to the school when the parent can't." This way, it's possible to unstick conversations through acknowledging the good things that people are doing on both sides of a potentially widening fault line.

Simply by being present and listening, therapists can learn a lot: how the child is seen by the school, the pressures school representatives may be experiencing, and what works to support effective collaboration. As one school psychologist said, "Therapists are less threatening than lawyers, and can do a lot as a result." In particular, therapists can help identify who's there for the child at school— which person steps in to offer suggestions, expresses affirmative thoughts about the child, continues to reach out to the parents, and so on. Another therapist said that, "In these meetings I do more listening, hear about what the school has tried, and get everything on the table before making suggestions."

Therapists can offer new ideas to help solve a problem. An experienced therapist said that by offering a concrete suggestion "It can make it tougher for the walls to go up." She spoke of how she might say, "There's one thought I just had. It's something we tried in another school and it was helpful to the child there." Such statements can normalize a situation, highlighting the fact that other kids have struggled similarly and solutions have been found.

Therapists can look closely at the data provided by the district documenting the child's progress. If data is missing or unclear, therapists can ask someone to provide additional information or clarify what is available (e.g., reading or math levels). Though most therapists are not educators and may not have experience working with such information, therapists can use common sense. And if the data or related goals do not make sense, the designated school representative can rewrite them so everyone on the team understands what they are working toward, including the child and parents.

Therapists can think "big picture," as one school psychologist said. They can ask questions about the child's future: is she heading to college or vocational or trade school? How might current plans be maintained over the summer? Looking ahead should be part of all IEP and 504 Plan meetings with older kids, certainly, and therapists can ask questions that move the conversation toward realistic goals and planning.

Therapists can help parents participate fully in the discussion, encouraging them to present their perspective and advocate for their child. When the child is present, therapists can support their self-advocacy, as well.

Therapists can summarize plans that were made and suggest that they be put in writing, if someone else has not picked up this responsibility in the meeting. Therapists can also see that the plans are then distributed to all the participants. Therapists can also suggest that everyone review the plan in the meeting rather than find issues with it later when they aren't able to jointly discuss them. Similarly, therapists can pull out their calendars to schedule a follow-up meeting, if unresolved issues stand in the way of coming to an agreement. Part of the planning consists of therapists informing others of their availability after the meeting. "Just call me," is what one therapist says at the close of every IEP meeting she attends.

Therapists can highlight the goodwill and perhaps the good feelings people have at the beginning, during, and at the end of the meeting, acknowledging that everyone is there to help and doing the best they can. Helping to identify common ground, co-constructing a team, and adding to a sense of hopefulness is a role therapists can not only play in their offices but also in meetings at school.

Therapists can identify significant problems in classroom placement. As one therapist said, "Sometimes, I might go in and say [to myself] 'I wouldn't have my kid here.' Now the parent really needs an educational advocate." Acknowledging that a situation is unworkable can help parents regroup and seek additional help and guidance from those with legal (or other) expertise, a topic that will be reviewed next.

Considerations Regarding Due Process Hearings

There are times when families and schools do not come to an agreement about the educational plan for a child. In those cases, the family may consider requesting a due process hearing in which the family, the school, and relevant witnesses present their views to a hearing officer in a formal setting with attorneys representing both parties. Parents may also choose one of five other options that may or may not involve an educational attorney.

Options to consider before requesting a due process hearing

Before deciding to request a due process hearing, there are both informal and formal ways to respond to a disagreement, listed below as five options. Parents can discuss these options with a therapist or may decide to seek the advice of an educational advocate when considering which is the best option.

Option 1: **Meet informally at the school.** School representatives can meet with the family informally to see if they can find common ground. This does not involve the introduction of legal representatives (on either side) and it's possible that a therapist might join the family to help explore what steps to take.

Option 2: **Request an Independent Educational Evaluation (IEE).** The school or family can ask for an IEE in order to gain an objective perspective on the problem and recommendations for services or placement. As mentioned before, the independent evaluator has no loyalty to the family or school. These evaluations are usually thorough and detailed.

Option 3: **Seek the support from the state department of education.** The family can seek help through a Facilitated IEP Meeting where a trained and unbiased facilitator assists in finding a resolution. Families can check with their school district to see if this is an option and, if so, can make a request in writing.

Option 4: **Request mediation.** The school or family can request mediation. The department of education provides an independent mediator to help resolve the conflict. Again, a letter must be written requesting this service.

Option 5: **File a complaint with the state department of education.** The family can file a compliant with the state department of education rather than request a due process hearing. This occurs when the family thinks that there has been a violation of state or federal special education law. It requires a letter to be written within 1 year of the possible violation.

When parents request a due process hearing

There are times when families decide to formally appeal a decision by requesting a due process hearing. At the hearing, parents or a special education lawyer present(s) their case, and the school district is expected to make a decision about the complaint. Like other requests, it must be filed in writing with the agency responsible for providing such hearings. The family and school are required to attend a mandatory meeting before the due process hearing to try to resolve the issue. If you are working with a family that has decided to formally appeal a decision, encourage the family to seek guidance from a special education attorney who is an expert on the regulations surrounding this decision. Sometimes, they may be able to avoid the due process hearing and negotiate an amicable resolution to the dispute.

The Place for a Special Education Attorney or an Educational Advocate

There are a number of reasons why parents might seek help from a special education lawyer or educational advocate, someone who can step in to represent the interests of students under IDEA and Section 504 of the Rehabilitation Act. Sometimes, a child is not making sufficient progress over a long period of time, or the child has received a significant number of suspensions, detentions, or disciplinary actions that seem punitive rather than helpful. At other times, a child may be struggling in school and the mandated services to which the child is entitled are not being provided. Or a parent's poor literacy skills or serious circumstantial problems prevent the parent from being able to advocate effectively. And, sometimes, parents' continuously negative and confrontational interactions with school staff lead them to conclude that it's time to contact an educational advocate for support and advice. As one lawyer said, "Often by the time a family seeks the help of an advocate, [the parents] are in no position to argue on behalf of their child."

Whatever the family's circumstances, you may be in a position to explore this issue with the family and recommend that the family seeks the help of an educational lawyer or advocate (see Appendix F). If so, encourage parents to be sure they are hiring an educational advocate who has experience and training in this area. Not all advocates are lawyers—some are former teachers, psychologists, social workers, special education administrators, and so on—and no certification authority exists for advocates. In most states, an educational advocate must also be a lawyer if the family needs legal representation in the form of a due process hearing. A skilled educational advocate may also be helpful but cannot pursue legal remedies that a lawyer has at his or her disposal.

Under IDEA, parents have the right to have a special education attorney represent them throughout the special education process, up to and including due process hearings and appeals. Keep in mind that this is a complex and technical area of practice and families will benefit greatly from having professional guidance. If it turns out the parent and attorney bring a claim and the hearing results in the parents' favor, under certain circumstances the attorney fees are paid for by the school district. This is a valuable tool for families, one that the IDEA makes available to try to level the playing field, so families without means can secure legal counsel along with those who have the resources to pay the fees themselves. In these instances, attorneys take the case contingently and, if they win, the school district pays for their services. Make note of the fact that special education advocates who are not attorneys are not covered by the IDEA.

One important thing to keep in mind is that there are some inherent tensions between educational advocates and school systems. Once parents hire a legal advocate, schools also have to enlist their own legal representation. As one advocate said, "the relationship [between the family and school] becomes more strained" once an advocate becomes involved. One way to reduce tension is for parents to select an advocate who not only knows the legal area well but also is a team player.

In some cases, children's unmet educational needs are so chronic or intense, or the relationship between the family and school is so frayed, that bringing in an advocate is not only an option to consider, but a necessary choice. Regarding these situations, one advocate said that, "It's wrong to wait until the very end to call an advocate," given the nature of the advice and services they can provide. Even though some of what educational attorneys and advocates do overlaps with a therapist's role—offering support to families seeking help, attending family–school meetings, advocating for the child—their expertise allows advocates to provide services that go beyond what most therapists can offer. The following list represents the range of services educational advocates and attorneys can offer.

- Advising and informing parents about their educational rights
- Meeting with parents to review school records and other relevant evaluations of the child
- Helping parents prepare for a number of different types of school meetings [Student Study Team (SST), IEP, Section 504, expulsion hearings, etc.], as well as accompanying them to the meetings
- Assisting parents in preparing an IEP for their child
- Collaborating and consulting with others who know and work with the child
- Helping parents seek reimbursement for outside services and school placement
- Referring families to a special education attorney (if the advocate is not one already) to negotiate an amicable resolution or file a due process legal proceeding when needed; an attorney brings expertise to the table that others cannot, such as being able to represent the child and family at due process hearings.

Though families can hire and pay for attorneys privately, educational attorneys can be found through small practices and educational and civil rights legal organizations (see Appendix F). As already mentioned, many attorneys take cases on a contingency basis.

In sum, special education attorneys and educational advocates can provide a number of important services to children and families.

Kids with Special Needs in Private Schools

There are times when a school district may place children with disabilities in a private school for children with disabilities at the school district's expense. This occurs only if the district cannot provide an appropriate education in the child's local school. Kids who need such specialized private school placement may be placed in a private school that is either licensed and approved or not approved by the school district. School districts may have a list of approved private schools to recommend to parents. For approved schools, the school's tuition is covered fully or in part by the school district. Keep in mind that when children are placed in a private school, all of the activities surrounding the maintenance of the IEP or 504 Plan will be maintained by the school district. In other words, the school district is still the agency in charge.

Sometimes, school districts will approve placement of a child in a nonapproved private school. Districts vary in their willingness and ability to pay for these placements. Due process hearings are required to get the district to pay for them. Sometimes, parents and the district can agree to split the cost of tuition.

Therapists working with kids in public schools whose specialized education needs cannot be met in the school district need to be aware of the private school option for students with disabilities. Therapists can encourage families or seek information themselves from the school district regarding the private school options that exist. In one case, a child in a large, bustling elementary school whose anxiety was so severe that she wasn't able to participate in class activities was placed in a local approved private school at the district's expense. The school had a small but robust student support team; classes with no more than 12 students made it possible for the therapist, support team, teachers, and family to help the child build up skills for managing her anxiety. Though progress was slow, the child eventually learned how to participate in classroom activities, ask for help, and, in short, become a student again. Once she reached middle school age, she returned to the public school system, where each grade was divided into smaller units of instruction that served her well. This is in keeping with the central goal of helping the child transition back to classrooms with typical peers whenever possible.

There is one other option for private school placement that is sometimes pursued by families who have determined that their child needs specialized education that the school district cannot provide. If parents can meet the legal requirements at a due process hearing, they have the right under IDEA to enroll their child in a private school themselves and seek reimbursement for the school's charges. The bill is not always reimbursed, however. In these cases, it is important for the parents to consult with a special education attorney in advance, since parents must provide prior notice and meet a certain legal standard for reimbursement.

It's also worth noting that private schools that are not paid for by the school district are not required by law to provide testing services for their students, though some schools do have in-house psychologists who administer testing.

When testing is not provided by a school, referrals for testing are made to outside practitioners or, as mentioned earlier, to the local school district. When outside testing is recommended for a student, private schools often draw from their list of recommended clinicians outside the school setting, clinicians whose work they respect and trust, the cost of whose services are covered by the family, not the school. They may be clinicians who practice privately, work in group practices, or are part of a clinic or hospital setting.

REVIEWING THE BASICS

When it comes to working with kids who have special needs, therapists can play an important role in helping families navigate the potentially daunting systems that provide all children with a free and appropriate education. Though it's difficult to know all the ins and outs of the relevant laws and regulations without formal legal training, there are a number of important points to keep in mind that can help you help families directly, help them advocate for themselves or seek the help of an educational advocate when needed:

- All public schools (including charter schools) must conform to the tenets of IDEA and Section 504 and create IEPs for children with special education needs, though schools vary in how they implement these policies due to factors like size, available resources, school culture, etc.

- Either schools or parents can initiate the testing of a child they think might be struggling, though parents must give consent if the school initiates it. The school can deny a parent's request for testing if the school deems it inappropriate.

- Parents are entitled to an Independent Educational Evaluation (IEE) if the school denies their request for testing or if they want a second, more objective opinion.

- Private schools do not have to guarantee appropriate educational environments for all children, but kids who attend private schools can access some services (e.g., testing, speech and language therapy, occupational therapy) through the school district in which they live.

- Therapists can help families explore the need for testing and, if qualified, conduct the testing themselves. Therapists should attempt to collaborate with the school beforehand to maximize what can be learned about a child's functioning in that setting.

■ Once testing reveals that a child is entitled to special education services, therapists can play an important role in IEP meetings by helping to set and implement realistic goals for the child and family.

■ If a family and school cannot come together and agree on an educational plan for a child, the parents can consider hiring an educational lawyer or educational advocate to represent their interests.

■ Therapists can work to help build connections between the family and school when disagreements arise by reminding each party of the other's good intentions and remaining focused on the best interests of the child.

CHAPTER 13

Conclusion

This book rests on a fundamental premise—that the school is a vital component in the lives of children and their families, and the most effective treatment of children's problems calls for a therapist to be school-savvy. As described in preceding chapters, there is a range of tools and approaches at your disposal. Based on the nature of your relationship with a school and the problem at hand, you may decide to assess a child's functioning by talking with a teacher, observing the child directly, recommending that the child be tested, attending a family–school meeting, or engaging in some other sort of ongoing collaboration with the school. It can be tempting to look for a consistent, well-defined role to play in a school's ecosystem. However, as explored in this book, you can see that it's not always so simple. The role you play may be different in every school and may evolve dramatically even within the same school, depending on the nature of the work you're doing. Ultimately, you may find the strategies you use less important than the mindset and spirit with which you proceed. What you think and believe to be true about schools will determine, in good measure, the relationships you have with the people inside them.

School-savvy therapists ask the sorts of questions that reveal a deep underlying respect for each particular school they encounter. Neither overly solicitous, nor presumptuous, the fundamental stance is always, "What do I need to know about your school in order to help this child?" When working with schools, you can foster hope and empathy by sensitively providing relevant information about the child and family, which will often bring new ideas to the table. You can promote self-advocacy on the part of parents and kids, knowing when to step back and let them take over. One of the most valuable qualities you can offer is the desire to harness the goodwill present in most situations. Simply communicating a sense of gratitude to those who are trying their best in the face of difficult circumstances can be, in itself, a lasting intervention.

Widening Your Scope of Interest and Influence

Part of developing a school-savvy mindset is to constantly seek out opportunities to educate yourself and apply your skills in ways that can make substantive contributions to the children and families you see as well as to the schools in your community. Consider becoming involved in programs, organizations, and partnerships that are linked to schools, some of which are identified below.

Offer your services to schools in the community. Many schools can benefit from support provided by local mental health professionals. You can offer to give presentations, workshops, or consultations to parents, faculty, and kids. You might offer services focused on particular *issues*, for example, homework, stress awareness and resilience, anxiety, bullying prevention, addiction, and social media. Or you might offer services focused around particular *groups*, for example, teachers facing a school crisis, families recovering from a natural disaster, and faculty and staff needing trauma-informed care.

Learn about the resources that are available in your local schools and communities. All schools have some resources available for families, even those that are the poorest. Federal, state and local funds support programs to improve student achievement and social-emotional learning, enhance parental involvement and parenting skills, prevent bullying, provide enrichment for English learners, maintain school-based health centers, establish after school programs and more. Some schools are the recipients of private charities and grants, as well. Therapists who are familiar with such programs can inform the families they see and the schools they work with, as well as share the information with colleagues.

Participate in school-community partnerships. Though hard to fund, many schools partner with organizations in the community, linking schools to programs and services that may be incorporated into the school environment. Schools partner with local businesses, arts venues, nonprofits, garden programs, libraries, scientific organizations, museums, colleges and universities, hospitals and clinics, and so on. For example, a public elementary school in Philadelphia partners with literally dozens of local agencies and businesses, including a local school of music that provides an artist in residence to teach violin lessons to the students. Therapists may be able to join in such partnerships, offering time, skills, and services in a collective effort to strengthen school-community ties.

Become involved with nationwide projects and activities that support schools. To help effect change at the broader, system-wide level, think about becoming involved in grassroots efforts or far-reaching programs on gun control, suicide prevention, school violence, school funding, and so on. Therapists can join with existing groups (e.g., parents, teachers, or policy-makers) to organize around shared concerns.

Seek support and collaboration from your professional organizations. Professional organizations can provide ongoing consultation and collaboration opportunities, not only to protect against misguided (if well-intentioned) actions and burnout, but also to enrich one's own sense of purpose in the field. For therapists who work with children who have school problems, there may be no better way to expand one's own field of vision than to collaborate with other professionals working on similar issues. Twenty-five years ago, for example, several therapists in the Philadelphia area came together to form a local organization, Specialists of Schools (SOS), creating a network of support for those who work with schools in the Delaware Valley. Today, it has over 300 members who come together to share resources and knowledge.

Looking Ahead

In his remarkable book *The Hidden Life of Trees*, Peter Wohlleben (2016) describes old beech forests where there are vast networks of trees—old and young, sick and healthy—that actively communicate and support one another when facing adversity, be it disease, insect invasions, drought, or other hardships. He writes, "A tree can only be as strong as the forest that surrounds it." As you go on and work with schools, it might be useful to think of yourself and your clients as part of a similarly vast network of relationships. Children—and therapists—are only as strong as the support figures that surround them. Embrace your role as an integral member of school communities.

The risk of writing a book comprised of dos and don'ts is that people will read it and be nervous about doing something wrong, embarrassing, or simply off base. Try to hold that anxiety at bay. Instead, I challenge you to let these ideas percolate. See where they take you. One of the things that happens when you give yourself permission to reach out to schools is that you start thinking more expansively and creatively. Add to this work. Talk about it with others. Help strengthen your own particular forest.

One of several Merriam-Webster definitions of the word "guideline" states that it is "a cord or rope to aid a passer over a difficult point, or to permit retracing a course." The guidelines in this book are offered with that spirit in mind. It is hoped that this collaborative framework can help guide you through difficult stretches and also allow you to retrace your steps as you reach out to schools over many years. We can use these tethers to lead children to healthier and more prosperous roads ahead, ones in which they feel a sense of purpose, self-determination, and belonging and, eventually, ones that allow them to move on from therapy. Sometimes, all of this begins with simply picking up the phone and calling a school.

APPENDICES

A BRIEF OVERVIEW OF SCHOOL TYPES AND PEDAGOGIES

Knowledge about different school types and pedagogies is helpful for working with schools effectively. The purpose of this appendix is to offer a brief look at the different types of schools and models of instruction so that you will be able to understand how the school you're working with fits into a larger context, and how the child you are seeing fits into a particular school. When therapists have done the work to understand the ins and outs of the schools in their area, they are much better equipped to help the families and children who come to their offices.

Types of Schools

Public Schools

Public schools educate the majority of children in America. Every school-age child in the United States has a legal right to a public school education, and every child's home is in a catchment area for a neighborhood school. Public schools do not charge tuition and are governed by a wide array of local, state, and federal regulations. Thus, public schools are inherently bureaucratic and complex institutions, especially in large or urban school districts. They can also be underfunded and subject to changes, both structural and pedagogical, based on political, social, or economic trends.

Therapists don't always realize that the local governance of schools means that policies may vary significantly from community to community and state to state. School boards are elected or appointed to oversee local public school districts, and the board determines school policies and practices. For example, every therapist is aware that schooling is compulsory in the United States, but some may not be aware that in some states, students can leave high school as early as 14 years of age, with parental permission. Other states require that students remain in school until the 18 years of age. These differences matter when considering options for students who are struggling and may want to opt out of formal education.

In general, public schools tend to be more racially and ethnically diverse than well-off private schools, especially in urban areas, where many immigrants reside (Musu–Gillette et al., 2016). These schools have more students who speak English as a second language, and often a more racially diverse faculty. On average, public school teachers are paid higher salaries than private school teachers and receive better benefits (Allegretto & Tojerow, 2014). In most places, public school teachers must adhere to state certification standards. Class sizes are typically larger and there may be more classes in each grade, depending on the density of the population. Public schools generally provide a wider range of student support services, both academic and health related (Ravitch, 2016). They are required to do this by federal law, which means that therapists may have more staff and resources to call upon when working with public schools.

Many of us see children from a wide range of economic backgrounds. It is important to be aware of the larger issues facing schools in our nation, because they directly affect the children we see. For example, policy-makers, educators, politicians, and others often claim that there are two public school systems—one in wealthy suburban and urban school districts, and the other in poor urban and rural school districts. Since public schools base their admissions on district boundaries, parents with financial means often choose where they live based on the boundaries of a high-achieving public school system. As a result, wealthier parents have much more control over finding the right school for their children to prepare them academically, socially, and, ultimately, vocationally. In addition, homeschooling or cyber-schooling options are growing, raising new issues around instructional design and the latest technologies.

When seen from an international perspective, even our better American public schools often lag behind those of other advanced industrialized nations in terms of learning assessments (Agasisti & Zoido, 2018). Furthermore, public schools are often at the forefront of national educational policy experiments such as the recent creation of the Common Core curriculum. When this curriculum was introduced, many children experienced stress due to the higher expectations and standards (Saeki, Pendergast, Segool, & Nathaniel, 2015). Therapists who understand some of the intricacies of public school trends and policies can more easily and immediately adapt to the specific problems that their clients experience.

Magnet Schools

Magnet schools are a type of public school that emerged in the 1960s. They offer specialized curricula for elementary, middle, and high school students across the country. Each magnet school tends to have a particular curricular focus, such as STEM (science, technology, engineering, and math), the performing arts, technical education, or languages. As with public schools, they are free for any child living in the school district, though most require a lottery system for admission and some require an entrance exam, interview, or audition. Therapists can encourage parents to seek information about magnet school options and their application process through the school district, including the lottery application time frame.

Like public schools, magnet schools are publicly funded and have to adhere to state requirements. It's important to note that magnet schools were a response to the problem of racial segregation in public schools. It was thought that by giving parents some choice in the school their child attended, educational inequities could be reduced. Today, the number of students in magnet schools nationwide (2.5 million) is slightly higher than the number of students in charter schools (about 2.2 million) (Berends, 2015; Polikoff & Hardaway, 2017).

Charter Schools

Many therapists are less familiar with charter schools, given that they've only existed since 1992 (Maranto, 2018). As the proverbial new kid on the block, they are also the subject of considerable controversy in school districts across the country. Some view charter schools as a way to repair a damaged public school system, while others think that they drain money from public schools.

Charter schools are public schools that have been created through a charter agreement between the community and the school. They are less dependent on the regulations and day-to-day supervision of the public school system. Thus, charter schools do not have to comply with district or state regulations, including testing. Charter schools do have to meet a set of mandated standards. They have been started by educators, parents, community leaders, school boards (local and state), colleges and universities, community groups, and in some cases, by national companies or statewide nonprofit organizations.

Each school is responsible for its own charter, which is based on a contract that outlines the school's principles, goals, governing structure, and system of accountability. In fact, one of the most important claims by charter school advocates is that they offer increased accountability—if the school fails to meet its standards, it can be closed down. Charter schools vary in their educational mission and assume many forms, in part because the competitive process of obtaining a charter requires them to differentiate themselves according to content and focus. Thus, there may be charter schools focused on the environment, bilingual education, the sciences, technology, and multiculturalism to name just a few. Like their public school counterparts, charter schools educate children in the core subjects of science, math, reading, and social studies, and they typically provide instruction in music, physical education, art, and other subjects.

Generally, charter schools require a significant level of parent involvement. Because of their relative autonomy, they can run a longer school day than private or public schools. If students want to play a sport or be involved with club activities, they are eligible to use public school resources that may not be available at their charter school. This is an important resource, as therapists often recommend afterschool activities for the children or teens they are treating. Therapists need to remember that charter schools are public schools, and that according to the law students have the same equity-based educational resources available to them that they would have in a traditional public school.

Gaining admission to a charter school is very different from the simple registration process of traditional public schools and can be stressful for parents and children. It often involves a lottery system that by law can't place restrictions on who is eligible to enter the lottery. The lottery system is meant to prevent corruption and favoritism and keep the charter system fair and democratic. Often there are many more students in the lottery system than any charter school can accommodate. Families can face keen disappointment when their child isn't selected. Where there are enough seats, students are generally admitted on a first come, first serve basis and, as in public schools, they cannot be discriminated against in the admission process.

Demographically, research has shown that over half of charter school students qualify for free or reduced lunches, and this is a common proxy for the number of low-income or "at risk" students enrolled in a given school (Epple, Romano, & Zimmer, 2016). Charters operate primarily in cities, especially those with low-rated school systems. Charter schools are often started with high hopes of improving education for the kids who need it most (Cookson, 2018). The dream of improving education is important but often comes up against a complicated funding system. Each state determines the level of funding for charter schools and, generally speaking, charter schools receive less funding per pupil than their local public school counterparts, though charter schools often raise private funds to expand their resources.

Private and Independent Schools

Roughly 10% of U.S. students attend private schools, also called independent schools, and this number includes religiously affiliated schools (Broughman, Restig, & Peterson, 2017). Many parents debate the relative value of private versus public school education. Naturally, families with greater means have greater potential access to and interest in private education However, there are many parents—irrespective of means and wealth—who extol the virtues of public school education as one way to provide children with real-world experience and potentially greater exposure to social and cultural diversity. In addition, some public schools offer more or different extracurricular activities—another attractive element. For most families, however, this debate doesn't even surface, since they don't have the means to pay private school tuition or may not be aware of scholarship opportunities that exist in private schools.

Private schools are generally funded by tuition fees, endowments, and fundraising efforts, though some schools also receive select, publicly funded benefits, such as textbooks or school bus support. Private schools actively seek money from alumni, businesses, and community organizations. Finally, in areas with a state-funded voucher system, some low-tuition private schools are primarily funded by vouchers from the state. It's important to realize that not all private schools are wealthy and well-funded schools; some are struggling and quite bare-bones.

However, because they are autonomous and do not receive tax benefits, private schools are able to offer curricula that have few regulations mandated by state and federal standards. For example, private schools can ignore the state and national testing regulations to which public schools must adhere. Their teachers don't have to "teach to the test," as the saying goes. As a result, private schools can offer students a specialized learning environment. They can build curricula around specific content areas, around religious ideas and values, and sometimes, around ambitious expectations of academic achievement. Private schools may also establish their own criteria for admission, enrollment requirements, and teacher qualifications. Private schools are usually accredited through an independent organization, or by a regional authority (NAIS, 2018). Accreditation ensures that the school meets regional or national standards set by a group of peers. It also ensures that the school's administration and academic programs undergo review by an outside group at least once every few years. Since the climate and culture of a private school is often attractive (small class size, etc.), private school teachers are often willing to accept a lower salary than teachers in public schools.

Faith-Based and Parochial Schools

Many of the private schools in the United States were founded by faith-based institutions, with the intention of incorporating religious principles and teachings into the educational foundation of their parishioners' lives. The Roman Catholic Church and early Quaker groups formed the first faith-based schools, which laid the groundwork for a wide range of educational institutions that now represent the diversity of religious beliefs—Protestant, Roman Catholic, Jewish, Muslim, and more. Students in faith-based schools make up roughly 5% of school-aged children in this country (Broughman, Restig, & Peterson, 2017).

Roman Catholic parochial schools make up the largest share of faith-based schools (nearly half of the five million private school students). The word *parochial* derives from the word *parish*, since early Roman Catholic schools were based in parishes. Today, not all parochial schools are attached to or associated with a local parish, but when they are, they're typically open to all children in that parish as well as children outside the parish. Most funding for parochial schools comes from donations to the parish or church. In the first half of the 20th century, Roman Catholic school systems modeled themselves on the expectations and curricula of public schools, and even today they typically use the same models. However, students attending a parochial school are expected to fully engage in the religious life of the school, which includes attending religious services during the school day and completing faith-based coursework that reinforces the school's values and beliefs (Waasdorp et al., 2018).

Other Christian schools, also privately founded and funded, represent many denominations including, though not limited to, the following: Quaker, Lutheran, Episcopal, Conservative Protestant denominations, Mennonites, Church of the Latter Day Saints, Seventh Day Adventists, and the Eastern Orthodox Church. In short, there are private schools representing most, if not all, religious groups in the United States. Certain faith-based schools (such as Orthodox Jewish schools) have grown substantially in recent decades (Schick, 2014).

Special Education Schools (Public and Private)

A special education school serves children whose needs cannot be met in a traditional classroom setting. Disabilities that require a special education environment might include any one of the following: autism, blindness, hearing or physical impairments, emotional and behavioral disorders, or cognitive and intellectual impairment. According to the Individuals with Disabilities Act (IDEA), public school systems are required to provide the needed educational services, either through a specialized private school or in a public school setting (see Chapter 12).

Nearly all public schools offer onsite special education services. Special education schools (public or private) offer these services in a separate school or section of a school. Typically, these institutions are small, and the ratio of students to teachers is much lower than that of a mainstream classroom. This ratio is one of the key reasons why parents seek out this more targeted approach to learning and find special education schools attractive, if not essential.

Special education schools are often oriented around a specific type of disability so that the curriculum and facilities can focus on very particular needs.

For example, a school for children with cerebral palsy in Philadelphia utilizes wide ramps rather than stairs to accommodate the students' wheelchairs, allowing them to be more independent. In addition, the school has a specialized nursing staff available to meet students' medical needs, even urgent ones.

There are special education schools in every state (e.g., APSESNJ, 2018), though the demand is often greater than the availability. Finding an appropriate school can be enormously time-consuming for parents. Therapists who work with children whose problems may necessitate going to a special school need to learn about or collaborate with those who know the different options in their area, understanding their missions, resources, staff, and facilities. Once a family identifies a school that might be a good fit for their child, they have to navigate the process of admission, including collaborating with their local public school district. As therapists, we can help the family and child through what can often be a time-consuming and challenging process or direct them toward educational experts and advocates who can do it with them (see Chapter 12).

Traditional and Progressive Pedagogies

When it comes to educating kids, controversy swirls around how and what to teach, as well as how to evaluate students' knowledge and teachers' performance. One of the ongoing debates in American education is that surrounding progressive versus traditional pedagogies. In practice, many, perhaps most schools mix these two approaches. Indeed, *progressive* schools may include more traditional practices, like a focus on test taking and outcomes. *Traditional* schools may incorporate practices such as consensus building and group projects, which are hallmarks of more progressive models. Understanding these pedagogies and where a particular school falls on the progressive-to-traditional spectrum can help you understand a school's inherent values, curriculum, and behavioral and academic expectations, and how these qualities affect the children you see (Spring, 2018).

Traditional Education

Some of what teachers do in their classrooms each day derives from pedagogical principles and practices that go back many centuries, if not millennia. These are the traditional educational approaches with which we're generally familiar.

Before there was a progressive movement in education, there was more or less a singular approach to teaching and learning, one that still endures. In this model, a learned person—a teacher—imparts information to students seeking knowledge. The imbalance in knowledge creates a relationship of hierarchy. Thus, educating means transmitting what was learned from the past to a new generation. Students enter classrooms to learn from their teachers and from the repositories of knowledge that are available at the time. In addition to acquiring knowledge and skills, students are expected to learn rules of social conduct, moral frameworks, and receptivity from someone in a position of authority. This was and is the traditional model of education.

Progressive Education

The ideals of progressive education took hold in the late 19th and early 20th century as a reaction to the perceived austerity and hierarchy of traditional educational systems (Dewey, 1916/2012). Turning the focus away from the teacher's authority, rote memorization, and the acquisition of knowledge, progressive educators saw the child as the necessary center of educational activities. The notion of a *child-centered* curriculum focusing on the *whole child* was introduced; it included many of the activities and subjects we take for granted today, such as music, art, physical education, and theater. Even though the tightening of public school budgets and shifting priorities threaten many of these extracurricular activities, most parents and educators agree that they are important if not essential elements of any educational system.

Progressive schools may include some of the following elements: block scheduling in which students have fewer but longer classes per day, multi-age classrooms that mix students from different grades, and curriculum integration, which promotes interdisciplinary study and connects a broad range of subjects—for example, art and music with social and physical sciences. Student choice allows students to pursue independent work that engages their unique passions and interests. Progressive schools or classrooms tend to have an egalitarian feel as a result of these policies.

Over time, some progressive ideas have taken hold in most classrooms (Tanner, 2015). These ideas include the innovation of classroom discussion as a way for students to develop critical thinking skills and the ability to articulate ideas, as well as learn from their peers rather than just a teacher or material resources. Progressive pedagogy established another important component of our educational framework: it saw the classroom as a necessary reproduction of the democratic principles of fairness and equality.

The interplay between traditional and progressive educational pedagogies.

One of the main distinctions between progressive and traditional schools that is discussed in therapists' offices relates to classroom structure, particularly structure that is visible and easily understood. One of the central ideas behind progressive education is that the child, as a learner, will be self-motivated, independent, and curious. Children who possess these qualities inherently or who can develop them may flourish in progressive schools and find rich opportunities there. However, many children have a need for external and more visible structures established by teachers. These are essential to their learning. Without them, they may fail to succeed.

When children are struggling to learn, therapists need to understand how progressive or traditional the school is. Sometimes this may be difficult for therapists to discern. For example, the more egalitarian feel of a progressive classroom can mask its underlying structure. When the structure is made clear to a child and family, that intervention alone might be sufficient for the child to succeed. Encouraging teachers to make the classroom structure explicit can sometimes provide just enough scaffolding to help the child make his or her way.

Progressive educational ideals can be found in most educational systems today. They have thrived in elementary schools and in private schools particularly. Yet, there are definite limits to how progressive educational principles can be applied, especially in large public schools. Imagine public high school teachers with over 100 students entering and exiting their classrooms each day; it's nearly impossible for them to individualize the curriculum and expectations for each child in regular education. Traditional educational practices make it possible to streamline curricula and reach a broad expanse of student needs without completely exhausting teachers and resources.

New Technologies

The rapid pace of technological innovation and its influence on kids and schools is another major area that is both energizing and unsettling for those who work in schools (Collins & Halverson, 2018). Educators think hard about students' instant access to information on the Internet, information that's vastly beyond the knowledge and expertise of any single teacher. Educators consider how that reality affects classroom planning, activities, and interactions. They worry about kids' limited attention span and their fascination if not obsession with online games and social media. These issues intersect with school pedagogies any number of ways including how to achieve educational equity (Darling-Hammond, 2015).

In addition, there are educational innovations such as flipped classrooms that reverse traditional teaching strategies by having students receive instructional content online, sometimes outside the classroom. In class, students are then expected to deepen their understanding of the material through class activities, peer-to-peer discussions, and interactions with the teacher. Another version of technology-based instruction is termed *blended learning*, where students have some control over the pace and timing of their learning by combining online with classroom instruction, either directed by the teacher or the student.

Technological innovation and other societal changes have prompted educators to reexamine teacher-student-text dynamics that may best foster knowledge acquisition and critical thinking skills that, ideally, lead to developing 21st-century skills. Educators hope these skills will better enable students to flexibly meet the vocational, educational, and life challenges ahead. For therapists, staying alert to changing trends in educational technology will be an enriching as well as an exciting dimension of our work.

WHO'S WHO AT SCHOOL

Knowing who's who in schools is an important part of collaborating with them. The following appendix lists some of the key personnel you'll likely encounter and the functions they each serve. The priorities for whom to contact are typically related to whoever the child or family designates, the presenting problem(s), whoever made the referral (if the referral came from the school), and the particulars of the school. School personnel are listed (roughly) in order of how frequently you may come in contact with them, though this varies widely depending on the specifics of the case at hand.

Types of School Personnel

Teachers

As discussed often and thoroughly throughout this book, teachers are the heart of any school. They typically are a child's primary source of adult contact throughout the day. Therefore, it's often helpful (and even essential) to get teachers' perspectives when evaluating a particular child's school problems. Most preschool and elementary school classrooms have one or two main teachers, making it easy to know whom to reach out to if you deem it necessary. Middle and high schools are more complex. Students typically move from class to class and have different teachers for each subject. Therefore, it may take time and energy to determine the best person to call. At these grade levels, often your first contact will be someone on the student support team or the student's advisor or homeroom teacher.

To become a teacher, certain certification or licensing requirements must be met. Teachers have bachelor's degrees and often graduate degrees as well. (Preschool teachers are an exception: they may hold an undergraduate degree, but it's not necessary for certification.) Once a teacher has met these requirements, he or she must also secure state or national certification and pass a criminal background check. Special education teachers must often seek additional education and certification. Private school is a different matter: many states do not require private school teachers to hold state certification. Private school special education teachers typically must have a bachelor's degree, but not necessarily a state license or certification.

School Counselors

As one school counselor asserted, "Our job is to talk with kids about their lives in a nonjudgmental and caring way." School guidance counseling emerged as an independent profession in the beginning of the 20th century and expanded greatly in the 1920s and 30's during the growth of the progressive education movement. However, it wasn't until the 1950s that the profession was officially established by the federal government through the creation of a Guidance and Personnel Services Section for public school systems. Late in the profession (1997), the American School Counselor Association (ASCA) established the National Standards for School Counseling, further strengthening the occupation's goals and standing. Today, school counselors work with children of all ages and provide a range of services, including working with families. School counselors help students meet their academic goals, support those struggling with social or emotional issues, and advise them regarding career options and college admissions. At times, school counselors facilitate support groups for kids with similar issues, such as those whose parents are divorced, those who are adopted, or those who have lost a loved one. They also work with kids in clubs and workshops, giving them a view of the range and dynamics in a given grade or class. When talking with school counselors, therapists can make a point of asking what support services exist at school, including the availability of such groups.

As one school counselor said, they are often the "adult of choice" for kids who are looking to speak with a person of authority at their school. This might be because: they typically don't grade or evaluate kids; they help normalize their experiences (since most fall within the normal range of behavior); and, at times, help them seek additional support. This is something therapists should keep in mind when considering whom to reach out to at a child's school and who might be able to provide extra support for certain students during the school day.

College and vocational guidance counselors, a subset of school counselors, are there to help high school juniors and seniors, as well as their parents, navigate the process of college applications and other career pathways. Many public school college and vocational counselors, especially in large urban public schools, carry a considerable caseload and cater to a large number of students. In smaller public and in private schools, especially schools with substantial resources, the ratio of college and vocational counselors to students is significantly lower and thus more time can be given to each student's particular needs. Either way, college and vocational guidance counseling entails looking at a student's course load and activities in light of their goals and steering them toward the careers or colleges that are right for them. This includes providing information regarding financial aid and scholarships, SAT or ACT preparation, and career planning; identifying job fairs and career coaches; helping find apprenticeship programs; and sharing resume tips, interview strategies, and other general support. Parents are usually brought into the process at some point. If not, therapists can encourage them to get involved.

School Social Workers

School social workers have been working in schools since 1907 and have been a powerful institutional force for fairness and equality since that time. Many of you reading this book are, in fact, practicing social workers and have a keen sense of the values underpinning the work you do. When collaborating with school social workers, you can be certain that they are trained to think of children as members of ever widening systems of influence that must be considered when evaluating children's needs and finding solutions to their problems. Social work, more than any other mental health profession, is firmly entrenched in systems thinking. Whatever the particular clinical orientation, a social worker's background is also deeply rooted in theories of social justice.

In the early years, school social workers were hired to help with the wave of immigrants entering the public school system, serving as advocates for the less fortunate and beginning what became a long tradition of home visits and other outreach efforts. Their presence and influence ebbed and flowed over the subsequent decades, but with the passing of the groundbreaking Public Education for All Handicapped Children Act in 1975, the role of school social workers gained strength. Today, one can become a school social worker by receiving a bachelor's degree in social work or, more typically, by earning a master's degree. In either case, supervised fieldwork must be completed in order to be granted a license.

A big part of a school social worker's job is to enhance the connection between the family and school, as well as help the child and family find resources (e.g., therapeutic, medical). As one therapist stated, "They check to see if the kids keep showing up in the same clothes each day, look for signs of problems, and keep an eye on kids who are struggling. They're good at it." School social workers can serve as important liaisons between the school and an outside therapist. As one school social worker said, "It makes a lot of sense for the therapist to reach out to the school, and the social worker can be that liaison." However, not all schools will have social workers on staff. Their numbers vary depending on the needs and resources of the school district.

School Psychologists

School psychology has a long history as well, going back to the late 19th century, though it didn't become a specialty until 1954, when psychologists at the Thayer Conference outlined the profession's specific functions and training requirements. From the field's inception, school psychologists have sought to solve children's learning problems through clinical interventions that build on their individual strengths, while simultaneously accommodating their weaknesses. Testing, of the right sort and done well, is instrumental in meeting these goals.

Today, school psychologists must be credentialed by the state and meet standards set by their professional organization, the National Association of School Psychologists (NASP), which requires either a master's (EdS or Masters in School Psychology) or doctoral degree. There has been enormous growth in the number of school psychologists working in the public schools nationwide, an increase of 220% from 1977 to 2010, mostly due to the rise in special education funding and requirements. Though testing kids to determine eligibility for services is an important part of their job, lately there has been a paradigm shift from the *test and place model* to one that incorporates a broader scope of work, including prevention, early intervention, and the use of other evidence-based methods (Ysseldyke et al., 2016).

School psychologists are trained in both psychology and education, and are typically part of a school's student support team. Individually or in groups, they screen students for mental health problems; work with kids who are struggling with emotional, learning, or behavioral problems; evaluate students for special education and other services; facilitate support groups for kids (on grief, divorce, social skills, etc.); collaborate with outside professionals; consult with families, teachers, and administrators; create school-wide programs and policies (e.g., on stress, social media, bullying, trauma); respond to crises; and more. As with other student support team professionals, state or school district guidelines determine some of the services that are provided, but other services arise because, as one school psychologist said, "needs bubble up that haven't been planned for."

Educational and Learning Specialists

Learning specialists, typically found at well-resourced or larger schools, carry out a wide range of duties including: working directly with students (individually and in groups, both within and outside the classroom) in particular areas (such as reading or math), helping students articulate their learning needs to their teachers, making sure students know what resources are available to them, helping students understand and implement their individualized learning plans, and helping students manage and prioritize workload demands. Learning specialists also coach teachers and administrators on how to adjust and refine their curricula or organizational structures and strategies based on the needs of individuals or groups of students. Some learning specialists work directly with families to answer questions they might have regarding homework, studying techniques, and so on or on implementing strategies that kids with learning challenges can use at home.

Educational or learning specialists typically have a master's in education degree (EdM) and teaching experience. Subsequently they may attain a specialist in education degree (EdS), where the focus would be on educational leadership, curriculum and instruction, school psychology and counseling, or reading and other specialized subjects. For those who seek further and more in-depth training, a doctoral degree (EdD or PhD) may be desirable.

Principals

Principals—also known as headmasters, chancellors, or school directors—assume overall responsibility for a school's students, faculty, staff, curriculum, and policies. They are accountable to multiple systems, including some type of higher authority (the district, school board, parish, religious community, parent cooperative, etc.). In public schools, they are in charge of meeting state, federal, and local educational guidelines, including those related to testing. They are the final decision makers, and there's no question that they make a real difference in how schools function.

Most schools require principals to have a master's degree in education administration or leadership. Though principals are not typically the therapist's first point of contact, you might connect with them under certain circumstances—when the school is small, when the principal made the referral, when the problem is serious or the child or family is in crisis, or when the circumstances require the principal to be the final mediator or authority (this may involve the principal attending IEP or 504 Plan meetings).

Vice or Assistant Principals

In larger school systems, principals often are assisted by vice or assistant principals who help with the overall administration. Should the principal be absent for any reason, the vice principal assumes responsibility for the school. However, vice principals typically don't have the same decision-making authority, unless designated by the principal. There can be more than one vice principal in larger schools, with their duties divided.

The responsibilities of vice principals vary, but they are often related to particular administrative areas of the school—student discipline and attendance issues, student support services, class schedules, recreational programs, transportation and cafeteria services, textbooks and supplies, or issues of health and safety. Given that vice principals often handle disciplinary issues, when kids come home from school and say, "I had to meet with the vice principal today," parents may feel a knot in their stomachs, assuming that their child was involved in some rule-breaking activity.

School Nurses

In 1902, the first school nurse was hired to help students and families with health care issues related to communicable diseases, given the rate of absenteeism in New York schools at the time. Since then, school nursing has become a specialized type of nursing that exists at the nexus of education and medicine, with expectations for understanding both worlds. The National Board of Certification for School Nurses (NBCSN) requires a bachelor's degree and an RN license, as well as the requisite number of hours of practice. Yet, each state has its own set of certification or licensing requirements with its affiliate organizations linked to the National Association of School Nurses (NASN).

Though not all schools have nurses, when they do, they are typically the first responders when someone needs medical attention. They work directly with kids, families, and physicians by administering medications, monitoring chronic health problems, and following up with kids who are returning to school after surgery or an illness. They also provide preventive care in the form of health classes and information about public health issues. In addition, school nurses are sometimes the people kids go to for nurturance and support. When faced with complaints of headaches or aching bellies, skilled and experienced nurses can sometimes help sort out the cause—perhaps an incipient virus or anxiety due to a history exam during the next class period.

If you work with kids who have medical problems, especially serious ones, consider reaching out to the school nurse, or asking someone in the family to do so. In one case, the school nurse became the key point person for a team working to support a child with chronic asthma. When the teenager, an eighth grader in a public school, started to experience an asthma attack, a plan was put in place for him to signal a teacher who would then text the school nurse, alerting her of his imminent arrival in her office. As a team member reported, "She understood completely that it was her job to triage the situation," thus making it possible for those at school to more comfortably and calmly maintain their respective roles.

Speech and Language Specialists

Speech and language specialists or pathologists (SLPs) are the professionals who assess and diagnose problems that children have regarding speech, language, and communication. In collaboration with families and other school staff, a speech therapist might identify problems having to do with speech sounds, literacy, feeding and swallowing, voice quality, stuttering, or articulation. These specialists may also be brought in when a child has an auditory processing disorder, dyslexia, a nonverbal learning disability, or other identified learning problem. Services may be provided individually or in small group settings and likely involve the child's teacher, with whom the speech and language specialist will collaborate and sometimes co-teach. Speech and language specialists are members of the school's student support team and also collaborate with outside professionals, including therapists.

Though private schools are not obligated to provide speech and language therapy, families have the right to ask their local public school to have their child evaluated. If problems are identified through an evaluation, the child may be entitled to receive services through the public school system.

Occupational Therapists (OTs)

School-based occupational therapy is a relatively new service that is often offered in larger, well-resourced schools, or shared by a cluster of schools. This profession began in 1917 when the Society for the Promotion of Occupational Therapy was founded; it is now called the American Occupational Therapy Association (AOTA). Originally designed to support the healing properties of human occupation, occupational therapists entered schools after the passage of the Education for all Handicapped Children Act (PL94-142) in 1975.

Occupational therapists help children perform the activities of daily life. School based occupational therapists provide assessment and therapy in the school setting (e.g. evaluating and strengthening a child's fine motor skills), collaborate with teachers and parents, and advise school personnel on how to best structure their classrooms to support every child's healthy growth and development. Interventions can involve one-on-one sessions with the occupational therapist that are then supplemented by exercises at home. Interventions can also include adapting a classroom's equipment to meet the needs of a particular child. Though much if not most of the work occupational therapists do in schools involves children with disabilities, not every student with a disability will receive such services (Rodger & Kennedy-Behr, 2017).

Physical Therapists (PTs)

Though not available at all schools, school-based physical therapists work with students with gross motor disabilities that are identified through IEPs or 504 Plans. Such disabilities include problems with strength, balance, endurance, mobility, or coordination that impact the student's ability to function in the school environment. For example, some students might struggle with maintaining enough postural strength and balance to sit upright in a chair during classroom instruction. Or some children may need assistance when using a wheelchair or getting on and off the bus. Interventions are focused on helping the child physically function in the school and the classroom. They can include the use of assistive technologies.

Physical therapists assess a child's situation by gathering information from parents, relevant school staff, and outside professionals, as well as through the use of their own standardized metrics. Sometimes, parents are provided with specific instruction for how to support their child in daily life at home, and feedback is sought to further refine interventions in both settings. In addition, physical therapists collaborate with outside professionals, often serving as the liaison between other health care providers, medical equipment vendors, and therapists.

School Parent Coordinator, Parent Liaison, or Outreach Coordinator

Parent coordinator roles vary widely, but coordinators often serve as the school's point person for families. They work with student support teams, parents' associations, and various community organizations to support families who seek help for their children or who seek information about their school's resources and policies. As members of the school staff (i.e., not volunteers) who are closely aligned with families, coordinators can help reduce family–school missteps and divisions. They can also serve as bilingual liaisons when language differences are a barrier to communicating. Parent coordinators often help families with pragmatic concerns: how to take public transportation to attend a parent-teacher conference, secure food stamps, find appropriate medical care, and so forth.

Behavioral Intervention Specialists (BIS)

Behavior specialists help individual kids whose problems significantly interfere with their functioning at school. To make assessments, behavior specialists observe children in their environment to see how frequently children misbehave or fail to meet the demands of the classroom, examining the *antecedent behavior* that preceded it. The specialist will then make a plan and work with a child's teacher to implement it, possibly instructing the teacher on a new technique or strategy. Behavioral intervention specialists are part of a school's multidisciplinary team and participate in IEP meetings and sometimes run group therapy sessions for kids with special needs or other problems, such as addiction. Most states require behavioral specialists to have a master's degree in education, behavioral analysis, or a related mental health field, such as social work or psychology.

Special Education Coordinator (or Director)

Special education coordinators oversee the services provided to students with cognitive, emotional, physical, learning, and behavioral disabilities. These coordinators collaborate with administrators, faculty and staff, work with individual kids to develop IEPs and 504 Plans, help coordinate and evaluate services, develop budgets, liaise with school boards, implement state guidelines, help train teachers and staff, and serve as representatives at district hearings. Special education coordinators typically have a bachelor's degree in education or special education, and many go on to earn master's or doctoral degrees. They often have additional advanced certification in special education and years of experience working with children with disabilities.

Box Appendix B.1:   # Who's Who at the School

- Teachers

- School Counselors

- School Social Workers

- School Psychologists

- Educational or Learning Specialists

- Principals

- Vice or Assistant Principals

- School Nurses

- Speech and Language Specialists

- Occupational Therapists (OTs)

- Physical Therapists (PTs)

- School Parent Coordinator, Parent Liaison, or Outreach Coordinator

- Behavioral Intervention Specialists (BIS)

- Special Education Coordinator (or Director)

DIRECT OBSERVATIONAL CODING SYSTEMS

The Disabilities Education Act (2004) insures that each child receiving disability status in schools must be observed at school, an observation that becomes part of the evaluation (and reevaluations) necessary to receive and maintain services. Even though direct observations of students are required under certain circumstances, there are no standard procedures or norms for collecting this data (Dombrowski, 2015). Typically, direct observations are conduced by school psychologists rather than psychologists or therapists outside the school. However, therapists might choose to use a direct observational coding system as a supplement to or replacement for naturalistic or qualitative observations. Two such coding systems are described briefly below.

Behavior Assessment System for Children (BASC-3) Student Observation System (SOS; Reynolds & Kamphaus, 2015) is designed for practitioners to be used in observing children at school. A recording form and timing device (used at 15-minute intervals) provides information about the child's behaviors, their frequency, and the degree of disruptiveness.

Behavioral Observation of Students in Schools (BOSS; Shapiro, 2004) is an observation system designed to corroborate a teacher's view of a problem and its severity and to supplement the evaluation of the effectiveness of interventions being implemented. Like the SOS, a form and timing device are required, using 15-minute recording intervals.

BEHAVIORAL RATING SCALES FOR KIDS

Behavioral rating scales are norm-based assessment tools that are completed by a parent, teacher, or child to rate a child's behavior based upon their observations and interactions (Campbell & Hammond, 2014). Some include structured developmental histories as well as observation systems; they are computer scored and interpreted using national norms. Those filling out the forms respond to questions about the child's behavior either using a scale with a broad basis for behavior (e.g., BASC-2 or ASEBA) or focused on a narrower dimension of behavior (e.g., Conners-3 or BRIEF). They are frequently used by school psychologists in their assessment of how kids are doing at school and are also used by therapists seeking information about a child when there is a need for comparative data. For many rating scales, multiple language versions are available. A sample of commonly used behavioral rating scales for parents, teachers, caretakers, and children is listed below.

Academic Competence Evaluation Scales: Teacher Form (ACES; Diperna & Elliot, 1999) is a standardized, functional assessment tool used to screen students ages 5–12 years for academic difficulties and interventions.

- **Teacher Form** for Grades K–12
- **Student Form** for Grades 6–12

Achenbach System of Empirically Based Assessment (ASEBA; Achenbach, 2009) offers a standardized approach to assessing a broad range of adaptive and maladaptive functioning in children and adults ages 1–5 through 90+ years.

- **Child Behavior Checklist (CBCL/1.5–5)** is used by parents to assess children ages 1.5–5 years.

- **Caregiver-Teacher Report Form (CBCL/TRF/1.5–5)** is used by caregivers and teachers to assess children ages 1.5–5 years.

- **Child Behavior Checklist (CBCL/6–18)** is used by parents for children ages 6–12 years.

- **Youth Self Report (CBCL-YSR/11–18)** is a self report measure used by children ages 11–18 years.

- **Teacher Report Form (CBCL-TRF/6–18)** is used by teachers to assess children ages 6–18 years.

Behavioral Assessment System for Children (BASC-3; Reynolds & Kamphaus, 2015) assesses behavior and self-perception for children ages 2 years and 6 months to 18 years.

- **Parent Rating Scales (PRS)** is used by parents to assess children ages 2 years and 6 months to 18 years.

- **Teacher Rating Scales (TRS)** is used by teachers to assess children ages 2 years and 6 months to 18 years.

- **Self Report of Personality (SRP)** is used by children.

Behavior Rating Inventory of Executive Functioning, Second Edition (BRIEF-2; Gioia & Isquith, 2011) assesses executive functioning and self-regulation in children ages 2–18 years.

- **Preschool Version (BRIEF-P)** is used by parents, teachers, and day care providers for children ages 2–5 years and 11 months.

- **BRIEF** is used by parents and teachers for children ages 5–18 years.

- **BRIEF-2 Screening Form** is used by parents, teachers, and children ages 5–18 years.

- **Self Report Version (BRIEF-SR)** is used by children ages 11–18 years.

Comprehensive Executive Function Inventory (CEFI; Naglieri & Goldstein, 2013) provides a comprehensive evaluation of executive function strengths and weaknesses for children ages 5–18 years.

- **Parent Form** for children ages 5–18 years.

- **Teacher Form** for children ages 5–18 years.

- **Self Report Form** for children ages 12–18 years.

Conners Comprehensive Behavior Rating Scales, Third Edition (CBRS-3; Conners, 2008) assesses a wide range of behavioral, emotional, social, and academic problems and disorders in children ages 6–18 years.

- **Teacher Form (CBRS-T)** is used by teachers to assess children ages 6–18 years.
- **Parent Form (CBRS-P)** is used by parents to assess children ages 6–18 years.
- **Conners Early Childhood (EC)** is used by parents, teachers, and day care providers to assess children ages 2–6 years.
- **Conners Self Report (CBRS-SR)** is used by children ages 8–18 years.

Devereux Behavior Rating Scale (DBRS; Naglieri et al., 1993) assesses moderate to severe emotional disturbances in children ages 5–18 years.

- **School Form (DBRS-SF)** is used by teachers to assess children ages 5–18 years.

Devereux Early Childhood Assessment, Second Edition (DECA-2; Powell et al., 2007) is a screening instrument used by parents and teachers to assess strengths and problem behaviors in preschoolers ages 2–5 years with significant behavioral issues.

Early Childhood Inventory-5 (ECI-5; Gadow & Sprafkin 2014) is a behavior rating scale that is used by teachers and parents to screen for DSM-5 emotional and behavioral disorders in children ages 3–5 years.

- **Parent Checklist**
- **Teacher Checklist**

Multidimensional Anxiety Scale (MASC 2; March, 2012) assesses the presence of symptoms related to anxiety disorders in children ages 8–19 years.

- **Parent Forms**
- **Self Report Forms**

National Institute for Children's Health Quality (NICHQ; Vanderbilt Assessment Scale, Second Edition, 2011) is used to help screen for impairments in academic and behavioral performance, in particular for symptoms of ADHD and inattention in children ages 6–12 years.

- **Vanderbilt Parent Rating Scale** has an extra section for conduct disorder.

- **Vanderbilt Teacher Rating Scale** has an extra section on learning disabilities.

SNAP-IV of Attention Deficit/Hyperactivity Disorder Symptoms (Swanson, Nola & Pelham, 1992) is a parent and teacher rating instrument that assesses symptoms of ADHD and other oppositional defiant disorders (ODD) in children ages 6–18 years.

AN ABBREVIATED GLOSSARY OF SPECIAL EDUCATION TERMS AND REGULATIONS

There are a number of terms and related acronyms commonly used when children enter the special education world in public schools. Therapists will do well to become familiar with the terms and regulations they represent listed below:

Appropriate Evaluation refers to the process by which all students who receive special education services are evaluated. The process must be appropriately conducted as established by IDEA, in that it must minimize misclassifications, prohibit a single evaluation as the criterion for placement, include a variety of assessment opportunities, and protect against racial or cultural discrimination in the assessment process.

Confidentiality of Information refers to the process of protecting the confidentiality of the student based on the Family Educational Rights and Privacy Act (FERPA).

Discipline of a Child with a Disability refers to the necessity of taking the child's disability into account when determining the appropriateness of disciplinary action.

Family Educational Rights Privacy Act (FERPA) is a federal privacy law that was created in 1974 that protects the privacy of student records and gives parents protections regarding their child's educational records.

Free Appropriate Public Education (FAPE) refers to the fact that individualized educational services are provided at the public's expense with public direction, must meet the standards of the state's educational practices, must cover preschool through secondary school education, and must conform to the standards set by the IEP.

Independent Educational Evaluation (IEE) is an evaluation administered by an independent practitioner for the purpose of determining a special education program when the parent(s) disagree with the results of an IEP. The IEE is paid for by the parents or the school system.

Instructional Support Team (IST) is a program designed to maximize learning potential in regular classrooms while also serving as a process for screening students who may require special education services. Members of the team may differ from school to school but they always include the principal, classroom teacher, and support teachers. Parents are encouraged to participate in the process.

Least Restrictive Environment (LRE) is a later regulation (2005) that determined that children must be educated in a setting most like the educational settings of typical children in which the child with the disability can succeed. Children with disabilities should be removed from regular educational settings only if the nature and severity of their disability makes them unable to achieve the goals established by their IEPs.

Local Education Agency (LEA) is another way of referring to the school district. The LEA representative is the principal, teacher, special education director, or any person who ensures that the special education services are provided and commits resources for doing so.

Multidisciplinary teams (MDT) are a group of people who represent various disciplines who evaluate or support students. These teams can include such representatives as school counselors, special education teachers, school psychologists, parents, and others. They are sometimes referred to as child study or student support teams.

Multitiered systems of support (MTSS) is based on Response to Intervention (RTI) practices and refers to a multidimensional system of support consisting of Tier 1 (a core curriculum designed to meet the needs of the majority of students), Tier 2 (supplemental support to those whose needs aren't met by the core curriculum), and Tier 3 (more intensive instruction, with or without special education services, including referrals to therapists).

Notice of Recommended Educational Placement (NOREP) is the written notice that the school must give to the parent to sign when it takes action regarding their child or does not respond affirmatively when the parent has made a request. Parents have three choices when signing the form: agree to the plan by signing the form, request a meeting at the school to discuss it, or disapprove the plan.

Parent and Teacher Participation relates to the belief that parent-teacher partnerships are essential for a child's success. This means that parents and teachers must collaborate on IEP teams to create goals, as well as ways of assessing interventions and modifying how they are implemented. Parents must provide input as well as be updated on decisions being made and both parents and teachers can disagree with or challenge these decisions.

Permission to Evaluate (PTE)-Evaluation Request Form is the form parents use to request an evaluation for their child.

Permission to Evaluate (PTE)-Consent Form is the form given to parents by the school, which they must sign. It explains the reason for evaluating a child, the timing of the evaluation, what records will be included, and the types of tests that will be used.

Procedural Safeguards protect children with disabilities and their families. These include the parental right to review educational records, participate in IEP meetings, receive prior written notice before anything is changed in an IEP, request an independent evaluation at the public's expense, due process rights, and more.

Prohibition on Mandatory Medication refers to an amendment that was made to the IDEA that prohibits schools from mandating medication as a condition of attending school, receiving an evaluation, or receiving special education services.

Response to Intervention (RTI) refers to a multitiered system of instruction and intervention designed to meet the needs of an individual child and to evaluate the progress the child is making in relation to the child's IEPs.

Specially Designed Instruction (SDI) refers to adapting to the unique educational needs of the eligible child by considering the content, method, or delivery of instruction.

Support Teacher is designated by the district and works under the principal's auspices. This teacher is responsible for coordinating and assisting school staff in meeting the instructional needs of students struggling with regular education.

Transition Services refers to the process of transitioning from school to postschool activities. These services necessarily involve the child who is age 16 years or older. (All children age 16 years or older are required to participate in IEP meetings.)

EDUCATIONAL ADVOCACY RESOURCES

There are a number of ways for families to find an educational advocate. First, there are local and state advocacy groups and individuals that provide services for free. School districts also have educational advocates they recommend for those families whose children attend one of the district schools. Finally, there are state hotlines that families can call for information about special education services and referrals for educational advocates. A sampling of the national organizations is listed below.

Commission on Mental and Physical Disability Law of the American Bar Association (ABA CMPDL) http://www.abanet.org/disabillity/disabilitydirectory/home.shtml

This organization promotes the American Bar Association's commitment to the application of the rule of law to those with mental, physical, and sensory disabilities. Its website provides a database for attorneys who work with disability issues.

Council of Parent Advocates and Attorneys (COPAA) http://www.copaa.net

This organization's mission is to be a national voice for special education rights and advocacy. The website offers guidelines for finding an attorney or educational advocate for children with disabilities.

National Parent Technical Assistance Center (NPTAC) https://healthfinder.gov/FindServices/Organizations/Organization.aspx?code=HR3898

Funded through the U.S. Department of Education under IDEA, this organization provides training and assistance to families of children with disabilities.

National Disabilities Rights Network (NDRN) http://ndrn.org/aboutus/pwd
.htm

This nonprofit, membership-based organization is the largest U.S. provider of
legally based advocacy services for individuals with disabilities.

ACKNOWLEDGMENTS

I'd like to begin by thanking my mentors and friends at the Philadelphia Child Guidance Clinic (PCGC): Salvador Minuchin, Braulio Montalvo, Carl Whitaker, Jay Haley, Theodora Ooms, Harry Aponte, Bernice Rosman, Henry Berger, and others. I am also grateful for my work and friendship with Marla Isaacs and her Families of Divorce Project clinical team—Braulio Montalvo, David Abelsohn, Jenny Simons—who gave me the opportunity to find ways to support children of divorce in the school setting. At the University of Pennsylvania, Ellen Sterling opened up new possibilities through a course we co-taught on Families and Schools. Jay Lappin and Bruce Buchanan brought their gifted teaching and supervision, as well as their wry humor and big heartedness to the joint PCGC-Penn's Graduate School of Education joint certification program in family therapy and school consultation. Harry Aponte, Theodora Ooms, and Jamshed Morenas, the principal architects of PCGC's school consultation services, generously shared their experience and knowledge of how to employ family systems therapy to school consultation in the surrounding community. Theodora's commitment to this work and believing that I had something to contribute to the field is how this all began. Both thrilling and humbling, she and others at the clinic set in motion a lifetime of work with their imprint on it.

I am grateful for the patience and generosity of all of the kids, families, teachers, administrators, and student support staff with whom I worked in the schools in west and southwest Philadelphia. In one small, public elementary school near the Philadelphia Child Guidance Clinic, a gifted school counselor, Florence Weinstein, graciously took me under her wing. Her wisdom and realpolitik grounded everything I did in the years that followed.

I am indebted to the faculty, staff, and students at Penn's Graduate School of Education, where I taught for 10 years, and to the Department of Psychology at Bryn Mawr College where I taught and supervised doctoral students for over 25 years. Through their commitment, creativity, and desire to learn how to help vulnerable kids and families, the Bryn Mawr students were instrumental in my decision to write this book.

Abington Friends School (AFS), where I worked for over 25 years as a consulting psychologist, was my school "home." It was the place where I learned how teachers, student support team members, and staff create environments in which children learn and grow, something that happens every single day. To all of you, I offer my profound gratitude.

I am also indebted to the children and families with whom I've worked over the years. The strength of their family bonds, and their resilience and resourcefulness, have been a continuing source of hope and inspiration.

There are many contributions made by colleagues that figured in key ways in writing this book. I first want to thank Martha Edwards and Fran Schwartz who invited me into this project; their contributions are the very foundation of the book. I'm additionally grateful to Fran for enriching my understanding of schools and doing so with unstinting good will, rigor, and realism.

I want to wholeheartedly thank the therapists, student support staff, school administrators, teachers, legal experts, and other professionals who generously gave their time and energy to be interviewed, many of them repeatedly. Their experiences working with kids, families, and schools inform every aspect of this book. These include: Lorraine Ball, Nancy Bare, Michael Basch, Leah Snyder Batchis, Eileen Bazelon, Martha Benoff, Becky Breed, Renie Campbell, Peter Capper, Elena Carlson, Michael Cassano, Tamar Chansky, Marissa Crandal, Eleanor DiMarino- Linnen, Tim Edge, Cameron Elliot, Mary Lynn Ellis, Maxine Field, Stephanie Fields, Shoshi Goldfus, Janice Gossman, Natalie Hilton, Abby Huntington, Rachel Kane, Linda Knauss, Jeff Knauss, Eliza Lee, Deanda Logan, Carol Moog, Suzanne Nangle, Rich Nourie, Theodora Ooms, Tom Power, Margaret Ann Price, Michele Reimer, Carol Roberts, Alexis Rosenfeld, Mary Rourke, Antonia Rudenstine, Kevin Ryan, Randy Schwartz, Abbie Segal-Andrews, Lynne Siqueland, Jeanne Stanley, Jana Stanton, Rob Staples, Debbie Stauffer, Juliet Sternberg, Susie Windle, Jed Yalof, Mary Zeman, and Kieran Zito.

For their generous participation in and astute contributions to a focus group, I want to thank Eleanor DiMarino-Linen, Tim Edge, Staci Heindel, Lynn Kaplan, Stephanie Fields, Emily Malcoun, Diane Sizer, and Julia Stein, as well as Abbie Segal-Andrews and Madelaine Nathanson for skillfully facilitating the discussions.

There are many others I want to thank for offering their insights and advice on the book and the very process of book writing, including: Halcy Bohen, Tamar Chansky, Jack Davis, Mary Dratman, Eva Gossman, Judy Greenwald, Larry Hirschhorn, David Rudenstine, Neil Rudenstine, Laurel Silber, and Zina Steinberg. I am also grateful to my dear friends who, sitting around the table one spring day, answered my question—"Should I write this book?"—in the affirmative, and provided guidance and encouragement throughout the project and my life. Thank you Halcy, Eva, Theodora, Angelica, and Carol.

Heartfelt thanks go to the wise and generous readers who reviewed chapters of the book. I am very grateful to Eliza Lee, Madelaine Nathanson, and Randy Schwartz for reading the book in its entirety with great skill, dedication and sensitivity, and also to Abbie Segal Andrews whose generous editorial input and support were invaluable throughout the project. I'm also grateful for the thoughtful and exacting feedback provided by those readers who read and commented on one or more chapters, including: Michael Basch, Leah Snyder Batchis, Martha Benoff, Eleanor DiMarino-Linen, Tim Edge, Mary Lynn Ellis, Eva Gossman, Linda Knauss, Jeff Knauss, Jay Lappin, Rich Nourie, Theodora Ooms, Michele Reimer, Leslie Rescorla, Mary Rourke, Fran Schwartz, Debbie Stauffer, Juliet Sternberg, and Kay Stewart. Additional thanks to Linda and Jeff Knauss who generously offered their guidance regarding ethical and organizational issues.

Many thanks go to the excellent editorial and marketing team at Norton, beginning with Andrea Costella for her original conception of and commitment to the book and who—along with Ben Yarling—enthusiastically shepherded the project through its initial phase. I am also grateful to Carol Collins for her advice, thoughtful critiques, and flexibility. I also want to thank Deborah Malmud, Megan Bedell, Nicolas Fuenzalida, and Kate Prince for their contributions. Special thanks go to Mariah Eppes and Sara McBride for their support in the project's final phase.

Miriam Peskowitz and Cecelia Cancellaro provided helpful editorial support early on, and Marilyn MacGregor, Lindsay Ladd, Marcy Coffey and her team offered their creativity and sound advice.

Elizabeth Baird, my principal editor, provided brilliant insights, analyses, and a fine eye and steady hand to revisions big and small, as well as an abiding sunniness and steady commitment to seeing the project through—she was truly indispensable.

Though I benefitted greatly from the help given by those mentioned above and others, any errors or omissions are mine alone.

There isn't an idea in this book that wasn't, in some way or another, shaped by the years of co-supervising doctoral students with Madelaine Nathanson at Bryn Mawr College. Her power of observation, sense of irony, wisdom, compassion, and abiding friendship gave rise to some of the most deeply fulfilling learning experiences of my life.

Enormous thanks goes to my family and friends who contributed in countless ways. Looking back, my parents, Del, Maxine, and Irma, modeled the values of persistence, common sense, and kindness. My older sister, Sue, instilled in me a love of reading—she'll always be the better writer. My brother, Steve and his wife, Cheryl, are a constant source of inspiration. I also want to express my gratitude to my extended family for their continued support: Krissy, Rob, Tom, Martha, Oliver, Jordana, Suzy, Mike, Neil, Angelica, Antonia, Nick, Sonya, David, Zina, Aaron,

Olivia, Sasha, Will and all of their children. Many thanks to Stephanie Campbell whose decades long, unwavering care brought order into my life.

With their inimitable enthusiasm, my Nebraskan childhood friends offered constant love and encouragement—Kathy, Judy, Nancy K., Kay, Elizabeth, and Mary Z. So many friends offered their support including Mary Ann, who followed the project on a nearly daily basis, Nancy M. and Eileen, as well as members of my book groups, avid readers all: Betsy, Rocky, Colleen, Court, John, Abbie, Sarah, Ledlie, and Mary D., Nancy F., Hope, Liz, Anna, and Joyce.

From start to finish, this book was a family affair. The constant refrain, "How's the book going?" brought into graphic relief the love and enthusiasm of my husband, Dan, my children, Jonah and Claire, and son-in-law, Josh. Jonah helped every step of the way by rigorously and compassionately applying his formidable analytical skills to the conceptual framework of the book, and for gently reminding me, when doubts arose, "It's *your* book, Mom." Claire showed her characteristic grit and determination in helping me see this project through and did so, along with her husband, Josh, with steady confidence and unflagging enthusiasm and love.

I could never have written this book without the tireless support of my husband, Dan, whose love, patience, unparalleled humor, companionship, and commitment were sustaining. Fortunately, he won the debates over organization and brevity, resetting my path countless times. He has always known how to say "no," thereby creating space to do what's most important in life.

As I was finishing the final edits on this book, I stumbled upon a yellowed newspaper clipping of a letter to the editor written by my father in 1983. He had taken it upon himself to write to Lincoln Nebraska's daily newspaper, *The Sunday Journal-Star*, in praise of his teachers at College View High School where his mother (my grandmother), Effie Kienhhoff Eno, was a teacher and the principal during the 1930s and 40s. He wrote: "[I] remember the many evenings mother stayed after school to help those for whom learning was hard, the hours spent on the phone in the evenings talking to parents working out problems with their children, the many hours spent correcting papers at home." With this recently discovered letter in mind, I also want to thank Effie for her many contributions to kids, families, and one small town high school, and the inexorable way her work may have led to mine.

REFERENCES

Achenbach, T. M. (2009). *The Achenbach System of Empirically Based Assessment (ASEBA): Development, Findings, Theory, and Applications.* Burlington, VT: University of Vermont Research Center for Children, Youth, & Families.

Adair, J. G. (1984). The Hawthorne effect: A reconsideration of the methodological artifact. *Journal of Applied Psychology, 69*(2), 334.

Agasisti, T., & Zoido, P. (2018). Comparing the efficiency of schools through international benchmarking: Results from an empirical analysis of OECD PISA 2012 data. *Educational Researcher, 47*(6) 352–362.

Allegretto, S. A., & Tojerow, I. (2014). Teacher staffing and pay differences: public and private schools. *Monthly Labor Review*, Bureau of Labor Statistics, *137*, 1–23.

Alliance of Private Special Education Schools of North Jersey (APSESNJ). (2018). *Information.* Retrieved from: https://specialeducationalliancenj.org/about-2/

Aponte, H. J. (1976). The family–school interview: An eco-structural approach. *Family Process, 15*(3), 303–311.

Ardelt, M., & Eccles, J. (2001). Effects of mothers' parental efficacy beliefs and promotive parenting strategies on inner-city youth. *Journal of Family Issues, 22*, 944–972.

Baumeister, R. R., & Leary, M. R. (1995). The need to belong: Desire for interpersonal attachments as a fundamental human motivation. *Psychological Bulletin, 117*, 497–529.

Bazelon, E. (2013). *Sticks and stones: Defeating the culture of bullying and rediscovering the power of character and empathy.* New York: Random House.

Benner, A. D., Boyle, A. E., & Sadler, S. (2016). Parental involvement and adolescents' educational success: The roles of prior achievement and socioeconomic status. *Journal of Youth and Adolescence, 45*(6), 1053–1064.

Berends, M. (2015). Sociology and school choice: What we know after two decades of charter schools. *Annual Review of Sociology, 41*, 159–180.

Biglan, A., Flay, B. R., Embry, D. D., & Sandler, I. N. (2012). The critical role of nurturing environments for promoting human well-being. *American Psychologist, 67*(4), 257–271.

Bonanno, G. A., Brewin, C. R., Kaniasty, K., & La Greca, A. M. (2010). Weighing the costs of disaster: Consequences, risks, and resilience in individuals, families and communities. *Psychological Science in the Public Interest, 11*, 1–49.

Bottiani, J. H., Bradshaw, C. P., & Mendelson, T. (2017). A multilevel examination of racial disparities in high school discipline: Black and white adolescents' perceived equity, school belonging, and adjustment problems. *Journal of Educational Psychology, 109*(4), 532–545.

Bowen, M. (1985). *Family therapy in clinical practice.* Lanham, MD: Jason Aronson.

Bronfenbrenner, U. (1979). *The ecology of human development: Experiments by nature and design.* Cambridge, MA: Harvard University Press.

Bronfenbrenner, U. (1992). Ecological systems theory. In R. Vasta (Ed.), *Annals of child development: Six theories of child development: Revised formulations and current issues* (pp. 187–250). London: Jessica Kingsley.

Brooks, R., & Goldstein, S. (2009). *Raising a self-disciplined child: Help your child to become more responsible, confident and resilient.* New York: McGraw-Hill Education.

Broughman, S. P., Rettig, A., & Peterson, J. (2017). *Characteristics of Private Schools in the United States: Results from the 2015-16 Private School Universe Survey. First Look. NCES 2017-073.* National Center for Education Statistics. U.S. Department of Education.

Brown, B. B., & Larson, J. (2009). Peer relationships in adolescence. In R. M. Lerner & L. Steinberg (Eds.), *Handbook of adolescent psychology: Contextual influences on adolescent development* (pp. 74–103). Hoboken, NJ: John Wiley & Sons.

Campbell, J. M., & Hammond, R. K. (2014). Best practices in rating scale assessment of children's behavior. In P. L. Harrison & A. Thomas (Eds.), *Best practices in school psychology: Data-based and collaborative decision making* (pp. 287–304). Bethesda, MD: National Association of School Psychologists.

Cantu, R. & Hyman, M. (2012). *Concussions and our kids: America's leading expert on how to protect young athletes and keep sports safe.* Boston: Houghton Mifflin Harcourt.

Carless, B., Melvin, G. A., Tonge, B. J., & Newman, L. K. (2015). The role of parental self-efficacy in adolescent school-refusal. *Journal of Family Psychology, 29*(2), 162–170.

Centers for Disease Control and Prevention. (2003). HIPAA privacy rule and public health. Guidance from CDC and the U.S. Department of Health and Human Services. *MMWR: Morbidity and Mortality Weekly Report, 52*(Suppl. 1), 1–17. Also: https://www.hhs.gov/hipaa/for-professionals/security/laws-regulations/index.html.

Chansky, T. E. (2014). *Freeing your child from anxiety: Revised and updated edi-*

tion: Practical strategies for parents of children and adolescents. New York: Harmony/Random House Books.

Christenson, S. L. (2004). The family–school partnership: An opportunity to promote the learning competence of all students. *School Psychology Review, 33*(1), 83–104.

Christenson, S., & Reschly, A. (Eds.), (2010). *Handbook of school-family partnerships.* New York: Routledge.

Christenson, S., & Sheridan, S. M. (Eds.). (2001). *Schools and families: Creating essential connections for learning.* New York: Guilford Press.

Clark, R. M. (2015). *Family life and school achievement: Why poor black children succeed or fail.* Chicago: University of Chicago Press.

Clarke, B. L., Sheridan, S. M., & Woods, K. E. (2010). Elements of healthy family–school relationships. In S. Christenson & A. Reschly (Eds.), *Handbook of school-family partnerships.* (pp. 121–136). New York: Routledge.

Clauss-Ehlers, C. S. (2017). In search of an evidence-based approach to understand and promote effective parenting practices. *Couple and Family Psychology: Research and Practice, 6*(3), 135–153.

Collins, A., & Halverson, R. (2018). *Rethinking education in the age of technology: The digital revolution and schooling in America.* New York: Teachers College Press.

Conger, R. D., Conger, K. J., & Martin, M. J. (2010). Socioeconomic status, family processes, and individual development. *Journal of Marriage and Family, 72,* 685–704.

Conners, C. K. (2008). *Conners Comprehensive Behavior Rating Scales* (Conner's CBRS). Toronto, Canada: Multi-Health Systems Inc.

Cookson, P. (2018). *Expect miracles: Charter schools and the politics of hope and despair.* New York: Routledge.

Cooper, H., Robinson, J. C., & Patall, E. A. (2006). Does homework improve academic achievement? A synthesis of research, 1987–2003. *Review of Educational Research, 76*(1), 1–62.

Craig, T., Brown, E., Larimer, S., & Balingit, M. (2018). Teachers say Florida suspect's problems started in middle school, and the system tried to help him. *The Washington Post,* February 18.

Cutler, W. W. (2000). *Parents and schools: The 150-year struggle for control in American education.* Chicago: University of Chicago Press.

Darling-Hammond, L. (2015). *The flat world and education: How America's commitment to equity will determine our future.* New York: Teachers College Press.

de Botton, A. (2016). *The course of love: A novel.* New York: Simon and Schuster.

Dewey, J. (1916/2012). *Democracy and education.* New York: Smith and Brown.

Dickson, D. J., Huey, M., Laursen, B., Kiuru, N., & Nurmi, J. E. (2018). Parent contributions to friendship stability during the primary school years. *Journal of Family Psychology, 32*(2), 217–228.

DiPerna, J. C., & Elliott, S. N. (1999). Development and validation of the academic competence evaluation scales. *Journal of Psychoeducational Assessment, 17*(3), 207–225.

Dodgen, D., Donato, D., Kelly, N. L., Greca, A., Morganstein, J., Reser, J., Ursano, R. (2016). Mental health and well-being. In A. Crimmins (Ed.), *The impacts of climate change on human health in the United States: A scientific assessment* (pp. 217–246). Washington, DC: U.S. Global Change Research Program.

Dombrowski, S. (2015). *Psychoeducational assessment and report writing.* New York: Springer.

Dowling, E. (2018). Theoretical framework: A joint systems approach to educational problems with children. In Dowling, E. & Osborne, E. (Eds.) *The family and the school: A joint systems approach to educational problems with children.* (pp. 1–29). New York: Routledge.

Downey, D. B., Condron, D. J., & Yucel, D. (2015). Number of siblings and social skills revisited among American fifth graders. *Journal of Family Issues, 36*(2), 273–296.

Duckworth, A. L. (2016). *Grit: The power of passion and perseverance.* New York: Scribner.

Dweck, C. S. (2016). *Mindset: The new psychology of success.* New York: Ballatine, 2008.

Eno, M. M. (1985). Children with school problems: A family therapy perspective. In Ziffer, R. L. (Ed.), *Adjunctive techniques in family therapy* (pp. 151–180). New York: Grune & Stratton.

Entwisle, D. R. (2018). *Children, schools, and inequality.* New York: Routledge.

Epple, D., Romano, R., & Zimmer, R. (2016). Charter schools: A survey of research on their characteristics and effectiveness. In *Handbook of the economics of education* (Vol. 5, pp. 139–208). Amsterdam: Elsevier.

Epstein, J. L. (1987). Toward a theory of family–school connections: Teacher practices and parent involvement. In K. Hurrelmann, F. Kaufmann, & F. Losel (Eds.), *Social intervention: Potential and constraints* (pp. 121–136). New York: DeGruyter.

Epstein, J. L. (1992). School and family partnerships. Encyclopedia of educational research. In Alkin, M. C., *Encyclopedia of educational research* (Vol. 3, pp. 1139–1151). New York: Macmillan.

Epstein, J. L. (2001). *School, family, and community partnerships: Preparing educators and improving schools.* Boulder, CO: Westview Press.

Epstein, J. L., Sanders, M. G., Sheldon, S. B., Simon, B. S., Salinas, K. C., Jansorn, N. R., Van Voorhis, F. L., Martin, C. S., Thomas, B. G., Greenfeld, M. D., Hutchins, D. J., & Williams, K. J. (2009/2018). *School, family, and community partnerships: Your handbook for action.* New York: Corwin Press.

Erdem, G., & Safi, O. A. (2018). The cultural lens approach to Bowen family systems theory: Contributions of family change theory. *Journal of Family Theory & Review, 10*(2), 469–483.

Espelage, D. L., Low, S., Van Ryzin, M. J., & Polanin, J. R. (2015). Clinical trial of second step middle school program: Impact on bullying, cyberbullying, homophobic teasing, and sexual harassment perpetration. *School Psychology Review, 44*(4), 464–479.

Fahey, T. (1995). Privacy and the family: Conceptual and empirical reflections. *Sociology, 29*(4), 687–702.

Felix, E. D., Green, J. G., & Sharkey, J. D. (2014). *Best practices in bullying prevention* (pp. 245–258). In A. Thomas & P. Harrison (Eds.), *Best practices in school psychology: Systems-level service*. Bethesda, MD: National Association of School Psychologists.

Finn, S. E. (2007). *In our clients' shoes: Theory and techniques of therapeutic assessment*. New York: Taylor and Francis.

Fu, C., & Underwood, C. (2015). A meta-review of school-based disaster interventions for child and adolescent survivors. *Journal of Child and Adolescent Mental Health, 27,* 161–171.

Gadow, K. D., & Sprafkin, J. (2014). *Early childhood inventory-5 screening manual*. Stony Brook, NY: Checkmate Plus. https://marketplace.unl.edu/buros/early-childhood-inventory-5.html

Garandeau, C. F., Vartio, A., Poskiparta, E., & Salmivalli, C. (2016). School bullies' intention to change behavior following teacher interventions: Effects of empathy arousal, condemning of bullying, and blaming of the perpetrator. *Prevention Science, 17*(8), 1034–1043.

Gioia, G. A., & Isquith, P. K. (2011). *Behavior rating inventory for executive functions* (pp. 372–376). New York: Springer.

Glosoff, H. L., & Pate, R. H. (2002). Privacy and confidentiality in school counseling. *Professional School Counseling, 6,* 20–27.

Gordon, M., & Siegel, D. J., (2009). *The roots of empathy: Changing the world child by child*. New York: The Experiment.

Grant, K. B., & Ray, J. A. (Eds.). (2018). *Home, school, and community collaboration: Culturally responsive family engagement*. New York: Sage.

Green, J. G., Felix, E. D., Sharkey, J. D., Furlong, M. J., & Kras, J. E. (2013). Identifying bully victims: Definitional versus behavioral approaches. *Psychological Assessment, 25*(2), 651–657.

Grolnick, W. S., Schreiber, M., Cole, V., Lochman, J., Ruggiero, K., Wong, M., Schonfeld, D. J., Cohen, J., Jaycox, L., Pfefferbaum, B., Wells, K., & Zatzick, D. (2018). Improving adjustment and resilience in children following a disaster: Addressing research challenges. *American Psychologist, 73*(3), 215–229.

Gupta, V. B. (2007). Comparison of parenting stress in different developmental disabilities. *Journal of Developmental and Physical Disabilities, 19,* 417–425.

Haley, J. (1976). *Problem-solving therapy.* San Francisco: Jossey-Bass.

Halikias, W. (2013). Assessing youth violence and threats of violence in schools: School-based risk assessments. In S. H. McConaughy (Ed.), *Clinical interviews for children and adolescents* (2nd ed., pp. 228–252). New York: Guilford Press.

Hallowell, E. M., & Thompson, M. G. (1993). *Finding the heart of the child: Essays on children, families, and schools.* Braintree, MA: Association of Independent Schools.

Heath, M. A. (2014). Best practices in crisis intervention following a natural disaster. In P. Harrison & A. Thomas (Eds.), *Best practices in school psychology: Systems-level services* (pp. 289–302). Bethesda, MD: National Association of School Psychologists.

Hiatt-Michael, D. B. (Ed.). (2004). *Promising practices connecting schools to families of children with special needs.* Greenwich, CT: Information Age.

Hill, N. E. (2010). Culturally-based worldviews, family processes, and family–school interactions. In S. L. Christenson & A. L. Reschly (Eds.), *Handbook of family–school partnership* (pp. 101–128). New York: Routledge.

Hill, N. E., & Tyson, D. F. (2009). Parental involvement in middle school: A meta-analytic assessment of the strategies that promote achievement. *Developmental Psychology, 45,* 740–763.

Hintz, J. M., Volpe, R. J., & Shapiro, E. S. (2002). Best practices in the systematic direct observation of student behavior. In A. Thomas & J. Grimes (Eds.), *Best practices in school psychology IV* (Vol. 2, pp. 993–1006). Bethesda, MD: National Association of School Psychologists.

Jacob, S., Decker, D., & Lugg, E. T. (2016). *Ethics and the law for school psychologists* (7th ed.). Hoboken, NJ: John Wiley & Sons.

Joseph, L. M., Wargelin, L., & Ayoub, S. (2016). Preparing school psychologists to effectively provide services to students with dyslexia. *Perspectives on Language and Literacy, 42*(4), 15.

Kahneman, D. (2013). *Thinking fast and slow.* New York: Farrar, Straus and Giroux.

Kalichman, S. C. (1993). *Mandated reporting of suspected child abuse: Ethics, law, & policy.* Washington, DC: American Psychological Association.

Kataoka, S. H., Nadeem, E., Wong, M., Langley, A. K., Jaycox, L. H., Stein, B. D., & Young, P. (2009). Improving disaster mental health care in schools: A community-partnered approach. *American Journal of Preventive Medicine, 37*(6), 225–229.

Kelly, K., & Ramundo, P. (2006). *"You mean I'm not lazy, stupid or crazy?!" The classic self-help book for adults with attention deficit disorder.* New York: Scribner.

Kohn, A. (2007). *The homework myth: Why our kids get too much of a bad thing.* Boston: De Capo Press.

Kosciw, J. G., Greytak, E. A., Giga, N. M., Villenas, C., & Danischewski, D. J. (2016). The 2015 National School Climate Survey: The experiences of lesbian, gay, bisexual, transgender, and queer youth in our nation's schools. *Gay, Lesbian and Straight Education Network (GLSEN).*

Kotchick, B. A., & Forehand, R. (2002). Putting parenting in perspective: A discussion of the contextual factors that shape parenting practices. *Journal of Child & Family Studies, 11,* 255–269.

Lareau, A. (2011). *Unequal childhoods: Class, race, and family life.* Berkeley: University of California Press.

Larson, J., & Mark, S. (2014). Best practices in school violence prevention. In A. Thomas & P. Harrison (Eds.), *Best practices in school psychology: Systems-level services* (pp. 231–244). Bethesda, MD: National Association of School Psychologists.

Lawrence-Lightfoot, S. (1978). *Worlds apart: Relationships between families and schools.* New York: Basic Books.

Lawrence-Lightfoot, S. (1983). *The good high school: Portraits of character and culture.* New York: Basic Books.

Lawrence-Lightfoot, S. (2003). *The essential conversation: What parents and teachers can learn from each other.* New York: Ballantine Books.

Lerner, H. G. (2009). Fear vs. anxiety: What's the real distinction between fear and anxiety? *Psychology Today* blogpost, October 11.

Lines, C., Miller, G. E., & Arthur-Stanley, A. (2011). *The power of family–school partnering (FSP): A practical guide for school mental health professionals and educators.* New York: Routledge.

Lippold, M. A., Greenberg, M. T., Graham, J. W., & Feinberg, M. E. (2014). Unpacking the association between parental monitoring and youth risky behavior: Mediation by parental knowledge and moderation by parent-youth warmth. *Journal of Family Issues, 35,* 1800–23.

Lopez, E. C., & Bursztyn, A. M. (2013). Future challenges and opportunities: Toward culturally responsive training in school psychology. *Psychology in the Schools, 50*(3), 212–228.

Lythcott-Haims, J. (2015). *How to raise an adult: Break free of the overparenting trap and prepare your kid for success.* New York: Henry Holt and Co.

Maranto, R. (2018). The death of one best way: Charter schools as reinventing government. In R. Maranto, S. Milliman, F. Hess, & April Gresham (Eds.), *School choice in the real world* (pp. 39–57). New York: Routledge.

March, J. S. (2014). *Multidimensional anxiety scale for children 2nd Edition*™ (MASC 2). New York: Pearson. https://www.pearsonclinical.com/psychology/products/100000735/mulitdimensional-anxiety-scale-for-children-2nd-edition-masc-2.html

McConaughy, S. H. (2013). *Clinical interviews for children and adolescents: Assessment and intervention* (2nd ed.). New York: Guilford Press.

Miller-Day, M. A., Alberts, J., Hecht, M. L., Trost, M. R., & Krizek, R. L. (2014). *Adolescent relationships and drug use*. New York: Psychology Press.

Minke, K. M., & Jensen, K. L. (2014). Best practices in facilitating family–school meetings. In P. L. Harrison & A. Thomas, A. (Eds.), *Best practices in school psychology: Systems-level services* (pp. 505–518). Bethesda, MD: National Association of School Psychologists.

Minuchin, S. (1974). *Families and family therapy*. Cambridge, MA: Harvard University Press.

Minuchin, S., & Fishman, H. C. (1981). *Family therapy techniques*. Cambridge, MA: Harvard University Press.

Miranda, A. H. (2014). Best practices in increasing cross-cultural competency. In P. L. Harrison & A. Thomas (Eds.), *Best practices in school psychology: Foundations* (5th ed., Vol. 2, (pp. 9–19). Bethesda, MD: National Association of School Psychologists.

Montalvo, B., & Gutierrez, M. (1983). Perspective for the use of the cultural dimension in family therapy. In J. C. Hansen & C. J. Falicov (Eds.), *Cultural perspectives in family therapy* (pp. 15–32). Rockville, MD: Aspen Publications.

Morrison, J., & Flegel, K. (2016). *Interviewing children and adolescents: Skills and strategies for effective DSM-5 diagnosis* (2nd ed.). New York: Guilford Press.

Musu-Gillette, L., Robinson, J., McFarland, J., KewalRamani, A., Zhang, A., & Wilkinson-Flicker, S. (2016). *Status and Trends in the Education of Racial and Ethnic Groups 2016*. NCES 2016-007. National Center for Education Statistics, US Department of Education.

Naglieri, J. A., & Goldstein, S. (2013). *Comprehensive Executive Function Inventory: Manual*. Multi-Health Systems.

Naglieri, J. A., LeBuffe, P. A., & Pfeiffer, S. I. (1993). *Devereux behavior rating scale: School form manual*. New York: Psychological Corporation. https://www.pearsonclinical.com/psychology/products/100000187/devereux-behavior-rating-scale--school-form.html

National Association of Independent Schools (NAIS). (2018). *Membership*. Retrieved from: https://www.nais.org/about/about-nais/

National Center for Education Statistics (2017). *Indicators of school crime and safety: 2017*. Washington, DC: U.S. Department of Education.

National Institute for Children's Health Quality (NICHQ; 2011). https://www.nichq .org/resource/nichq-vanderbilt-assessment-scales.

Nock, M., & Kurtz, S. (2005). Direct behavioral observation in school settings: Bringing science to practice. *Cognitive Behavioral Practice, 12*, 359–370.

Okonofua, J. A., & Eberhardt, J. L. (2015). Two strikes: Race and the disciplining of young students. *Psychological Science, 26*(5), 617–624.

Olweus, D. (1996). Bullying at school: Knowledge base and an effective intervention plan. *Annals of the New York Academy of Sciences, 794*, 265–276.

Olympia, D. E., Jenson, W. R., & Hepworth-Neville, M. (1996). *Sanity savers for parents: Tips for tackling homework*. Longmont, CO: SoprisWest.

O'Malley, M., Voight, A., Renshaw, T. L., & Eklund, K. (2015). School climate, family structure, and academic achievement: A study of moderation effects. *School Psychology Quarterly, 30*(1), 142.

Patrikakou, E. N., & Weissberg, R. P. (2000). Parents' perceptions of teacher outreach and parent involvement in children's education. *Journal of Prevention & Intervention in the Community, 20*(1-2), 103–119.

Patterson, K., Grenny, J., McMillan, R., & Switzler, A. (2011). *Crucial conversations: Tools for talking when stakes are high* (2nd ed.). New York: McGraw-Hill.

Pellegrini, A. D., Symons, F., & Hoch, J. (2012). *Observing children in their natural worlds: A methodological primer*. New York: Psychology Press.

Perren, S., Corcoran, I., Cowie, H., Dehue, F., Garcia, D., McGuckin, C., Sevcikova, A., Tsatsou, P., & Vollink, T. (2012). Tackling cyberbullying: Review of empirical evidence regarding successful response by students, parents, and schools. *International Journal of Conflict and Violence, 6*, 283–293.

Pfohl, W., & Jarmuz-Smith, S. (2014). Best practices in using technology. In P. L. Harrison & A. Thomas, A. (Eds.), *Best practices in school psychology: Foundations* (pp. 475–487). Washington, DC: National Association of School Psychologists.

Poland, S., Samuel-Barrett, C., & Waguespack, A. (2014). Best practices for responding to death in the school community. In P. L. Harrison & A. Thomas (Eds.), *Best practices in school psychology: Systems-level services* (pp. 303–320). Bethesda, MD: National Association of School Psychologists.

Polikoff, M., & Hardaway, T. (2017). Don't forget magnet schools when thinking about school choice. *Brookings Institution Report*, March 16.

Powell, G., Mackrain, M., LeBuffe, P., & Lewisville, N. C. (2007). Devereux early childhood assessment for infants and toddlers technical manual. *Lewisville, NC: Kaplan Early Learning Corporation*.

Power, T. J., Karustis, J. L., & Habboushe, D. F. (2001). *Homework success for children with ADHD: A family–school intervention program*. New York: Guilford Press.

Pullen, P. C. (2017). Prevalence of LD from parental and professional perspectives: A comparison of the data from the National Survey of Children's Health and the Office of Special Education Programs' reports to Congress. *Journal of Learning Disabilities, 50*(6), 701–711.

Ratts, M. J., Singh, A. A., Nassar-McMillan, S., Butler, S. K., & McCullough, J. R. (2016). Multicultural and social justice counseling competencies: Guidelines for the counseling profession. *Journal of Multicultural Counseling and Development, 44*(1), 28–48.

Ravitch, D. (2016). *The death and life of the great American school system: How testing and choice are undermining education.* New York: Basic Books.

Reamer, F. G. (2013). Social work in a digital age: Ethical and risk management challenges. *Social Work, 58*(2), 163–172.

Reijntjes, A., Kamphuis, J. H., Prinzie, P., & Telch, M. J. (2010). Peer victimization and internalizing problems in children: A meta-analysis of longitudinal studies. *Child Abuse and Neglect, 34,* 244–252.

Reinhardt, D., Theodore, L. A., Bray, M. A., & Kehle, T. J. (2009). Improving homework accuracy: Interdependent group contingencies and randomized components. *Psychology in the Schools, 46*(5), 471–488.

Reynolds, C. R. & Kamphaus, R. W. (2015). *Behavior Assessment System for Children, Third Edition (BASC-3).* New York: Pearson. https://www.pearsonclinical.ca/en/products/product-master/item-33.html

Robinson-Wood, T. (2016). *The convergence of race, ethnicity, and gender: Multiple identities in counseling.* Los Angeles: Sage.

Rodger, S., & Kennedy-Behr, A. (Eds.). (2017). *Occupation-centred practice with children: A practical guide for occupational therapists.* Hoboken, NJ: John Wiley & Sons.

Rudenstine, S., Wright, L., Morales, A. M., & Tuber S. (2018). The value of integration: Psychoanalytic psychotherapy meets ego psychology in a psychotherapy group for children. *Journal of Infant, Child, and Adolescent Psychotherapy, 17(4), 346–363.*

Saeki, E., Pendergast, L., Segool, N. K., & Nathaniel, P. (2015). Potential psychosocial and instructional consequences of the common core state standards: Implications for research and practice. *Contemporary School Psychology, 19*(2), 89–97.

Sansone, R. A., Leung, J. S., & Wiederman, M. W. (2013). Having been bullied in childhood: Relationship to aggressive behavior in adulthood. *International Journal of Social Psychiatry, 59,* 824–826.

Sarason, S. (1971). *The culture of the school and the problem of change.* Boston: Allyn and Bacon.

Sarason, S. (1996). *Revisiting "The culture of the school and the problem of change."* New York: Teachers College Press.

Saul, J. (2013). *Collective trauma, collective healing: Promoting community resilience in the aftermath of disaster.* New York: Routledge.

Schick, M. (2014). *A census of Jewish day schools in the United States 2013–2014.* New York: Avi Chai Foundation.

Schultz, J. J. (2011). *Nowhere to hide: Why kids with ADHD and LD hate school and what we can do about it.* Hoboken, NJ: John Wiley & Sons.

Shapiro, E. S. (2004). *Academic skills problems workbook.* New York: The Guilford Press.

Sheridan, S. M., Knoche, L. L., Edwards, C. P., Bovaird, J. A., & Kupzyk, K. A. (2010). Parent engagement and school readiness: Effects of the Getting Ready intervention on preschool children's social-emotional competencies. *Early Education and Development, 21,* 125–156.

Sheridan, S., & Kratochwill, T. (2010). *Conjoint behavioral consultation: Promoting family–school connections and interventions* (2nd ed.). New York: Springer.

Sheridan, S. L., & Reschly, A. L. (Eds.) (2010). *Handbook of family–school partnerships.* New York: Routledge.

Sirrine, E. H. (2014). Childhood Grief: Interventions for Working with Bereaved Children and Adolescents. *Digital Seminar.* Eau Claire, WI: PESI. Retrieved from: https://catalog.pesi.com/item/childhood-grief-interventions-working-bereaved-children-adolescents-8439

Smith, C. P., & Freyd, J. J., (2014). Institutional betrayal, *American Psychologist, 69*(6), 575–587.

Spring, J. H. (2014). *The American school, a global context: From the Puritans to the Obama administration.* Boston, MA: McGraw-Hill.

Steiner-Adair, C. (2013). *The big disconnect: Protecting childhood and family relationships in the digital age.* New York: Harper.

Stevenson, H. (2014). *Promoting racial literacy in schools: Differences that make a difference.* New York: Teachers College Press.

Sulkowski, M. L., & Lazarus, P. J. (2016). *Creating safe and supportive schools and fostering students' mental health.* New York: Routledge.

Swanson, J., Nolan, W., & Pelham, W. E. (1992). *The SNAP-IV rating scale.* Irvine, CA: University of California, Irvine.

Tanner, D. (2015). *Crusade for democracy, revised edition: Progressive education at the crossroads.* SUNY Press.

Teti, D. M., Cole, P. M., Cabrera, N., Goodman, S. H., & McLoyd, V. C. (2017). Supporting parents: How six decades of parenting research can inform policy and best practice. Research-practice partnerships: Building two-way streets of engagement. *Social Policy Report, Society for Research in Child Development*, Vol. 30, No. 5.

Thompson, M., (2009). *The paradox of the anxious parent.* ISACS conference handout. Retrieved from http://www.isacs.org/misc_files/Paradox%20of%20 the%20Anxious%20Parent--Original.pdf

Thompson, M. G., & Mazzola, A. F. (2005). *Understanding independent school parents: An NAIS guide to successful family–school relationships.* Washington, DC: National Association of Independent Schools.

Tucker, B. Z., & Dyson, E. (1976). The family and the school: Utilizing human resources to promote learning. *Family Process, 15*(1), 125–141.

Underwood, M. K., & Ehrenreich, S. E. (2017). The power and the pain of adolescents' digital communication: Cyber victimization and the perils of lurking. *American Psychologist, 72*(2), 144-158

U.S. Department of Education (2001). *Family Educational Rights and Privacy Act (FERPA).* Washington, DC: GPO. Retrieved from https://www2.ed.gov/policy/ gen/guid/fpco/ferpa/index.html

U.S. Department of Education, National Center for Education Statistics, Common Core of Data (CCD). (2016). *Local Education Agency Universe Survey,* 2013–14 and 2014–15. Retrieved from https://nces.ed.gov/fastfacts/display.asp?id=372

U.S. Department of Education, Office of Planning, Evaluation and Policy Development, Policy and Program Studies Service (2017). *Issue brief: Student support teams* (January). Retrieved from https://www2.ed.gov/rschstat/eval/high -school/student-support-teams.pdf

Van Harmelen, A. L., Kievit, R. A., Ioannidis, K., Neufeld, S., Jones, P. B., Bullmore, E., Dolan, R., The NSPN Consortium, Fonagy, P. and Goodyer, I. (2017). Adolescent friendships predict later resilient functioning across psychosocial domains in a healthy community cohort. *Psychological Medicine, 47*(13), 2312–2322.

Waasdorp, T. E., Berg, J., Debnam, K. J., Stuart, E. A., & Bradshaw, C. P. (2018). Comparing social, emotional, and behavioral health risks among youth attending public versus parochial schools. *Journal of School Violence, 17*(3), 381-391.

Wachtel, E. F., (2004). *Treating troubled children and their families.* New York: Guilford Press.

Wald, J., & Losen, D. J. (2003). Defining and redirecting a school-to-prison pipeline. *New Directions for Youth Development, 2003*(99), 9–15.

Wallace, J. M. Jr., Goodkind, S., Wallace, C. M., & Bachman, J. G. (2008). Racial, ethnic, and gender differences in school discipline among U.S. high school students: 1991–2005. *The Negro Educational Review, 59*(1–2), 47–62.

Walsh, F. (2016). *Strengthening family resilience* (3rd ed.). New York: Guilford Press.

Webb, N. B. (2001). Strains and challenges of culturally diverse practice. In N. B. Webb (Ed.), *Culturally diverse parent-child and family relationships* (337-350). New York: Columbia University Press.

Webb, N. B. (Ed.). (2003). *Mass trauma and violence: Helping families and children cope.* New York: Guilford Press.

Weiss, H. M., & Edwards, M. E. (1992). The family–school collaboration project: Systemic interventions for school improvement. In S. L. Christenson & J. L. Connolly (Eds.), *Home-school collaboration: Enhancing children's academic and social competence* (pp. 215–243). Silver Spring, MD: National Association of School Psychologists.

Wentzel, K. R., Russell, S., & Baker, S. (2016). Emotional support and expectations from parents, teachers, and peers predict adolescent competence at school. *Journal of Educational Psychology, 108*(2), 242–255.

Werner, E. E. (2013). What can we learn about resilience from large-scale longitudinal studies? In S. Goldstein & R. B. Brooks (Eds.), *Handbook of resilience in children* (pp. 87–102). Boston: Springer.

Williams, K. R., & Guerra, N. G. (2007). Prevalence and predictors of internet bullying. *Journal of Adolescent Health, 41*(6), S14–S21.

Wohlleben, P. (2016). *The hidden life of trees: What they feel, how they communicate—Discoveries from a secret world.* New York: Greystone Books.

Ysseldyke, J. E., Burns, M. K., Dawson, M., Kelly, B., Morrison, D., Ortiz, S., & Telzrow, C. (2006). *School psychology: A blueprint for the future of training and practice III.* Bethesda, MD: National Association of School Psychologists.

INDEX